GREAT MYTHS OF INTIMATE RELATIONSHIPS

D0746333

Great Myths of Psychology

Series Editors
Scott O. Lilienfeld
Steven Jay Lynn

This superb series of books tackles a host of fascinating myths and misconceptions regarding specific domains of psychology, including child development, aging, marriage, brain science, and mental illness, among many others. Each book not only dispels multiple erroneous but widespread psychological beliefs, but provides readers with accurate and up-to-date scientific information to counter them. Written in engaging, upbeat, and user-friendly language, the books in the myths series are replete with scores of intriguing examples drawn from everyday psychology. As a result, readers will emerge from each book entertained and enlightened. These unique volumes will be invaluable additions to the bookshelves of educated laypersons interested in human nature, as well as of students, instructors, researchers, journalists, and mental health professionals of all stripes.

www.wiley.com/go/psychmyths

Published

50 Great Myths of Popular Psychology
Scott O. Lilienfeld, Steven Jay Lynn, John Ruscio, and Barry L. Beyerstein

Great Myths of Aging
Joan T. Erber and Lenore T. Szuchman

Great Myths of the Brain
Christian Jarrett

Great Myths of Child Development
Stephen Hupp and Jeremy Jewell

Great Myths of Intimate Relationships
Matthew D. Johnson

Great Myths of Education and Learning
Jeffrey D. Holmes

Forthcoming

Great Myths of Personality
M. Brent Donnellan and Richard E. Lucas

Great Myths of Autism
James D. Herbert

50 Great Myths of Popular Psychology, Second Edition
Scott O. Lilienfeld, Steven Jay Lynn, John Ruscio, and Barry L. Beyerstein

GREAT MYTHS OF INTIMATE RELATIONSHIPS

DATING, SEX, AND MARRIAGE

Matthew D. Johnson

WILEY Blackwell

This edition first published 2016
© 2016 John Wiley & Sons, Inc

Registered Office
John Wiley & Sons, Ltd, The Atrium, Southern Gate, Chichester,
West Sussex, PO19 8SQ, UK

Editorial Offices
350 Main Street, Malden, MA 02148-5020, USA
9600 Garsington Road, Oxford, OX4 2DQ, UK
The Atrium, Southern Gate, Chichester, West Sussex, PO19 8SQ, UK

For details of our global editorial offices, for customer services, and for information about how to apply for permission to reuse the copyright material in this book please see our website at www.wiley.com/wiley-blackwell.

The right of Matthew D. Johnson to be identified as the author of this work has been asserted in accordance with the UK Copyright, Designs and Patents Act 1988.

Library of Congress Cataloging-in-Publication Data

Names: Johnson, Matthew D., 1978– author.
Title: Great myths of intimate relationships : dating, sex, and marriage /
    Matthew D. Johnson.
Description: Hoboken : Wiley, 2016. | Series: Great myths of psychology |
    Includes bibliographical references and index.
Identifiers: LCCN 2015049854 (print) | LCCN 2016002202 (ebook) |
    ISBN 9781118521281 (hardback) | ISBN 9781118521274 (paper) |
    ISBN 9781118521267 (pdf) | ISBN 9781118521311 (epub)
Subjects: LCSH: Love. | Sex. | Interpersonal attraction. | Dating (Social customs) |
    Marriage. | BISAC: PSYCHOLOGY / Psychotherapy / Couples & Family.
Classification: LCC BF575.L8 .J626 2016 (print) | LCC BF575.L8 (ebook) |
    DDC 306.7–dc23
LC record available at http://lccn.loc.gov/2015049854

A catalogue record for this book is available from the British Library.

Cover image: © Stock Illustrations Ltd / Alamy

Set in 10/12.5pt Sabon by SPi Global, Pondicherry, India
Printed and bound in Malaysia by Vivar Printing Sdn Bhd

1   2016

For Deanne, with love

CONTENTS

ACKNOWLEDGMENTS

In October 2010, it was my turn to give a talk to the faculty and students of the Psychology Department at Binghamton University, my academic home. We usually give and hear talks that are heavy on methods and data, and I've given many such talks. However, in October of 2010, I felt like having fun. My dad had died a few months earlier, and I had grown weary of being heavy and serious. I wanted to give a talk that was light and fun. So, on that day in 2010, I gave a talk titled "30 Interesting Empirical Findings about Intimate Relationships in 60 Minutes." It turned out to be the light and fun talk I had hoped for. Sitting in the audience that day was my friend and colleague Steven Jay Lynn, Distinguished Professor of Psychology. Afterward, he invited me to write a book for a series that grew out of his book *50 Great Myths of Popular Psychology* that he wrote with Scott O. Lilienfeld, John Ruscio, and the late Barry L. Beyerstein. This book is the product of that invitation. Therefore, I begin my acknowledgments by thanking Steve. Were it not for him, this book literally would not have been written. Steve has been a supportive and wonderful colleague since he first picked me up from the airport for my job interview in the winter of 1999 in his red sports car. At every step of my career at Binghamton University, Steve has been ready with advice, insight, help, and care. He has made me a better psychologist. For that, he has my deep gratitude.

The psychology faculty at Binghamton University is truly great. I am proud to be a part of it. A few colleagues in particular were instrumental in helping me think about and write this book. Nicole Cameron helped me understand issues involving animal models of sexual and parenting behavior. She is a smart, enthusiastic, and patient teacher. Pete Donovick is always ready to talk with me about any subject. Peter Gerhardstein, Brandon Gibb, and Celia Klin were excellent leaders of the various academic units to which I belong. All of them were patient and kind as I let other aspects of my work slide while writing this book. I hope each will continue in leadership positions. Ken Kurtz was always interested in my work and wanted to talk about it, even when I didn't. It is nice to have a colleague ask about one's work, thank you. Richard Mattson is the principal investigator on a research project where I am one of the co-investigators. He has been patient and understanding in the face of my professional distraction and disarray. Chris Bishop, Meredith Coles, Cindy Connine, Terry Deak, Gina Fleming, Mary Ellen Gates, Jennifer Gillis, Courtney Ignarri, Albrecht Inhoff, Sarah Laszlo, Mark Lenzenweger, Don Levis, Stephen Lisman, Barbara Luka, Ann Merriwether, Ralph Miller, Vladimir Miskovic, Joe Morrissey, Ann Paludi, Ray Romanczyk, María-Teresa Romero, Lisa Savage, Linda Spear, Skip Spear, Greg Strauss, Pam Turrigiano, Cyma Van Petten, Dave Werner, and Deanne Westerman are all wonderful colleagues who have helped me in ways too numerous to recount here.

To my non-psychology friends and colleagues at Binghamton University (Anna, Benita, Dave, Dean, Doug, Elisa, Elizabeth, Frank, Howard, Jim, John, Julia, Kelly, Kevin, Melissa, Michael, Michelle, Nancy, Paul, Rebecca, Robert, Scott, and Steve), thank you for not throwing things at me when I started lecturing on topics that I included in this book. I'm especially grateful for the tolerance of my friends (as well as the people sitting near us and assorted restaurant staff members) who had to endure more than one of my "lectures" on female sexuality. Your mercy will not be forgotten and I promise to never again mention bonobos.

While I tried to put my students' work ahead of this book, they no doubt felt that I was pulled away from them the last two years. This is especially unjust because they continue to teach me and bring tremendous joy to my work as a professor. I'm grateful to my current and former graduate students: Karen Aizaga, Davis Brigman, Zachary Collins, Lauren Fishbein, Hayley Fivecoat, Laura Frame, Richard Mattson, Jared McShall, Tarah Midy, Rebecca Osterhout, and Dawnelle Paldino. Binghamton University enjoys a reputation that allows it to attract the best undergraduate students of any public university in New York. This means that I have had many amazing undergraduate students over the years. While there are too many to list here, a few have been particularly helpful in working on this book. Naquan Ross helped me with my thinking about a few of the myths and some of my primary source references. Meghan Axman, Thomas Costello, Karina Hain, and Andrea Joanlanne helped me with proofreading and indexing. Finally, the students in my intimate relationships seminars helped to teach me what I didn't know.

Outside of Binghamton University, I received assistance from Laura Bishop, M.D., who is a physician specializing in obstetrics and gynecology. She read over my chapters on sexuality and offered important revisions. Rebecca Allerton is the Executive Director of Rise (http://rise-ny.org/), which offers comprehensive domestic violence services to the Greater Binghamton, New York region. I have worked with Rebecca as a board member of Rise for several years and I am very appreciative to her, Mike Cox (Chief of Police in Endicott, NY), and the staff of Rise for teaching me about what it's like to be on the frontline of domestic violence services. The team from Wiley has been especially patient and helpful throughout this process. I am especially appreciative to Kathy Atkinson, Danielle Descoteaux, Gunalan Lakshmipathy, Anna Oxbury, Karen Shield, and the art department who developed the beautiful cover design.

I have been lucky to have truly great teachers throughout my life. Dudley Weiland was my sixth-grade teacher at Peck Elementary in Arvada, Colorado. His intensity and integrity inspired me then and now. In college at the University of Denver, I had the good fortune to work with Bernard Spilka and Howard Markman. Professor Spilka (Bernie) taught me the importance of having a broad education. In his classes and office hours, he wove together philosophy, literature, and science in a way that cemented my path as a psychologist. I started working in Howie's lab as a work-study student coding video tapes of one of his landmark studies. I was immediately hooked on studying intimate relationships. Howie is smart, driven, and generous. Whether we were working in lab (with Mari Clements and Scott Stanley) or playing intramural hockey, I was always learning from Howie (and I still am).

My graduate training at UCLA allowed me to have the career (and life) I have today. In particular, my clinical supervisor Andy Christensen, my fellow students, and my mentor Tom Bradbury ingrained a profound respect for science (i.e., the truth). Andy taught me how to do couple therapy and what I know about Myth 23 and the coda I learned from him. One could not have a better teacher of psychotherapy than Andy. The friendship of Aaron Benjamin, Edith Chen, Jennifer Christian-Herman, Victor Chavez, Becky Cobb, Cathy Cohan, Rose Corona, Joanne Davila, Brian Doss, Chris Furmanski, Chris Gipson, Colleen Halliday, Stan Huey, Ben Karney, Norman Kim, Anna Lau, Erika Lawrence, Cari McCarty, Emily McGrath, Greg Miller, Phoebe Moore, Lauri Pasch, Antonio Polo, Ron Rogge, Liza Suarez, Kieran Sullivan, Sylvia Valeri, Steve Wein, Shannon Whaley, Patsy White, and Will Yost taught me how to work hard. They modeled going into the lab even though it was always sunny and we all lived near the beach. Finally, my mentor, Tom Bradbury is truly my academic hero. He has set the bar as a professor, writer, and scientist to which I aspire. What I owe him can never be repaid.

The loss of my father left a hole in my heart and an even bigger hole in my mother's heart. Their marriage continues to inspire me and my mom's resilient grace continues to humble me. My brothers, Steve and Ted, are excellent writers and modeled beautiful prose for me. My sister, Jolene, is a scientist, law enforcement officer, national park ranger, and a trusted confidant. Finally, I should say forthrightly that I was not a good husband while I wrote this book. I spent too many nights and weekends brooding and fretting over it. Perhaps Myth 26 should have been "writing a book about intimate relationships will help you with your own." To Deanne, I say thank you for being with me through difficult times and good times, but mostly thank you for just being present. Being with you calms me, educates me, inspires me, and exhilarates me. Therefore, it is to my wife Deanne that I dedicate this book.

– Matt Johnson

INTRODUCTION

Overall, how satisfied are you with your life?

How you answer that question is more likely to be predicted by your satisfaction with your current intimate relationship than your satisfaction with any other part of your life. Let me repeat that. Our happiness in life is most closely aligned with our happiness (or lack thereof) with our intimate relationships. So, we had better pay attention to those relationships!

Let me pause for a moment and clarify that by "intimate relationships" I mean close relationships that have, at minimum, the potential for sex, such as one's relationship with a spouse, girlfriend, or boyfriend. So, I am not talking about parents, children, friends, or coworkers. That being said, some principles of intimate relationships may be applied to other types of relationships. Now that we've defined intimate relationships, let's get back to their importance.

Not only is intimate relationship satisfaction associated with overall life satisfaction (Diener, Gohm, Suh, & Oishi, 2000; Diener, Suh, Lucas, & Smith, 1999), it's associated with nearly everything we care about. The quality of our intimate relationships is associated with …

… physical health. The association between intimate relationship quality and physical health is consistent, whether it is measured molecularly (e.g., G. E. Miller, Dopp, Myers, Stevens, & Fahey, 1999) or in terms of morbidity (e.g., Langhinrichsen-Rohling, Snarr, Slep, Heyman, & Foran, 2011). Put simply, the quality of our intimate relationships is a matter of life and death. For example, if you have heart disease, you are

Great Myths of Intimate Relationships: Dating, Sex, and Marriage,
First Edition. Matthew D. Johnson.
© 2016 John Wiley & Sons, Inc. Published 2016 by John Wiley & Sons, Inc.

more likely to live longer being in a good relationship than a bad one (Coyne et al., 2001). Not only is the association between physical health and relationship quality strong, it's consistent across races and ethnicities (McShall & Johnson, 2015b).

... mental health. As with physical health, relationship satisfaction is correlated with mental health. This finding is so strong that marital dysfunction is associated with all but one of the 11 most common mental illnesses (Whisman, 2007), a finding that (like the findings involving physical health) is consistent across racial and ethnic groups (McShall & Johnson, 2015a).

... job performance. Relationship distress is associated with multiple job performance measures, such as tardiness and absenteeism (e.g., Forthofer, Markman, Cox, Stanley, & Kessler, 1996; Leigh & Lust, 1988). This means that there are significant and meaningful monetary correlates of relationship dysfunction at both an individual level and a societal level.

In other words, it's clear that relationships matter. Yet, despite all of the empirical and anecdotal evidence of the importance of intimate relationships, confusion reigns. We can see this confusion in the media and in the ways our friends go about trying to solve their relationship problems.

Goal of the book

The goal of this book is to put a dent in some of the confusion about intimate relationships by tackling 25 persistent myths about these relationships. You will see throughout the book that I have attempted to emphasize data from high-quality scientific articles. There's always a temptation when writing about human behavior to fall back on our own experiences, insights, and judgments. However, these can mislead us. Although there are times to listen to intuition (see Myth 22), some of the most important and fundamental lessons learned in psychology tell us that intuition can mislead. Just as I implore you not to trust your own intuition, I will also implore you not to trust a voice of authority (including mine). There are many supposed experts on intimate relationships, men and women who have written compelling books and made a lot of money talking about relationships. Most of these folks are well meaning and some are quite knowledgeable, but, as with any claims related to science, your mantra should be "show me the data." Therefore, this book is filled with citations. I have tried to back up nearly every claim by citing a source in which you can check out the scientific support for what I have written. No doubt that by the time this book goes into print, some of the findings I have described will have been upended by new studies or new data that will necessitate a revision of my conclusions. That's OK; in fact that is part of the fun of science, including relationship science. Another fun part of my job is listening to what others think of relationships. So, I encourage you to share your thoughts about the book or about intimate relationships more generally with me by visiting my lab website at marriage.binghamton.edu.

Structure of the book

I organized the book to approximate the developmental course of intimate relationships from myths about sex – the true starting point of development – to myths about attraction and courtship; online dating; same-sex relationships; predictors of relationship success; and, finally, myths about gender differences, discord and dissolution. Each chapter has a brief introduction followed by a discussion of each specific myth. Occasionally, there are side boxes with definitions, theoretical concepts, or marginally related asides. The chapter introductions and side boxes are meant to give a bit more context to the myths and my discussion of the myths.

I hope you find the book helpful.

1 SEX

"Sex." The very word is loaded. After all, "everything in the world is about sex except sex. Sex is about power." This quote, which is widely but improbably attributed to Oscar Wilde, captures the sway this topic has on us. Yet, it's also a topic that is steeped in lore, misunderstanding, and ignorance. More than once, I've urged couples in my practice to engage in a course of self-education on the topic of sex because they often report wanting to know more about sex and do more with each other, but are flummoxed by the plumbing and wiring of the human body (to these couples, I recommend Paul Joannides' excellent 2012 book, titled "Guide to Getting it On," which is comprehensive and entertaining). Of course, with all of the ignorance and misinformation about sex, there are also myths.

For this chapter, I have selected four myths that are specific to intimate relationships. The first myth is about the persistent belief that women are less sexually minded than men. The second myth is about the "hook-up culture" among college students and young adults. In the third and fourth myths of this chapter, I write about marriages that haven't been consummated and intimate relationships with very little sexual activity.

There are – of course – other myths about sex in intimate relationships. For example, many are surprised to learn that more than half of men and women in their 60s, 70s, and 80s report being sexually active two or three times a month (Lindau, Schumm, et al., 2007). In fact, there are growing concerns about sexually transmitted diseases spreading among older adults (Caffrey & O'Neill, 2007; cf. Lindau, Laumann, & Levinson, 2007). In any case, the reluctance to talk about sex in the context of

Great Myths of Intimate Relationships: Dating, Sex, and Marriage,
First Edition. Matthew D. Johnson.
© 2016 John Wiley & Sons, Inc. Published 2016 by John Wiley & Sons, Inc.

intimate relationships, even among couples therapists (B. W. McCarthy, 2001), leads to myths that need busting.

Myth #1   Men have a stronger libido than women

The strength of the belief that men are more libidinous than women is so ingrained that its validity is assumed (e.g., Mann, 2014). Silly cartoons showing the brain of the man thinking mostly about sex versus the brain of the woman thinking mostly about chocolate or commitment or shopping (see Figure 1) capture this sentiment (see also Myth 21). We've also all heard unsubstantiated facts, such as men think about sex every seven seconds (for a discussion of this myth, see Lilienfeld, Lynn, Ruscio, & Beyerstein, 2009). Of course, this is not true; however, men do think about sex more often than women and men seek out sex even when it's unwise or illegal (Baumeister, 2000; Baumeister, Catanese, & Vohs, 2001). Nevertheless, there are compelling data that we may be underestimating the strength of women's libidos and that our belief in this gender difference is steeped in culture (Lippa, 2009).

The repression of women's sexuality

No discussion of this topic can begin in earnest without talking about the history of women and their sexuality. Throughout history men have described women's sexuality in a way that revealed both the exciting and threatening nature of it. Because men have written most of the texts from the ancient to modern eras, the historical perspective on women's sexuality is necessarily viewed from a detached and masculine point of view. Even in historical writings that describe women as libidinous, one can detect the male perspective. In Paul's first letter to the Corinthians, he makes the point that "the husband should fulfill his wife sexually" (1 Cor. 7:3 New Living Translation). In Greek mythology, Tiresias – who was a man but lived for seven years as a woman – settles a marital argument between Zeus and Hera about who enjoys sex more. Hera claimed it was the man and Zeus claimed it was the woman. Tiresias said that men experience only 10% of the pleasure that women experience. On a side note, Hera was so angry with Tiresias for siding with Zeus that she cursed him with blindness, and Zeus, feeling bad about that, allowed him to live for seven generations and gave him clairvoyance. So it goes with being a marital therapist.

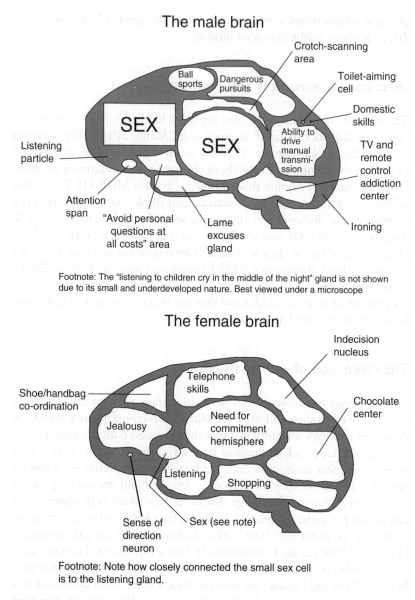

The male brain

Ball sports

Dangerous pursuits

Crotch-scanning area

Toilet-aiming cell

Domestic skills

SEX

SEX

Ability to drive manual transmission

TV and remote control addiction center

Listening particle

Attention span

"Avoid personal questions at all costs" area

Lame excuses gland

Ironing

Footnote: The "listening to children cry in the middle of the night" gland is not shown due to its small and underdeveloped nature. Best viewed under a microscope

The female brain

Indecision nucleus

Telephone skills

Shoe/handbag co-ordination

Chocolate center

Jealousy

Need for commitment hemisphere

Listening

Shopping

Sense of direction neuron

Sex (see note)

Footnote: Note how closely connected the small sex cell is to the listening gland.

Figure 1 This drawing from an unknown source (found in many places on the internet) is perpetuating the myth about male versus female libidos, as well as several more blatantly sexist stereotypes.

The ancient emphasis on women's sexual pleasure was not limited to religions and mythology. The famous Greek physician Galen of Pergamum (born in 129 CE) believed that women had to have an orgasm for conception to occur. Remarkably, the medical community held this belief for 1,500 years! Stop and think about the reasonable consequences of such a line of thought. As Daniel Bergner (2013) points out, this led to the medical establishment trying to understand the "certain tremor" that women experienced during sex and how that enabled procreation. This erroneous assumption had men began thinking even more about their own genitalia. For example, there were theories that a small penis might not lead to enough pleasure for the woman to conceive. Even the discovery of the Fallopian tubes by Gabriele Falloppio in the sixteenth century didn't stop him from describing how the shape of a man's foreskin might prevent the woman's orgasm and, consequently, conception (Laqueur, 1990).

Despite these and other examples from antiquity that women enjoy sex, there are many more examples throughout history of women's sexuality being minimized or denied. Again starting with the Bible and with Greek mythology, both Eve and Pandora embody the danger of lust unleashed. Thus, it's unsurprising that over time the female Eros (i.e., libido or sexual love) was presented as permissible only in the marriage bed, and sometimes not even there. The Victorian era was a time when Eros in women was denied (Dabhoiwala, 2012). Certainly, no God-fearing Christian lady of the Victorian era would enjoy sex. Rather, the following description of sex usually attributed to Lady Hillingdon captures the sentiment regarding female Eros at that time: "When I hear his steps outside my door I lie down on my bed, open my legs and think of England." Women of the 19th century were often seen as a temperate, if prudish, counterweight to men's lustful and intemperate nature. This denial of women's sexuality can be found today in many cultures.

The point here is that even when men wrote about women experiencing Eros, it usually comes across as naive or even silly. Of course, to say that women experience ten times the pleasure of men is as daffy as saying that they take no pleasure in sex. Therefore, I have written about this myth acutely aware that I am yet another man writing about women's sexuality. As with all myths in this book, I provide links to the primary sources and urge you to read these sources on your own to see if your interpretations are similar to mine. In particular, this myth should be considered carefully because, when it comes to women's sexuality, men have been getting it wrong for as long as men have been working on it. In addition, I also urge you to consider this myth in light of the crushing repression women have felt because of men's assumptions about their sexuality. This repression can come in the form of a jealous boyfriend who sees his girlfriend dancing with someone else and responds with violence, or it can come in the form of genital mutilation done to prevent women from enjoying sex. The research that I discuss involving women's libidos must be considered against the backdrop of both my gender and the ongoing repression of women based on their perceived sexuality (Baumeister & Twenge, 2002). With those qualifiers, let's look at the research.

The dubious nature of self-report data

One of the main ways psychologists collect data is by simply asking their study participants questions. These questions can come in many forms, but the answers to these questions are referred to as *self-report data*. There are many ways in which researchers try to ensure the validity of that self-report data. For example, we can ask the same question in multiple ways or, in relationship research, we can pose the question to both partners. Another way of measuring the validity of self-report data is to ask the questions, but also to observe the behavior in question. Meredith Chivers has done this by asking men and women what turns them on and by observing how turned on they are by various sexual stimuli. As I discuss in greater detail in Myth 11 (on the fluidity of female sexuality), the observation of sexual arousal has been measured for many years using a device that measures blood flow to the genitalia. The rapid increase in blood flow to the penis or vaginal walls indicates sexual arousal. In men, the increased blood flow is part of the physiological process leading to an erection. In women, the increased blood flow leads to increases in the secretion of moisture in the vagina that serves as a lubricant. These measurements are done with a plethysmograph, which measures changes in volume in either the vaginal walls or the penis (Burnett, 2012). So, Chivers compared how sexually aroused people said they were versus the rate of blood flow to their genitalia in response to various stimuli.

In a series of studies, Chivers showed video clips of erotic scenes to men and women (again, for more of a discussion on this line of research comparing gay and straight men and women, see Myth 11). She showed clips of men having sex with women, men having sex with men, women having sex with women, men alone masturbating, women alone masturbating. She also showed videos without sex, like videos of landscapes, of an attractive woman walking around naked, of an attractive and well-built (in every way) naked man walking on a beach alone with a flaccid penis, and of a naked man with an erection. Then there was the kicker: she showed participants a video of bonobos (a type of primate) having sex. During each of these videos the subjects were hooked up to the plethysmograph and were asked to rate their own feelings of sexual arousal on a handheld device. Thus, she was able to compare participants' reported arousal versus their arousal as observed in the amount of blood flowing to their genitalia.

With men, the videos of landscapes and primates having sex resulted in little arousal and the scenes that you would expect – depending on the sexual orientation of the man – resulted in a substantial arousal. Furthermore, the men's ratings of their own arousal matched pretty closely to their arousal as measured by the blood pulsing through their penises.

With women, it was a very different picture. Women rated their own arousal as you might expect. For straight women, there were higher ratings when they saw a man with a woman and lower ratings when they saw men with men and women with women. For lesbians the ratings were high for women with women and lower for men with men. All of the women rated their arousal as being low for the landscapes and primates. The blood flowing to their vaginal walls told a much different story! Women – straight and lesbian – seemed to be pan sexual. The women had blood flow when watching the sexual videos regardless of who was with whom and there was a large discrepancy between their subjective ratings and their vaginal ratings. Interestingly, women even experienced moderate blood flow when watching the bonobos copulating. In fact, there was more vaginal blood flow when watching the primate sex than when watching the handsome naked man strolling on the beach with his well-endowed but limp penis swinging from side to side. Clearly, there's a large gap between the arousal that women report and the arousal they feel.

Chivers has replicated her findings repeatedly (Chivers & Bailey, 2005; Chivers, Rieger, Latty, & Bailey, 2004; Chivers, Seto, & Blanchard, 2007; Chivers, Seto, Lalumière, Laan, & Grimbos, 2010; Chivers & Timmers, 2012; Suschinsky, Lalumière, & Chivers, 2009). In addition, research from Terri Fisher suggests that women are willfully denying their sexual arousal. In a series of studies, she demonstrated that women more than men will try to hide their sexuality. For example, women are less likely than men to report how frequently they masturbate if they think someone – even a stranger – will see their answer (e.g., Alexander & Fisher, 2003; Fisher, 2013). Therefore, it seems women experience much more arousal than they're willing to disclose. In an interview, Fisher explained that "being a human who is sexual, who is *allowed* to be sexual, is a freedom accorded by society much more readily to males than to females" (emphasis in original; Bergner, 2013, p.17).

The downside of monogamy

If women are feeling more sexual than they are letting on, why are couples in committed relationships not having more sex? As a couple therapist, one of the chief complaints I hear involves the desire for more sexual intimacy. Even when it's not the primary reason for a couple to come into therapy, it's an issue that's raised frequently (and delicately). In my practice, I have found that it's raised about equally often by men and by women. Lack of sex has been an issue with couples in my practice whether they're in a straight, gay, or lesbian relationship (see Myth 12). Being troubled by a lack of Eros in a committed relationship seems to know no gender or orientation barriers. So, women are more libidinous than they let on and men are just as libidinous as they've said; yet, I hear quite frequently that couples would rather watch television or read than have sex.

For women, it appears that they're sexually bored. When married women think about sex with someone other than their partner, they can become quite aroused. Researchers who study the role of female orgasm believe that it may have developed to encourage sex with multiple partners. The theory put forward by Blaffer Hrdy, as described by Bergner (2013), is that men reach orgasm much faster than women. The fact that women tend to need protracted stimulation from their partner means that women are ideally suited to having multiple partners, even within one session of sex. Although this contradicts the perspective of some prominent evolutionary psychologists (e.g., Buss & Schmitt, 1993), Hrdy posits that it makes evolutionary sense and can be seen in other species, both close to (Wallen, 1982) and far from (Erskine, 1989; McClintock & Anisko, 1982) humans on the phylogenetic tree. In several primate species, females have sex with multiple males and they're the initiators of sex (Wallen, 1995). There are also scorpions in which the female will not have sex with the same male again within 48 hours, but will have sex with another male within an hour of the last copulation. As Bergner points out, there are several explanations for this and researchers haven't coalesced around the primary function of this behavior, but scientists have speculated about the advantages of this type of mating strategy. Nevertheless, you may be asking, are there data about *human* females?

Figure 2 In the scene pictured above, the characters Claire (Julie Bowen) and Phil (Ty Burrell) from the ABC television show *Modern Family* (season 2, episode titled "Bixby's Back") are role-playing two strangers who are meeting for the first time in a hotel bar in an effort to spice up their sex life on Valentine's Day. ©American Broadcasting Companies, Inc./Karen Neal.

Research into the sexual fantasies of women – or to put it more bluntly – what they think about while they masturbate has provided additional insight. Women fantasize about sex with strangers quite often and tend to find it especially arousing. Indeed, even fantasies about taboo, coerced, or violent sex tend to be quite common among women (Critelli & Bivona, 2008). At this point, I must emphasize the word "fantasy" here. A fantasy is not the same as an actual desire and most certainly not the same as permission. Nevertheless, many women in long-term relationships talk about the ways in which the familiar aspects of their partners are no longer a turn on and that their fantasies about new partners who feel a strong attraction to them is arousing.

Conclusion

So, does this mean it's time to chuck monogamy out the door? Does it mean that for the sake of increasing the sexuality in your marriage you should join a swingers club or invite the neighbor over for a threesome?

Nobody is suggesting this. Rather, it's worth noting that a waning libido in a committed relationship is normal (see Myth 4), even among couples who had frequent and satisfying sex early in their relationship. It may be liberating to know that it's not necessarily you or your partner who is at fault. If you're waiting for the key to rebuilding the Eros in your relationship while keeping it monogamous, I am afraid I have no easy answers. Some couples have suggested treating sex like exercise. Just do it. Even when you don't feel like doing it, you will feel better afterward and be glad that you did. Other couples talk about ways to see their partner as a stranger, whether by role playing (as the characters Phil and Claire Dunphy are doing in Figure 2) or simply arriving separately when meeting at a restaurant.

In any case, two things seem clear: most people overestimate the sex-drive gender difference (Hyde, 2005; Oliver & Hyde, 1993; Petersen & Hyde, 2010) and women's attraction to "strange" (to borrow a colloquialism) seems to be at least as strong as that of men. For further reading, see Bergner (2013); Baumeister, Catanese, and Vohs (2001); Hite (2004); and Hrdy (1999). For somewhat different perspectives on this issue, read Meston and Buss (2009) and Thornhill and Gangestad (2008).

Myth #2   Hooking up in college is bad for women

She got the text a little after midnight: "Want to hang out?" She knew what that meant. It was from her friend (with benefits), Jim. There was only one reason that he would be texting her late on a weekday during midterms. She and Jim were both majoring in tough disciplines and took their classes seriously. The hard work was paying off because they both had good grades. Unlike a lot of their classmates, they had their plans in place and knew what it would take to get into graduate school. So, there was no way that Jim wanted to go to one of the bars or fraternity parties. He had the same test she had in about 12 hours. She looked at the text again and noticed that her eyes were blurry from studying without a break for the last three hours. She was tired and needed sleep, but she also knew that she was keyed up and anxious about the test.

She liked Jim. He was smart and occasionally funny. He was thin in the way that some people are thin despite horrible eating habits. Overall, she liked the way he looked. She knew that she was better looking than he – not to mention smarter and wittier – and that she could do better.

However, Mr. Better-than-Jim wasn't texting her, Jim was. She thought that hooking up with Jim might be the perfect way to wind down. It would be fun and she would probably be asleep faster than if she just went home alone. So, she wrote back: "In library. Are you home?" She liked her phrasing because it made her intentions clear: There will be sex, and I will not be spending part of tomorrow washing sheets. His response was quick: "Come over." So she did.

Quite a bit has been written about the hook-up culture among young adults and how it has replaced more traditional forms of courtship. This culture is especially prevalent on college campuses. I first realized the extent of the college hook-up scene from the students in my undergraduate seminar. I was not so naive as to think that they were still using terms like "courtship" or "date." Nevertheless, I had assumed that the change was one of semantics more than actual behavior. I asked my students to tell me the modern term for going on a date. Blank stares followed. So, I tried again.

> OK, I said, "What words would you use to describe a young man asking a young woman to dinner and a movie?"
> This led the students to ask follow up questions. "Are they meeting friends there?"
> "No," I said "it's just the two of them."
> "Are they in an exclusive relationship?"
> "No, this would be what we used to call a 'first date.'"
> "Have they already hooked up?"
> Now I was the one with questions. "What?! No! This would be their first time together. For goodness sakes, he's simply asking her to go to dinner and a movie. What does your generation call that?"

It was beginning to dawn on all of us that we were shouting to each other across a wide generation gap. As far as they were concerned, I may as well have been talking about "goin' a courtin' with a sword and pistol by my side" (from the 16th-century song, "Frog Went A-Courtin;" Wedderburn, 1549/1979). So it was that – for neither the first nor the last time – my students patiently explained the way things are to me, their professor.

They told me that many college relationships begin with sexual behavior prior to getting to know the other person. Not necessarily sex, but anything from kissing to coitus. The sexual experiences may or may not be followed up with conversation and getting to know each other. Thus, my assumption that someone would ask another person to dinner and a movie seemed to reverse the order of current college courtship operations. Even if they know each other first, they will most likely move their relationship to a more intimate level first through sexual experiences and later through more emotional connections and nonsexual shared experiences. My students were quick to make three points. First, many of them, including both men and women (gay and straight), indicated that they didn't like the change from (what I will call) dating culture to hook-up culture. They seemed to like the idea of taking someone to dinner and a movie as a way to get to know the other person and to decide whether to engage in sexual activities together. The second thing that they wanted me to know was that they themselves didn't engage in hook-ups. Whether they were all lying or whether my class on intimate relationships drew more students who eschewed hooking up, I cannot say. Interestingly, they didn't seem concerned about their own reputation or what their classmates (or I) thought of them. They seemed to be making the point that many students did *not* hook up on a regular basis and that the ones who were engaging in frequent casual sexual encounters were a particularly visible minority. Furthermore, they argued that the perception of the hook-up culture was making it harder for those who longed for meaningful intimate relationships. Finally, the third point that the students made was that the hook-up culture seemed to be good for some heterosexual men and not-so-good for heterosexual women. Since my students educated me, much more has been written about hooking up and what it means for men and women. So, let's look at the data.

Prevalence of sex in college

Others have noticed the cultural changes that my students told me about. These changes have led to a great deal of attention from journalists and commentators who are writing about the prevalence and dangers of hooking up – especially for women. For example, Laura Sessions Stepp, author of *Unhooked: How Young Women Pursue Sex, Delay Love, and Lose at Both* (2007), wrote about the dangers that women expose themselves to when they engage in casual sex. In another example, Jill Weber, author of *Having Sex, Wanting Intimacy: Why Women Settle for One-Sided Relationships* (2013), coins a new term, *sextimacy*, and defines it as "the effort to find emotional intimacy through sex" (p. ix). Several other journalists and authors have also written about the dangers of casual sex. Others have indicated that the problem is not that women are having casual sex; rather, the problems is the reaction of older generations to the apparent prevalence of casual sex (e.g., Valenti, 2009). A third group of authors has taken a different approach by writing about the shift in women appearing to be more and more interested in pleasing men than in worrying about their own sexual fulfillment. For example, Ariel Levy has written about this in *Female Chauvinist Pigs: Women and the Rise of Raunch Culture* (2005), noting that young women seem too concerned with how men view them than with concerns about themselves. As you can imagine, stories about the hook-up culture on college campuses and other places where you find young men and women have garnered a great deal of media attention. This has led to some myths involving the prevalence of sex among young adults.

Much of the reporting about the hook-up culture has led, as Elizabeth Armstrong, Laura Hamilton, and Paula England (2010) put it, to the impression that "young people are having more sex at earlier ages in more casual contexts than their Baby Boomer parents" (p. 23). Using data from the best resource for information on the sexual practices of Americans, the National Health and Social Life Survey, they note that Baby Boomers (those born after 1942) did have more sex and at younger ages than their parents' generation. However, those born between 1963 and 1972 showed no increases in sexual activity and even a little decrease. Other data back the conclusion that the amount of sexual activity among adolescents and young adults is either stable or decreasing. However, it seems that the handwringing in the media is not because sexual activity is increasing or that adolescents are starting to become sexually active at younger ages. Rather, it seems that the consternation of older generations is caused by the apparent casual nature of sexual behavior in this generation.

Indeed, the rate of casual sex among college students has increased. Paula England, Emily Fitzgibbons Shafer, and Alison Fogarty (2008) conducted a study of college students at more than 19 universities and found that 72% of both men and women reported having had at least one hook-up by their senior year. This number is reasonably consistent with smaller samples (e.g., Garcia & Reiber, 2008). What may be lost in these raw numbers are the frequency and intensity of these hook-ups. The large survey data revealed that college students don't hook up as much as older generations think they do. By their senior year, when college students who indicated that they had hooked up were asked how often, 40% said they had done so three or fewer times, 40% said between four and nine times, and 20% said ten or more times; and 80% of students said they had done it less than once a semester. Therefore, it seems that some of the more provocative images and headlines that portray casual sex among college students as ubiquitous are off the mark.

Beyond the frequency of casual sexual activity, the college students that England and colleagues surveyed indicated that the intensity of their experiences was less than what has been portrayed in the media. The respondents indicated that in their last hook-up, one third of them had intercourse, one third didn't go beyond oral sex, and one third didn't go beyond kissing and non-genital touching. In addition, hooking up with strangers was uncommon compared with repeated hook-ups with the same person. These types of hook-ups have various labels, such as "friends with benefits" or "fuck buddies,"[1] and often involve socializing before or after sexual encounters. In all of this discussion about rates and descriptions of casual sexual experiences in college, it's important to remember that 20% of college seniors report having never had penile–vaginal intercourse (Armstrong et al., 2010). In other words, for all of the handwringing about sexual behavior in college, the rates, frequency, and intensity of college sexual experiences is flat or declining, and a sizable minority of college students have eschewed sex outside of marriage altogether (see Myths 3 and 4 for rates of married couples who don't have sex).

Before getting to whether hooking up is bad for women, here are three other facts to keep in mind as you watch or read breathless stories about the hook-up culture. First, casual sex isn't new. The sexual revolution of the late 1960s, advances in the availability and effectiveness of birth control, and the decline of the paternalistic nature of college administrators (known as *in loco parentis*) all led to an increase in casual sex (Armstrong et al., 2010). The second point to remember is that hook-ups haven't replaced relationships. By their senior year, 69% of heterosexual college students reported having been in a relationship that lasted at least six months. Although there appears to be some fluidity between referring to someone as a boyfriend/girlfriend and a hook-up – with some relationships preceding or following hook-up-type relationships – it's clear that college students are still engaging in relationships (England et al., 2008). Third, the tendency for women to engage in hook-ups is somewhat stronger for White women and wealthier women. All of this seems to confirm that the students in my class were fairly typical of college students around the country, because many of them emphasized their desire for relationships, their distress about navigating the current social landscape, and they seemed to deemphasize the importance of multiple sexual experiences. That being said, my students and I agreed that something fundamental about the nature of intimate relationships had changed during the 20-year gap between our collegiate experiences.

What's bad about hooking up for women?

Having established what the hook-up culture in college does and doesn't entail, the question remains whether it's good or bad for women. I focus on women because there are more potentially negative consequences for women compared to men, and because I haven't seen or read books about the negative consequences of casual sex for men in college, as I have for women (see Stepp, 2007; Weber, 2013). As with some of the other myths in this book, this one is partially true. There are clearly some downsides for women hooking up.

The most direct and dangerous consequences of hooking up are the increased likelihood of contracting a lifelong or life-threatening disease and becoming a victim of violence. College men and women often feel invincible, and this includes discounting their chances of acquiring a sexually transmitted disease (Centers for Disease Control and Prevention, 2012). This partially explains why a quarter of all new HIV diagnoses are among women under age 25 (Centers for Disease Control and Prevention, 2011), and nearly half of the newly diagnosed sexually transmitted diseases are among men and women under age 25 (Weinstock, Berman, & Cates, 2004). In addition to increasing vulnerability to disease, hooking up increases women's chances of being victims of violence. In fact, women between the ages of 20 and 24 experience nonfatal intimate partner violence more than any other group, and casual sexual encounters create additional opportunities for such assaults (Catalano, 2007). These statistics were brought home for me in a discussion I had with a gynecologist who has a lot of college students as patients. She noted that she treats a lot of students for sexually transmitted diseases (mostly herpes, chlamydia, and gonorrhea as well as syphilis and HIV); moreover, she was shocked by how much violence her patients have experienced – both reported and unreported as well as acknowledged and unacknowledged (for more on intimate partner violence, see Myth 22). While increasing the likelihood of illness and violence may be direct consequences of sexual encounters, there are also indirect and psychological consequences.

Armstrong et al. (2010) argue that the pervasiveness of the sexual double standard is behind some of the most commonly cited negative consequences for women engaging in casual sex. One of the women interviewed for their article noted that "guys can have sex with all the girls and it makes them more of a man, but if a girl does then all of a sudden she's a 'ho' and she's not as quality of a person" (p. 25). In addition, they note that the social stigma and labeling that comes with hook-ups is often predicated on the erroneous assumption that most hook-ups involve intercourse, with one of the women interviewed noting that she was called a "slut" when she was still a virgin. In addition to social stigma, many researchers have described the dangers of college campuses on which fraternities represent the primary venue for college students (especially underage ones) to access alcohol. This access provides the members of the fraternity with many opportunities for undermining women's ability to provide consent for sexual activities, ranging from spiking drinks, to blocking exits, to refusing safe transportation upon departure; therefore, it's no surprise that sexual assault is one of the risk factors associated with college hook-up culture (see also Flanagan, 2014). To their credit, student activists, campus administrators, policy-makers, researchers, and journalists are now paying attention to how the culture of a campus may further endanger women.

Despite the serious potential consequences I've already outlined, in interviews of college women (for methodological details, see Hamilton & Armstrong, 2009), women's biggest complaint about hook-ups was that the sex wasn't very good compared to sex in relationships. Indeed, follow-up studies have demonstrated that women aren't enjoying sex in hook-ups as much as sex in relationships because men in hook-ups are far less likely to sexually perform so as to pleasure the women. For example, in hook-ups, women are more likely to perform oral sex than to receive it. As a result, women having relationship sex report enjoying sex more and having more orgasms than women having hook-up sex (Armstrong, England, & Fogarty, 2012). This state of affairs (no pun intended) is also confirmed when men are interviewed. They report having much more concern about the sexual pleasure of their relationship partner than their hook-up partner (Armstrong et al., 2010). Thus, it seems that one of the most common downsides of casual sex for women is that the sex is simply not as good as sex in a relationship.

What is good about hooking up for women?

So, if hook-up sex is not as good as relationship sex, what's in it for women? The answer seems to lie in the downside of relationships. Many of the women interviewed in the studies cited above and in an article for the *New York Times* (K. Taylor, 2013) talked about the costs and benefits of having a relationship in college and decided that the costs outweigh the benefits. In extensive interviews, women talked about the fact that relationships tend to be time sinks that they can't afford. For example, one woman at the University of Pennsylvania interviewed in the *New York Times* said "I positioned myself in college in such a way that I can't have a meaningful romantic relationship, because I'm always busy and the people that I am interested in are always busy, too" (p. 1).

In addition to time, there are other dark sides of relationships. Some women Hamilton and Armstrong interviewed indicated that they viewed college as a time to meet a diverse group of people, and they feared that being a relationship would detract from that goal. Other women complained about relationships having a negative impact on schoolwork and how their boyfriends were unsupportive of their work ethic in college. Still other women talked about the jealousy and abuse that can take place in relationships. Abuse in college relationships is far more common than many people realize, with one study conducted by the Centers for Disease Control and Prevention reporting that 10% of students were hit or worse by their boyfriend or girlfriend in the last 12 months (see Myth 22 on violence in intimate relationships). Qualitative interviews with women in college who experienced abuse revealed that such abuse had profound consequences for their academic performance, their social and familial relationships, as well as their careers. To quote Armstrong, Hamilton, and England (Armstrong et al., 2010, p. 26): "The costs of bad hook-ups tend to be less than the costs of bad relationships: bad hook-ups are isolated events, but bad relationships wreak havoc with whole lives."

Given the costs of relationships to women in college, it's easier to understand why it doesn't seem to be the case that men are the only ones pressing for a culture of casual sex in college. In addition, there are now significantly more women in college than men, and that means that there are also women who wanted to have a relationship in college, but who haven't done so. Some of these women talked about adapting to this reality and thinking that if they aren't going to have a relationship in college, at least they can have some fun. After all, whereas hook-up sex is not as good as relationship sex, 50% of women said they enjoyed the sexual aspects of their most recent hook-up "very much." That number jumped to 59% if their most recent hook-up involved intercourse (Armstrong et al., 2012).

Conclusion

In the end, the change in the norms of sexual activity among college students has been significant in terms of a greater willingness to have casual sex and at least some of this change seems to be the result of women initiating hook-ups. This shift appears to be a consequence of the cost of relationships to young women, both in terms of time and risk. Therefore, a portion of college women have decided that the benefits of hooking up are preferable to the alternatives (despite the fact that sex in relationships is more pleasurable for women than sex in hook-ups). Nevertheless, it's important to remember that for all of the media attention that the hook-up culture has received, nearly one-third of college seniors have never hooked up, and 40% report either never having had intercourse or only having had one partner.

Myth #3 All marriages have been consummated

For a marriage to be considered legitimate by many faith and cultural traditions, it must be consecrated by an official in a public ceremony and consummated through sexual intercourse. For example, a marriage may be annulled by the Pope if the marriage is *ratum et non consummatum* (Code of Canon Law, n.d.) and can be voided by many governments if it's not consummated (e.g., in the United Kingdom; Matrimonial Causes Act, 1973). As you can imagine, there's often a deep sense of shame, anxiety, and alienation for couples who haven't consummated their marriage. Thus, it's difficult to estimate how many couples haven't consummated their marriages, but it's believed that approximately 1.5% of marriages aren't consummated within a year of the wedding and 0.75% of marriages remain unconsummated for the remainder of the marriage (B. W. McCarthy & McCarthy, 2003).

Of course, the idea of a marriage not being consummated is not new. Mary Shelley's *Frankenstein* (1831) describes one of the briefest fictional marriages that wasn't consummated. Victor and Elizabeth are unable to consummate their marriage because the monster apparently rapes and definitely murders Elizabeth on their wedding night honeymoon in the Alps. In *Middlemarch* (1872), George Eliot captured the sadness, frustration, and anger that can occur when the hopeful expectations of a Roman honeymoon are met with the disappointment of being in a sexless marriage. In the novel, Eliot describes the bride, Dorothea, alone in Rome trying to understand what this means for her marriage and her life:

> However, Dorothea was crying, and if she had been required to state the cause, she could only have done so in some such general words as I have already used: to have been driven to be more particular would have been like trying to give a history of the lights and shadows; for that new real future which was replacing the imaginary drew its material from the endless minutiae by which her view of Mr [sic] Casaubon and her wifely relation, now that she was married to him, was gradually changing with the secret motion of a watch-hand from what it had been in her maiden dream. (p. 144)

We'll not dwell on the fact that a visitor who interrupted her crying would become her next husband.

In real life, George Eliot was no stranger to the unconsummated marriage. At the age of 60, she married John Cross, who was 20 years her junior. The story goes that when it came time to consummate their marriage, while honeymooning in Venice, the groom leaped from their hotel room into a canal rather than have sex with his bride. The story that he preferred to jump into a canal (and asked the passing gondoliers not save him from drowning) because he wasn't up to the sexual demands Eliot placed on him makes for a better – if apocryphal – story than that he was suffering from depression. We may never know his real reasons for jumping off their balcony. In any case, scholars seem to agree that their marriage remained unconsummated for the entirety of their six-month marriage, which ended with Eliot's death (Maddox, 2009).

Setting aside the infamous leap into the canal, the prize for most famous unconsummated marriage goes to John Ruskin and Effie Gray, who were married on April 10, 1848. Following their wedding, they went to honeymoon in the Scottish Highlands. As Gray noted in a letter to her father, "I had never been told of the duties of married persons to each other and knew little or nothing about their relations in the closest union on earth" (James, 1947, p. 220). However, as Helena Michie (2006) noted, it was one thing for a lady of this time to be ignorant of the mechanics of sex, but Ruskin was more worldly. So, what caused him to refuse to consummate their marriage? As it happens, there's a surprisingly large literature on their marriage and the reasons Ruskin gave Gray for not consummating it. These included, the fact that, as an art critic, Ruskin was used to the idealization of women's bodies, including most representations of nude women having no pubic hair (this could also be said of representations of women's bodies today, e.g., Schick, Rima, & Calabrese, 2011). Gray described Ruskin's reaction to her body on their wedding night in the same letter to her father:

> For days John talked about this relation to me but avowed no intention of making me his Wife [by consummating their marriage]. He alleged various reasons, hatred to children, religious reasons, a desire to preserve my beauty, and finally this last year told me the true reason (and to me this is as villainous as all the rest) that he had imagined women were quite different to what he saw I was, and that the reason he did not make me his Wife was because he was disgusted with my person [on our wedding night].

Scholars have debated the six-year marriage between Ruskin and Gray that ended in divorce in 1854. Some have argued that he was put off by her pubic hair and other features of sexual maturity that were inconsistent with the perfect and pubescent forms that Ruskin studied in his scholarship of fine art, while others felt he simply didn't want to have children (Lutyens, 1972). While it's tempting to spend more time understanding the reasons why a couple in Victorian times might have an unconsummated marriage (for a detailed account of the Ruskin–Gray honeymoon as well as that of another Victorian couple, see Michie, 2006), let's move on to the present.

Reasons for unconsummated marriages

As with Victorian times, there are still marriages that remain unconsummated. One of the earliest studies I could find on the reasons for unconsummated marriages was from a book with a title that reflected a focus on finding fault with wives rather than husbands: *Virgin Wives: A Study of Unconsummated Marriages* (Friedman, 1962). Two years later, another study with almost the same name (Blazer, 1964) was conducted in which 1,000 married women who reported being virgins (corroborated by a gynecological exam and their husbands) and who were physically capable of vaginal intercourse were asked "Why are you still a virgin?" The most common answer was fear that intercourse would be painful (see Figure 3 for all of the answers displayed proportionally). The fear of pain during intercourse (known as *dyspareunia*) is consistently ranked as the primary reason for unconsummated marriages in other studies (C. Ellison, 1968), including in studies conducted in other cultures (Al Sughayir, 2004; Bayer & Shunaigat, 2001; Özdemir, Şimşek, Özkardeş, İncesu, & Karakoç, 2008). For many women this fear is based on their suffering from *vaginismus*, which is when vaginal penetration is painful or impossible. For some women, this occurs exclusively during sex, but other women can't insert tampons or have vaginal examination (for more on the diagnosis of vaginismus, see Reissing, Binik, Khalifé, Cohen, & Amsel, 2004). The good news is that there are empirically supported treatments for vaginismus and dyspareunia (e.g., Gindin & Resnicoff, 2002; Van Lankveld et al., 2006).

Although fear of vaginal pain is the primary reason cited for not consummating marriages, men aren't off the hook. Erectile dysfunction and premature ejaculation are also cited in nearly all of the studies of unconsummated marriages (e.g., Ribner & Rosenbaum, 2005). In fact, prior to the "married virgin" studies, one researcher in India concluded that problems with the men accounted for nearly all of the cases in which the

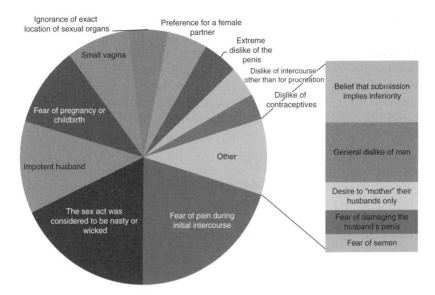

Figure 3 The reasons 1,000 wives stated for not consummating their marriage (adapted from Blazer, 1964, p. 214).

lack of sex was unintentional (Pillay, 1955). Again, here the news is good. There are effective treatments for both erectile dysfunction and premature ejaculation (Metz & McCarthy, 2003, 2004).

Although I have broken down the reasons for unconsummated marriages into female and male sexual problems, it's a fool's bargain to treat sexual problems in intimate relationships as either his problem or her problem. It's clear that the effective approaches to working with couples who haven't consummated their marriage is to treat it as an issue within the couple, not one partner or the other (B. W. McCarthy & McCarthy, 2003; Rosenbaum, 2009).

Finally, it's also worth noting that there are cultural and contextual influences at work here. Growing up in a culture that is strident in prohibiting premarital physical contact or even communication between genders appears to put people more at risk of being in an unconsummated marriage. Such cultures are also likely to reinforce perceptions of sex as dirty and sinful. Similarly, conservative cultures are less likely to have comprehensive sex education and more likely to have arranged marriages. People in conservative cultures also tend to marry at a younger age. All of these factors can produce spouses with little or no idea as to what to expect sexually from marriage. The anxiety and psychologically wrought experience of having sex with a spouse for the first time becomes all the more intense in situations when one or both of the partners lack the knowledge and experience to make sex an enjoyable experience. The problem can be even more intense for adolescent girls who end up in arranged marriages to older men. Worse still, there are some cultures that require some evidence that the marriage has been consummated (Bayer & Shunaigat, 2001). So the pressure on young brides and grooms in these cultures is enormous. In many conservative and religious cultures, a couple having difficulty consummating their marriage for more than a few weeks are encouraged to seek help from a member of the clergy, who may not have the expertise to deal with these issues. Thus, while not new, the problem of unconsummated marriages in conservative cultures has begun to receive more attention and been labeled a "crisis" by some (Al Sughayir, 2004; Özdemir et al., 2008; Ribner & Rosenbaum, 2005).

Conclusion

Although there are relatively few unconsummated marriages, there are more than most people realize. What are the factors that lead a minority of couples to fail to consummate their marriages? Couples who marry young, whose marriages were arranged, who had little or no contact prior to their wedding, who have genital pain or other physical impairments, who have little sexual knowledge, and whose communities require proof of consummation are more likely to delay consummation for weeks or permanently. The internal and external pressure of being in an unconsummated marriage can lead to anxiety, anger, and shame. This type of pressure is perhaps what prompted George Eliot's groom to leap from their honeymoon suite into a Venetian canal rather than consummating his new marriage with his famous wife.

Myth #4 — All marriages are sexually active

Marriages in which the couple's sex life has withered are much more common than unconsummated marriages (see the previous myth). Couples who have ceased being sexual altogether are referred to as being in "no-sex" intimate relationships, and couples who have sex once or twice a month at most are referred to as having a "low-sex" relationship. If this describes your relationship, you have a lot of company. It's estimated that there are more than 20 million marriages in the United States that meet the criteria of being no- or low-sex marriages. Yet one would not be able to tell this from the media. Just spend a little time watching television and you will see married couples being sexually active, no matter how "sexually repellent" the husband may be (Hollywood still rarely puts sexually repellent women on television; M. Feeney, 2005).

For some people, being in a no- or low-sex marriage isn't a problem – or at least not a problem that they feel needs to be addressed in a forthright manner. Consider the following account from a woman who responded to a questionnaire for the *Hite Report*:

> Having sex isn't very important to me for the most part. I lived with one man for most of seven and a half years; our sexual relationship was only active for about the first two and a half of those years. After that it dissolved almost completely – I don't think we fucked more than twice in the last year of it. During all that time I never had or actively desired an affair with another man (or woman), and the relationship with this one man was otherwise sufficiently satisfying and nourishing that I was able to imagine living with him for the rest of my life quite sexlessly. We were not unsensual – we did kiss and hug, and this physical contact was (I now understand) exceedingly important to me. I didn't relish the idea of no sex forever, but it seemed quite livable-with, given the importance of the rest of the relationship, to me. (Hite, 2004, p. 391)

I have heard many of my clients talk about their relationships in similar terms. Many of the couples who are seeing me for problems in their relationship will tell me that they want to work on other issues.

For other couples, experiencing a loss of intimacy and vitality because of the lack of sex or sexuality in relationship is of primary importance to them. They talk wistfully about their sex life when they were dating or before they had children. They use terms that evoke a longing to rekindle a fire that they fear is down to the last embers. Partners who are especially open and willing to be vulnerable will talk about the impact the decreasing intimacy is having on them. These partners use terms like "lonely," "hurt," and "unloved." Other partners speak in more angry terms, even threatening to have an affair or revealing that they have had some one-night-stands because of their frustration with the lack of sex in the relationship.

Working with problems of sexual desire is difficult because there are no easy answers and often those who turn to pills, potions, or lotions as a solution end up disappointed and more frustrated than before. My work with these couples is guided by the work of Barry McCarthy who developed a program for integrating sexual therapy into couples therapy (B. W. McCarthy, 2001). For those couples who seem ready to address the issue of desire directly, I recommend the book *Rekindling Desire: A Step-by-Step Program to Help Low-Sex and No-Sex Marriages* by McCarthy and his wife Emily McCarthy (2003). In their excellent book, they write about the four components of sexual functioning as being (1) desire, (2) arousal, (3) orgasm, and (4) satisfaction. While each of these components influences the others, all of them play a role in how couples can end up in a low- or no-sex relationship.

Desire

When thinking about sexual desire in a committed relationship, people often see a contradiction in the idea that one can maintain sexual desire for the same person over the course of a long relationship. George Bernard Shaw describes the vow of marriage as follows: "When two people are under the influence of the most violent, most insane, most delusive, and most transient of passions, they are required to swear that they will remain in that excited, abnormal, and exhausting condition continuously until death do them part" (Shaw, 1920, p. 25). While Shaw was writing about marriage more generally, his words can easily be applied to sexuality in marriage more specifically. In her book, *Mating in Captivity*, Esther Perel (2006) writes about the difficulty of maintaining sexual desire when a couple has deep affection for one another. As couples become more caring for each other, their love becomes safe, affectionate, and comfortable, or as Perel puts it, "like a flannel nightgown" (p. 32). Others have colorfully described sex in committed relationships as having the "flaccid safety of permanent coziness" (Goldner, 2004, p. 388), whereas in essence eroticism is about "otherness" and the need for distance to distinguish that your partner is someone "other" than you (de Beauvoir, 1953; see also Myth 20).

So, how can couples overcome this and keep the romance alive? The process begins by owning the problem. By the time many couples have arrived at the point where they want to work on the sexual desire in their relationship, there's usually been some blaming. It's not always spoken aloud. In fact, it's often difficult to talk about it. Most people would like to be seen as sexually alive, including by their partner. To talk openly about one's lack of desire or wanting to be more desirable puts one in a vulnerable position. It can also be difficult to talk about it out of fear of making matters worse or hurting the partner's feelings. Think of all of the one-liners about the fragile male ego or endless jokes about women being sensitive about their looks. These bits of comedy hit home because one's sexual self-image is as delicate as a Fabergé egg. Nevertheless, the blaming – even if it's self-blame – starts early for no- and low-sex couples. Barry and Emily McCarthy (2003) make the point that it's not his problem or her problem, but it's "our" problem. By this, they mean that even if the problem appears obvious, for example erectile dysfunction or vaginismus, it's still a problem for the couple to work on together. Framing the sexual issues in a relationship as a couple problem is likely to lead to a better understanding and prognosis.

To give an example of how this can work, I will describe a couple I treated. Andy and Erin were in their mid-sixties. Erin had been retired from her job as a hospital nurse for about a year. Andy still worked as a partner in a successful accounting firm. As always, I asked about their family (they were empty-nesters), their stresses outside the marriage (his job required long hours and lots of stress), and what initially attracted them to each other (they both seemed stable and caring). They didn't seem to be in serious distress, but they said they were arguing more. Erin was the more upset of the two, while Andy seemed shocked that, after nearly 40 good years of marriage, he found himself in my office. After successfully launching their children and seeing their parents through terminal illnesses, he thought things were now settling down, so why was Erin upset? After a few sessions discussing some seemingly minor incidents, Erin started talking about how much she missed "being intimate" with Andy.

"By intimate, you mean …" I asked, knowing the answer but wanting her to say it rather than me.

"I mean sex," she answered. "I go to bed while he's still watching TV – or more likely while he's sleeping in front of the TV – and I lay there thinking about when we used to have sex. I miss it." She started crying, paused, and continued softly. "I miss Andy."

Andy looked distraught and bewildered. He was clearly a loving husband, a good father, a pillar of his community who went to church and volunteered his time. Now he was realizing that he had been hurting his wife. Worse still, he was hurting her by relaxing in the evening after a long day of work. During the silence, he seemed to be working on how to understand it all. If he was angry or sad, those were secondary to a feeling of confusion and helplessness. Finally, as my gaze told him it was time for him to say something, the accountant in him reviewed the books:

"It has been a long time since we had sex." I could almost see him sifting through the ledger in his mind to see how he ended up in debt to his wife. "We really haven't had much of a sex life since the kids were born."

"I know," Erin said softly. "Let's change that."

Over the course of the session, we came to realize that Erin, having retired from her hospital job, discovered what it was like to not feel fatigued all the time. In the last year, she started sleeping normal hours; consequently, she regained her energy and, with it, her interests in new activities. She wanted one of those new activities to be sex with her husband. The problem was Andy was still working as hard as ever. They both felt he should be able to pull back at work, but it never seemed to happen. In addition, they had developed different sleep schedules over the years, so they had little time in bed together when they were both awake.

By looking at the problem from the perspective of it being "our" problem, not Andy's because he falls asleep watching TV and comes to bed after Erin is asleep and not Erin's because she was the one who changed, it became their issue to work on together. Happily for them, they were in good health and had no physiological challenges to overcome.

Arousal and orgasm

Although it was not the case with Andy and Erin, many couples experience problems with arousal and orgasm. As discussed in the previous myth, there are a variety of treatments for particular issues of arousal and orgasm that have demonstrated efficacy. Whether the treatments include working with a therapist, a medication and a therapist, or just a self-help book, they usually will involve tackling the issue as a team. In my experience, the couples who are the most successful are the ones able to approach sexual challenges with an open mind and a lot of humor. There is a lot that can be awkward in working on sexual problems with a partner. Accepting that and being ready to laugh and have fun with lowered expectations seems to be how couples are able to stick with programs to treat issues like erectile dysfunction, premature ejaculation, and vaginismus.

Satisfaction

Barry and Emily McCarthy (2003) talk about finding bridges to sexual desire. In the case of Andy and Erin, I learned that they had a standing date night on Saturday nights. They both enjoyed that time together. It was often the only night of the week that they went to bed at the same time. They used that as a bridge to include time in bed to reacquaint themselves with each other's bodies. I made a point of forbidding sexual touching. At this point they were to simply get used to the feeling of being together and attending to each other. While my motive was genuine, I had an alternative motive as well. I wanted to take the pressure off. Nothing ramps up performance anxiety like saying "OK, on Saturday at 10:35 p.m. you need to engage in coitus." Rather, I wanted there to be no pressure so I forbade sexual touching. It's not that having your therapist forbid sex turns you into Mr. and Mrs. Casanova, but it allows space to begin the process of feeling less awkward and having more fun. If the couple doesn't break the rules by having sex (they often do – making my job easier), I will work through the stages of change in McCarthy and McCarthy's book in an effort to improve their sexual satisfaction.

Erin and Andy's date nights started to include sex on a regular basis. This feeling of closeness permeated their relationship, which led to more shared interests and joint activities. They seemed to remember that they not only loved each other, but that they really liked each other too. Eventually, they were planning for Andy's retirement and discussing their shared goals. They both seemed hopeful and happy.

Conclusion

There is an adage that a good sex life can add 15–20% to relationship satisfaction and a bad sex life can detract 50–70% from relationship satisfaction (B. W. McCarthy & McCarthy, 2003). I've not found that to be quite true in my practice. Instead, I've found that sexual satisfaction and relationship satisfaction are moderately correlated (e.g., Sprecher & Cate, 2004, found a correlation of .45). A moderate correlation means that for some couples an unhappy sex life goes hand-in-hand with an unhappy marriage, but for other couples there may be dissatisfaction with their sex life while being generally happy in the relationship (I've also known couples who seemed deeply distressed and dysfunctional while enjoying an active and satisfying sex life). In any case, there are effective treatment options available to those who want to improve their sexual functioning.

Note

1 For a detailed description of the nuances of various terms used to describe sexual partners not in a committed relationship, see Shannon Claxton and Manfred van Dulmen's (2013) article titled "Casual Sexual Relationships and Experiences in Emerging Adulthood."

2 ATTRACTION AND COURTSHIP

Jennifer Aniston and David Beckham were recently named the "hottest" woman and man by the editors of *Men's Health* (2013) and *Marie Claire* (2014) magazines, respectively. Would you accept an invitation from one of them for a date or a romantic rendezvous? If the magazine editors are right, and you are unencumbered by a committed relationship, I suppose you would say yes (take a look at Figure 4 and think it over). After all, what could be more attractive than someone who is hot? It turns out attraction is a bit more complicated than physical beauty (although it's a major factor). For example, people place a very high premium on finding a partner who is honest and trustworthy (Anderson, 1968), but this still doesn't capture the complexity of how and with whom we fall in love. This chapter (and to a large degree the next one) is about myths involving attraction and falling in love.

Of all of the aspects of intimate relationships, the topics surrounding attraction and courtship are the ones in which my students are most interested. I expected college students' interest in this topic given their developmental stage, but I was surprised by the topic's pull across all audiences with whom I've discussed it, including retirees. It seems people of all ages and marital statuses are interested in how to attract and woo someone. Perhaps this is for the best. Even after decades of marriage, people still want to know that their partners are attracted to them.

There are three myths involving attraction and courtship. In the first myth, I discuss the benefits and detriments of being – as Sade put it – a smooth operator. I do my best in this myth to describe psychological principles that will give readers the best chance of getting with that special someone. In the second myth, I address a question I am asked

Great Myths of Intimate Relationships: Dating, Sex, and Marriage,
First Edition. Matthew D. Johnson.
© 2016 John Wiley & Sons, Inc. Published 2016 by John Wiley & Sons, Inc.

Figure 4 Would you turn down a date with Jennifer Aniston or David Beckham, who were recently named the "hottest" woman and man by the editors of *Men's Health* (2013) and *Marie Claire* (2014) magazines, respectively? © Corbis Images.

frequently: Do opposites attract? Third, I explore the extent to which people know what they want in a partner and whether what we say we want correlates with how we behave (a topic I will revisit in the online dating chapter). So, let's learn how to be a smooth operator.

Myth #5 Being smooth is the best way to pick someone up

"I couldn't help but notice that you look a lot like my next girlfriend." This is an example of an unsmooth pickup line from the movie *Hitch* (2005), which is about a relationship consultant who helps men woo women. The line is said by David Wike's character to Eva Mendes' character. It doesn't work. Then, Will Smith's character comes in to rescue her from the unsolicited interaction by using some smooth lines of his own. Of course, women are also able to be smooth, such as when Ingrid Bergman's character says to Humphrey Bogart's character in the movie *Casablanca* (1942): "Was that cannon fire, or is it my heart pounding?" So, the question behind this myth is whether being smooth – as Will Smith's character tries to teach hapless men, such as Kevin James' character, to be – is the best way to initiate an interaction with someone in whom you are interested. Alternatively, would a line like the one uttered by Russell Crowe's character to Jennifer Connelly's character in *A Beautiful Mind* (2001) be the better way to go? Here is his line: "I don't exactly know what I am required to say in order for you to have intercourse with me. But, could we assume that I said all that. I mean essentially we're talking about fluid exchange right? So, could we go just straight to the sex?" The answer to this question is almost always no, but this fact has not stopped people from looking for shortcuts.

Books on how to find and land a partner, whether it's for a few hours or for a lifetime, have spent many weeks on the best-seller list. For example, *The Rules: Time-Tested Secrets for Capturing the Heart of Mr. Right* (Fein & Schneider, 1995), which gave women advice about dating, sold over 2 million copies in 27 languages (Witchel, 2001). This was followed up by the best-selling *Rules of the Game* (Strauss, 2007), which did the same for men. The success of these and other books has led to an entire industry of seduction gurus and dating coaches (Swarns, 2012; Yuan, 2013) and even led to a VH1 television series called *The Pickup Artist*. The demand for advice on meeting and seducing others means that people want to know one thing: "What's the secret?" To answer this question, let's begin by simply reviewing the process of meeting potential mates.

Making the first move

As Russell Crowe's character figured out, certain steps cannot be skipped, meaning that he couldn't "go just straight to the sex." As with humans, animals must also follow certain steps if they are to reproduce. There are some steps that are nearly universal across animals and humans prior to intercourse. For all primates (our closest relatives in the animal kingdom), three behaviors are essential to making the first moves (Eibl-Eibesfeldt, 1979). The animal must do something to announce its presence to potential mates. The animal must make its sex evident. Finally, the animal must indicate its availability and willingness to have sex. Even well beyond primates, these are behaviors that are deemed essential to most animals. But, do they apply to humans?

David Givens (1978, 1983) set out to answer this question by examining humans in the places where they go to select mates (their natural habitat, if you will). He went to bars where people went to meet others. In the 1970s these were called singles bars, but – depending on your age – you might know them as dance halls, discotheques, or nightclubs. While observing humans in this habitat, Givens noticed the same three behaviors. Showing up was necessary. This point is so obvious, I will let the lyrics from the Tony-award-winning musical *Avenue Q* (2003) make the point:

> There is life outside your apartment.
> I know it's hard to conceive.
> But there's life outside your apartment.
> And you're only gonna see it if you leave.
>
> There is cool shit to do,
> But it can't come to you,
> And who knows, dude
> You might even score!

Beyond simply showing up, Givens noticed that people announced their presence by bumping into others or speaking loudly. In addition, he noticed that their behaviors seemed designed to emphasize their gender, meaning that the men acted more masculine and the women more feminine than in other settings. These two behaviors are, of course, necessary but not sufficient. The third step involves sending a signal that you are interested in a particular person.

It's generally thought that men make the first move and that women sit back and await their potential partners to offer themselves. However, there are many animal species in which females approach males for sexual purposes (for a review, see Wallen, 1995). As with animal models, women in singles bars tend to be the first to indicate their receptiveness to particular men (Cary, 1976; de Weerth & Kalma, 1995; Kendon, 1975; Kendon, Harris, & Key, 1975; McCormick & Jones, 1989; Perper & Weis, 1987). The term for the subtle behaviors that comprise women's first moves that indicate a willingness to be approached, for example briefly making eye contact, is *proceptivity* (Perper, 1989). Proceptivity allows a woman to initiate contact while maintaining plausible deniability and acting as if she's hard to get (see side box).

The problem with the subtle nature of proceptivity is that it can be misperceived or missed. For example, a partial smile from someone might mean that that person is open to being approached or that he or she is trying to hide a burp. On the receiving end, proceptive behaviors

Bonus myth: Women should play "hard to get"

Women are often told that they should "play hard to get" in order to be found more attractive to men and in order to find a more desirable man. So common is this advice that "Socrates, Ovid, Terence, the Kama Sutra, and Dear Abby all agree that the person whose affection is easily won is unlikely to inspire passion in another" (Walster, Walster, Piliavin, & Schmidt, 1973, p. 113). To determine whether this is good advice, let's go back to the first empirical article (that I could find) on this subject. Elaine Walster, G. William Walster, and Ellen Berscheid (1971) tested the effectiveness of playing hard to get in two studies with adolescents. In their studies, they paid high school students $2 each to rate the social desirability of two people. The participants saw a picture of both people and read a description of them. The key variable that was changed was that sometimes the description ended by describing one of the people as either very interested, very disinterested, or having unknown interest in the other person described (they provided no information about how the other person felt). Being good scientists, the experimenters included descriptions and pictures of both attractive and unattractive people so they could check their manipulations. If the advice to play hard to get was correct, the high school students should have rated the disinterested people as more socially desirable. However, in the first study, there was no statistically significant difference and, in the second study, the people who were interested in the other person were rated as more socially desirable. This is the opposite of the outcome that would occur if playing hard to get were good advice.

Following up this study, Elaine Walster, G. William Walster, Jane Piliavin, and Lynn Schmidt (1973) did five more experiments – this time with college students – that replicated the findings of the previous article. In each of these experiments, there was no support for the hypothesis that playing hard to get made someone more desirable. Happily, they didn't leave it alone at that point. They conducted a sixth experiment in which they manipulated how hard to get a woman was for the participant and how hard to get she was for other men. It turns out that women who were portrayed as easy for the participant to get but hard for other men to get were viewed as the most desirable. But, it gets better. Consider both the assets and liabilities of women who are generally hard to get and women who are easy to get. Men seemed to think the women who were easy for them and hard for others to get had all of the positive qualities of both generally hard-to-get and generally easy-to-get women, while none of the negative qualities.

Charlene L. Muehlenhard and Richard M. McFall (1981) took a slightly different approach. They asked 106 college men to think of four different women: one whom they wanted to date, one whom they liked as a person, one about whom they felt indifferent, and one whom they disliked. For each of these women, the men were asked what their reactions and behaviors would be if the woman did one of the following: directly asked him for a date, hinted about going out (e.g., telling him about a movie she wanted to see or letting him know that she had no weekend plans), or did nothing (in other words waited for him to ask her out). Almost all of what determined men's reactions was how they felt about her. So, there appeared to be no benefit to playing hard to get; in fact there was some cost because a sizable portion (30%) of the men indicated that, if a woman he was interested in did nothing, he would take that as a sign that she was not interested in him.

To summarize, it seems that there's a great deal of support for women *not* to play hard to get with a man in whom they are interested. However, they are wise to appear to be hard to get for other men. For an accounting of some of these benefits, see Jonason and Li (2013). Their data make it clear that there are benefits to women who appear to be hard to get. For example, they note that men will probably take them to a more expensive restaurant. In any case, ladies, there's no reason to play hard to get with a specific man you want to get!

can be missed completely or over-interpreted. In one study, only 36% of men and 18% of women accurately detected when someone was flirting with them (Hall, Xing, & Brooks, 2014). The sender versus receiver distinction is important because receivers tend to infer more specificity and rejection than senders mean to imply when it comes to nonverbal communication (Fichten, Tagalakis, Judd, Wright, & Amsel, 1992). Such is the nature of subtle communication, and the bad news is that these problems continue through courtship and marriage (see Myth 16: Good communication is the key to a happy relationship). This problem is compounded by a sex difference in which men tend to view interactions between men and women as having more sexual tension than women (Abbey & Melby, 1986; cf. Perilloux & Kurzban, 2014). Nevertheless, there are multiple studies that suggest that in heterosexual venues, men need quite a bit of encouragement before they risk approaching a woman. While being observed in singles bars, men tend to approach women only after repeated eye contact followed by smiling (Walsh & Hewitt, 1985; see also Perper, 1985). For a review of this line of research, see Moore (2010).

The challenge of initiating interaction

Once proceptivity has been perceived (or even if it has not been), someone has to make the first move to actually initiate conversation. Some have referred to these initial moves toward conversation as "opening gambits" (e.g., M. R. Cunningham, 1989). The use of the term "gambit" is telling because the word refers to move in chess in which one player offers a sacrifice of material (usually a pawn but sometimes a piece of greater value) to the opponent in the hope that the sacrifice of the piece will lead to a more advantageous position. As in singles bars, gambits in chess can either be accepted (meaning the opponent took the offered material) or declined (meaning the opponent didn't take the material). In chess, declining a gambit can either be done by offering a different gambit or by fortifying a defense. This imperfect analogy can be applied to opening lines between potential mates. If, for example, a man approaches a woman and offers to buy her a drink, she may accept with the knowledge that he may be looking to put himself in an advantageous position later. She may decline but offer to buy him one or invite him to sit down (offering her time and attention to him in a counter gambit). She may decline while turning to a friend, thereby strengthening her position that she's not interested and not alone. In any case, the opening gambit requires a willingness to sacrifice – time, money, or ego – in the hope that it pays off. As such, opening gambits require a certain amount of self-esteem or – barring that – a situation that precludes social risk (Cameron, Stinson, & Wood, 2013).

This is where the question of being "smooth" comes into play. While it's not clear that everyone would agree on the definition of "a smooth operator," most would agree that we're talking about someone who is suave. In other words, someone who makes the gambit seem natural.

However, this is still not specific enough for scientific study. It's easier to study variables when they are isolated, so, to examine this myth, I have broken the idea of a person being "smooth" into nonverbal and verbal components.

Nonverbal smoothness

How people walk, how they use touch, and how they use eye contact are all behaviors that contribute to their perceived attractiveness. In the movie *Hitch*, Will Smith's character spends a great deal of his time coaching Kevin James' character in the art of nonverbal behavior. For example, on kissing, he says "the secret is to go 90% of the way and hold," going on to indicate that she will come the last 10% of the way. So, does this sort of behavior matter? The data are mixed on the degree to which being nonverbally "smooth" matters. One way to be smooth is to subtly mimic the movements of the other person. This is called *behavioral synchrony*, and it's usually a behavior that two people who like each other and are having a pleasing interaction do without thinking about it (Crown, 1991; Grammer, 1990). These types of nonverbal behaviors go both ways as well. To understand the nonverbal behaviors that women use to express their interest in a particular man during initial conversations, researchers had college students watch video tapes of a man and a woman having a conversation in a public place and asked them about the likelihood of the woman accepting the man's invitation to go out based on her behavior. They were able to identify the following nonverbal behaviors that indicate interest in a man (Muehlenhard, Koralewski, Andrews, & Burdick, 1986, p. 413):

- Eye contact
- Smiling
- Leaning toward him
- Shoulders oriented toward him
- Being around 18 inches apart
- Touching while laughing
- Touching while not laughing
- Catching his eye while laughing at someone else's humor
- Attentiveness
  - She stops what she's doing.
  - She doesn't look around.
  - She doesn't look at other men.

- Avoiding public grooming
- Using animated speech

You will notice that I have listed some complex nonverbal behaviors. This is a lot to keep track of, and we've not even started thinking about what to actually say. Of course, most people do these things without consciously thinking about them. In fact, when we do start to think about them they can come off as awkward or forced. So, if someone can perform all of these nonverbal behaviors at the right time and in the proper proportion, we might call that person "a smooth operator" or simply "socially skilled."

Verbal smoothness

Michael Cunningham (1989) examined how different opening gambits work with members of the other sex (it's unclear whether his research will extend to opening lines on members of the same sex; see Myth 12: There are no differences between same-sex and heterosexual relationships). In a series of studies, he divided opening lines into three categories based on previous work examining preferences for opening lines (Kleinke, Meeker, & Staneski, 1986): direct, innocuous, and flippant (i.e., cute). In one of these experiments Cunningham went to three bars in suburban Chicago and had a White man of "medium attractiveness" (1989, p. 29) approach 63 different women using one of six lines. Four lines (two direct and two innocuous lines) were rated very highly in

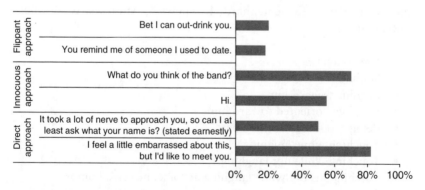

Figure 5 This graph shows the percent of women who reacted positively when a moderately attractive White man approached them in a Chicago bar and uttered the lines shown on the left side of the graph. The direct and innocuous lines appear to be the most effective (adapted from M. R. Cunningham, 1989, p. 29).

prior research by Kleinke and colleagues, and two were rated near the bottom (two flippant lines). The male experimenter was not told of the hypotheses and was instructed to deliver the lines earnestly. The women were selected at random (as long as they were not with a man and not deeply involved in conversation) and the line to be delivered was randomly assigned. The responses of the women were rated using both verbal and nonverbal cues (e.g., maintaining eye contact or looking away). The raters were 93% consistent in their positive versus negative ratings. The results? In the end, women reacted more positively to the direct and innocuous lines compared to the flippant lines. Specifically, each of the lines and the percent of women who reacted positively are shown in Figure 5.

Cunningham did another experiment with both men and women being approached (always by an experimenter of the other sex), with similar results for women. The men, however, reacted positively to essentially all of the approaches (this is called a ceiling effect), which made it difficult to draw very many conclusions other than that men aren't very discriminating when it comes to opening lines. Therefore, it seems that if your definition of smooth is one who uses flippant or cute lines, the smooth operators lose big time; however, if your definition of smooth is someone who uses direct or innocuous lines, then smooth men do well. Women it seems can use nearly any opening gambit on men.

Perhaps you are wondering if the most important part of being smooth might be neither what was said nor how it was said, but rather in wearing down the target of your desire. In other words, might it be the case that persistence is the key to being smooth. For example, is it possible to wear down someone to the point that they simply say yes? Using the same three categories of opening gambits, researchers set out to see if women's responses would change if they were mentally worn out. This is a concept that researchers call *ego-depletion*, meaning that self-regulation diminishes after an extended period of self-control (e.g., working when you would rather be playing) or mental work (e.g., decision-making or difficult mental tasks). So, in theory, maybe smooth operators can pick out the women who have worn out their self-control mechanism and move in – even with a flippant line that rarely works. Nope. It turns out that women are even less interested in flippant lines when they are ego-depleted, thus less likely to hide their contempt for such lines. There were no differences for direct or innocuous opening gambits (Lewandowski, Ciarocco, Pettenato, & Stephan, 2012).

Being smooth is not everything

Alright, so the data on being smooth are far from clear. Let's look at the question from another angle. Are there other factors that can improve your chances of winning the heart of that special someone who may or may not even know you exist? Here, I am happy to report, I have some good news even for the decidedly unsmooth. There are other effects that are more likely to influence the receptiveness of your potential sweetheart than how smooth you are during your opening gambit. Here are a few examples.

The mere exposure effect

We, as humans, tend to like what is familiar to us (Zajonc, 1968). For example, the more you hear a song played on the radio, the more you will like it. The more you use a certain type of product, the more you will like it. There are certainly exceptions, but this outcome is one of the fundamental findings of psychology. It has implications for many aspects of our lives and has been applied to a great many other areas of research from prejudice to memory (e.g., Bornstein & D'Agostino, 1994; Reber, Schwarz, & Winkielman, 2004; Westerman, 2008). The term for our liking of the familiar is the *mere exposure effect*, as in one merely has to be exposed to something more to elicit more positive feelings about it (for a review, see Garcia-Marques, Mackie, Claypool, & Garcia-Marques, 2013). As you can imagine, knowledge of this effect may also be applied to intimate relationships. I often tell my students that if they are interested in someone, they should start exposing themselves to that person more. Wait, that didn't come out right! I mean they should endeavor to be seen by them more. So, I tell my students that they might take the same classes or go to the cafeteria at the same time as their would-be lover. Simply running into the person more (i.e., exposing yourself more – with your clothes on) will increase the person's feelings of positive regard for you. When I mention this to students, they usually follow up with a question along the lines of "isn't that considered stalking?" Yes, if the person has indicated disinterest and you continue to show up, you are stalking. Aside from disrespecting the wishes and rights of this person to not be around you, it is likely that your attempts will become an annoyance. Furthermore, as we just learned, if the object of your desire is not interested in you, her or his exercise and depletion of self-control will reduce the likelihood of a positive response to your continued presence. In other words, there really is a line at which it becomes stalking and, therefore, irritating and counterproductive (and possibly illegal). And, this line can be found by believing and accepting another person's disinterest in your company.

The influence of proximity

One predictor of people we fall in love with is whether they are physically close to us. Part of this is likely related to the mere exposure effect, but logically it simply makes sense. You are more likely to fall for someone you know than someone you don't know, and you are more likely to know people who live and work near you (Festinger, Schachter, & Back, 1950). In other words, even if your perfect soulmate is out there, you probably won't end up together if she or he lives in a small village in Tibet while you live in suburban St. Louis. Of course, this is an extreme example, but the influence of proximity has been repeatedly demonstrated as an important predictor of who gets together (Ebbesen, Kjos, & Konecni, 1976). So, practically speaking, this means that it's less likely you will find a good match if you don't interact with other people.

The pratfall effect

Finally, there are data that suggest that the opposite of being smooth is attractive. In a clever demonstration of this, experimenters set up a fake trivia game show. The participants listened to fake audiotapes of people supposedly trying out for the show and rated how attracted they were to each of the contestants. The first contestant got most of the answers wrong and came off as uninteresting and unaccomplished, the second got most of the answers correct and came off as interesting and accomplished, the third was like the first (uninteresting, unaccomplished, and often wrong) but spilled a drink at the end, and the fourth was like the second (interesting, accomplished, and mostly correct) but also spilled a drink. Again, the question for the participants in the study was whom did they find most attractive? The winner was contestant four who was interesting, accomplished, and mostly correct, but who spilled a drink (Aronson, Willerman, & Floyd, 1966). This would be the opposite of smooth. So, it would seem that the most attractive person would be the one who has a lot of positive features, but who is decidedly not smooth. In other words, people tend to be attracted to near perfection rather than perfection. Being clumsy or prone to pratfalls is an easily dismissed – or even desired – imperfection.

Conclusion

In the end, people probably have different definitions of smooth. However, a few things seem clear. In order to meet the right person, one has to go out at some point and make it somewhat clear that one is available. When it comes to initiating conversation, having social skills is a good thing (notice the word skills – meaning these can be learned, practiced, and improved). In addition, being direct or innocuous is much better than being cute or flippant (at least for men trying to meet women). Finally, putting too much effort on being smooth may come off as inauthentic and – worse still – may mean that you're concealing an adorable clumsiness.

Myth #6

Opposites attract

One of the questions I am asked most often – regardless of whether the audience consists of college students, middle-aged adults, or older adults – is whether opposites attract. The assumption that opposites attract is so deeply ingrained in our understanding of relationships that the vast majority (85.7%) of people who are actively seeking a partner claim to be looking for someone with opposite traits (Dijkstra & Barelds, 2008). Couples in long-term relationships are even more convinced that opposites attract because it's easy to see contrasts. When two people are in a relationship for a long period of time their differences will stand out more than their similarities. Similarly, if you think about your friends who are in relationships, the differences jump out at you. In marital therapy, I spend a great deal of time helping couples work through "their differences," not their similarities. I am not the first counselor to have noticed this, and some have centered their work with couples on the assumption that opposites attract (e.g., Baron, 2011; Hendrix, 2004; LaHaye, 1998; Mayhall & Mayhall, 1990). So, clearly most people believe that opposites attract, but do they really?

Relationship scientists refer to this as a question of *homogamy* versus *heterogamy*. Do people tend to select spouses who are similar to themselves (homogamy) or do they tend to select spouses who are different from themselves (heterogamy)?[1] Not surprisingly, this is one of the oldest questions to be addressed by relationship science. The clear winner between homogamy versus heterogamy – by a country mile — is homogamy. There's consistent support that birds of a feather flock together, not that opposites attract. In this myth, I will review the support for homogamy, the lack of support for heterogamy, and discuss why this myth is so persistent.

Support for homogamy

One of the first to address the question of whether similarity leads to attraction was Theodore Newcomb (1956), at the University of Michigan. He rented a house near campus and had 17 men (this was long before men and women shared college housing) who were transferring to the university that semester stay in the house for free as long as they agreed to spend four to five hours a week answering questionnaires. They were all strangers from different cities, and they all arrived within 24 hours. They were able to care for the house and themselves as they wished (within the rules of the University of Michigan at the time). Across two cohorts over two years, Newcomb found that the more individual pairs of men were similar, the higher they rated their liking of each other. The effect was strong enough for Newcomb to end his article by exclaiming "Vive la similarité!" (p. 586). Since then, loads of data have been collected to support the theory that similarity leads to attraction. In fact, in their meta-analysis (a study of multiple studies of a specific research questions) of 240 laboratory studies of the effect of similarity on attraction, Matthew Montoya and Robert Horton (2013) spend little time on the overall strength of the association between similarity and attraction, which is $r = .59$ ($r = .49$ for male–female pairs), opting instead to examine competing theories about the mechanisms that drive the association. In addition, the effect appears to be cross-cultural, perhaps even stronger in Eastern cultures (Chen, Luo, Yue, Xu, & Zhaoyang, 2009). So, similarity clearly leads to increased attraction, but does it predict improved relationship outcomes?

Similarity as a predictor of relationship quality
Whether similarity between spouses predicts better relationships is more difficult to determine. Let's start with an example based on personality. Consider two people, both of whom always seem to be unhappy. They meet and fall in love. Both of them are what we would consider neurotic or, in other words, high in negative affectivity. This means that even when things are going well, they are anxious or

depressed and they let everyone know by wearing the emotional distress on their metaphorical sleeves. People with this type of trait – think of Woody Allen as an archetype – tend to have worse relationships than other people (here again, think of Woody Allen as an archetype). This finding is very clear in the literature (e.g., Beach & Fincham, 1994; Davila, Karney, Hall, & Bradbury, 2003; Karney & Bradbury, 1997; Pasch, Bradbury, & Davila, 1997). So, would it be better if, instead of one person in a couple being neurotic, both people were neurotic? It's hard to imagine the answer to this question being yes. Indeed, the answer is no (Whisman, Uebelacker, & Weinstock, 2004). In fact, when it comes to similarity of personality, the type of personality partners have is far more important than their match (Dyrenforth, Kashy, Donnellan, & Lucas, 2010; Montoya, Horton, & Kirchner, 2008).

If matching on personality is not predictive of better relationships, what about matching on variables other than personality? When it comes to similarity in other domains, the findings are more promising but still mixed. As I have noted, there's a strong empirical case to be made for people being attracted to others who are similar to them, and this is true as well for variables other than personality, like attitudes and values (see Montoya et al., 2008) There's also consistent evidence that married couples tend to have shared attitudes and values (e.g., D'Onofrio, Eaves, Murrelle, Maes, & Spilka, 1999; Nagoshi, Johnson, & Honbo, 1992). Nevertheless, there's less consistent support for the notion that these similarities are associated with higher levels of marital satisfaction. Indeed, there are studies that describe there being no association (e.g., D. Watson et al., 2004); studies that describe an association for one partner but not the other, husbands but not wives (Houts, Robins, & Huston, 1996); studies in which the association was there for similarities in some domains but not others (again, only for husbands; Gaunt, 2006); and one study of Chinese couples in which similarities in values were associated with marital satisfaction (Luo et al., 2008). In thinking about more specific attitudes and values, there are studies that demonstrate that the couples who have similar views regarding traditional gender roles within families – for example, which parent is mostly responsible for child care and which is mostly responsible for earning income – have more satisfying relationships (Houts et al., 1996; Lye & Biblarz, 1993; Overall, Sibley, & Tan, 2011). Unfortunately, there's no easy and clear answer to the question of whether similarities between partners predict better relationship outcomes.

It certainly is clear that similarity is associated with attraction and that couples tend to be similar across multiple domains (sometimes called *assortative mating*), but whether being similar leads to better relationships is not at all clear. Nevertheless, the myth is "opposites attract." Sticking to the question of whether similarities attract, the answer is clearly *yes*! But, that doesn't necessarily mean that opposites don't attract because both could be true. So, let's examine those studies.

Lack of support for heterogamy

Often when people say idea that opposites attract they are referring to complementarity – or the idea that people seek out partners who seem to have traits that they lack. In this way, they will be especially compatible. For example, in my practice, I often have couples in which one of the spouses is known as the outgoing and jocular spouse and the other is thought of as the shy and serious spouse. It's easy to see how an outgoing and jocular woman would benefit from searching out a shy and serious man and vice versa. Indeed, their friends and relatives may have been rooting for such a pairing. The question before us is whether this is actually what happens. In other words, do people seek out complementary partners? In still other words, is there support for heterogamy?

No. There's essentially no evidence that differences lead to greater attraction or improved relationship outcomes. For example, Eva Klohnen and Shanhong Luo (2003) examined what led to greater attraction when a potential mate was similar to the research subject versus similar to the research subject's ideal self, versus someone who would complement the research subject. They found support for both types of similarity, but none for complementarity. This is similar to other findings as well (Klohnen & Mendelsohn, 1998; Markey & Markey, 2007; Till & Freedman, 1978). For example (as discussed by Finkel, Eastwick, Karney, Reis, & Sprecher, 2012), introverts are no more attracted to extraverts than to others (Hendrick & Brown, 1971).

OK, OK, so people who are dissimilar are not attracted to each other, but aren't they more likely to have successful relationships? No. As reviewed by Finkel and colleagues (2012), relationship satisfaction is not associated with complementary interests (Houts et al., 1996), attitudes (Aube & Koestner, 1995), or spending behaviors (Rick, Small, & Finkel, 2011). Indeed, there are no reviews of the literature that conclude that complementarity leads to better relationship outcomes (e.g., S. G. White & Hatcher, 1984). This is even true when we think of sex roles. In other words, if a very masculine man and a very feminine woman marry would they have a better relationship? No. The best case is when both partners are feminine (Antill, 1983). For a longer discussion of this finding, see Myth 21: Men are from Mars, Women are from Venus. To summarize, opposites don't attract, and to the extent that opposites find themselves in intimate relationships, there's no evidence that they do better than people who are similar.

Thoughts on why the myth of heterogamy persists

Despite the overwhelming evidence for homogamy and against heterogamy, this myth is incredibly resilient (there's even a self-help book based on this myth; Baron, 2011). So, why – in the face of all of the contrary evidence – is the myth of heterogamy so entrenched in our understanding of relationships? There are probably a few factors at work here. As I have noted before, contrasts tend to stand out. So, even if you match a couple on many dimensions, they and others will likely notice the areas in which they are different.

Beyond that, there's evidence that spouses will begin to complement each other over time, even when they start out as quite similar (Levinger, 1986). Neil Jacobson and Andrew Christensen (1996) describe how it makes sense for two people to move into roles that are complementary through a system of conditioning (i.e., rewarding and punishing experiences). For example, if one member of a couple is slightly more dominant than the other, the couple may settle into a pattern in which that person becomes much more dominant because competing for dominance leads to conflict (a punishing experience), and acquiescing to these roles leads to an end to the conflict (when something unpleasant ends, the behavior that preceded it is considered to have been *negatively reinforced* – meaning the cessation of a noxious stimulus). Indeed, the experience of new couples growing more complementary has been demonstrated empirically (e.g., Dryer & Horowitz, 1997; Markey, Lowmaster, & Eichler, 2010). In addition, established couples are more likely to display complementary behavior when they are placed in a laboratory situation that is meant to evoke competition between the two of them (Beach, Whitaker, Jones, & Tesser, 2001). Of course, as Jacobson and Christensen are quick to point out, developing complementary roles within a marriage can also lead to conflict. In fact, one of the main themes of their treatment for marital discord addresses the issue of problems associated with the development of complementarity within intimate relationships (see Myth 23: Marital therapy doesn't work).

Conclusion

In summary, partner differences are small compared to partner similarities. To the extent that couples experience complementarity, it appears to develop over time. Thus, the notion that opposites attract is not supported by the research literature. Rather, similarity is attractive and – in some aspects – satisfying.

Myth #7

People know what they want in a partner

One of the most fundamental aspects of intimate relationships is the ability to decide and describe what you do and don't want in a partner. From an early age children talk about their ideal partners and in doing so are describing the characteristics that they seek in their future spouses. Adults do much the same. Most are able to describe what they are looking for in a partner (and they rate the importance of these characteristics very highly; e.g., Stewart, Stinnett, & Rosenfeld, 2000). For example, Frank Sinatra is widely quoted as saying "I like intelligent women. When you go out, it shouldn't be a staring contest." In another example, Anaïs Nin is quoted as saying "I, with a deeper instinct, choose a man who compels my strength, who makes enormous demands on me, who doesn't doubt my courage or my toughness, who doesn't believe me naive or innocent, who has the courage to treat me like a woman." While few of us are as eloquent as Ms. Nin, the question remains whether we actually know what qualities in a potential intimate partner will lead to a satisfying and fulfilling relationship.

What do people say they want in a partner?

Before we discuss whether people know what is best for them in a relationship partner, let's first look at what people actually want. The sociologist Reuben Hill was the first person to systematically ask young adults what they preferred in a mate. He conducted a study that found that women and men tended to emphasize similar traits, with dependability, emotional stability, personality, health, and desire for children near the top. There were only a few differences between men and women, with ambitiousness and having good financial prospects being more important to women, and physical attractiveness and cooking ability being more important to men (R. Hill, 1945).

David Buss (1989) surveyed 10,047 participants in 37 different cultures and found similar results: men valued physical attractiveness more than women, and women valued potential income and wealth more than men. Buss and colleagues followed this study with one that looked at the changes in stated mate preferences in various regions in North America over the span of 57 years. Specifically, they examined sizable data sets from 1939 ($N = 628$), 1956 ($N = 120$), 1967 ($N = 566$), 1977 ($N = 316$), 1984/1985 ($N = 1,496$), and 1996 ($N = 607$) that were collected at various locations. They found that the preferred characteristics were evolving over time, such that the gender differences were diminishing. The importance of both physical attractiveness and financial potential increased substantially for both men and women. In particular, the importance placed on financial potential increased dramatically over time for men, more so than women's increases. Thus, it seems that the two values with the biggest gender differences in the first half of the 20th century moved up in importance for both genders. Of the values that dropped over time, the biggest drops were for chastity, which dropped six ranks for men and seven for women; domestic skills (e.g., cooking and housekeeping), which dropped six ranks for men only; ambition, which dropped four ranks for women only; and refinement/neatness, which dropped four ranks for both genders. In contrast, the value of the following attributes increased over time: as mentioned above, financial prospects increased significantly for men (four ranks); physical attractiveness, which moved up in the rankings six slots for men and four for women; education/intelligence, which moved up six slots for men and four slots for women; sociability, which moved up five slots for men and three slots for women; mutual attraction/love, which moved up four slots for women and three for men; and similar educational background, which moved up three slots for men only. In terms of geographical differences, there were only a few minor disparities. For example Texans appear to value chastity more than respondents from other parts of the country. Nevertheless, regional effects were quite small and most regions were very similar. In the end, the overall picture was of the two genders coming closer and closer to a shared perspective on the ideal mate. For a rank order of the mate preferences, as adapted from Buss and colleague's article, see Table 1 (Buss, Shackelford, Kirkpatrick, & Larsen, 2001).

Table I Rank ordering of values sought in a mate in 1939 and 1996, by participant gender

	Women		Men	
Rank	1939	1996	1939	1996
1	Emotional stability, maturity	Mutual attraction love	Dependable character	Mutual attraction love
2	Dependable character	Dependable character	Emotional stability, maturity	Dependable character
3	Ambition, industriousness	Emotional stability, maturity	Pleasing disposition	Emotional stability, maturity
4	Pleasing disposition	Pleasing disposition	Mutual attraction love	Pleasing disposition
5	Mutual attraction love	Education, intelligence	Good health	Education, intelligence
6	Good health	Desire for home, children	Desire for home, children	Good health
7	Desire for home, children	Ambition, industriousness	Refinement, neatness	Sociability
8	Refinement, neatness	Sociability	Good cook, housekeeper	Good looks
9	Education, intelligence	Good health	Ambition, industriousness	Desire for home, children
10	Chastity	Similar education background	Chastity	Ambition, industriousness
11	Sociability	Good financial prospect	Education, intelligence	Refinement, neatness
12	Similar education background	Refinement, neatness	Sociability	Similar education background
13	Good financial prospect	Good looks	Similar religious background	Good financial prospect
14	Similar religious background	Similar religious background	Good looks	Good cook, housekeeper
15	Favorable social status	Favorable social status	Similar education background	Similar religious background
16	Good cook, housekeeper	Good cook, housekeeper	Favorable social status	Chastity
17	Good looks	Chastity	Good financial prospect	Favorable social status
18	Similar political background	Similar political background	Similar political background	Similar political background

Note. Ns = 628 & 607 for 1939 and 1996, respectively. These data are based on Table 6 of Buss et al. (2001) and Todd K. Shackelford (personal communication, July 27, 2013).

Beyond the research by Buss and colleagues (2001), other studies have offered similar data and trends. For example, these findings have been extended temporally with more recent data (Henry, Helm, & Cruz, 2013), extended to younger populations (Regan & Joshi, 2003), and to other cultures (Saroja & Surendra, 1991). Some of the findings on preferences for good financial prospects have been explored in greater detail to see what is behind this preference in both genders (Jonason, Li, & Madson, 2012). In much of this work two themes have been emphasized – gender differences and evolutionary explanations, which have been a source of some debate in the field, with some scientists arguing that both the gender differences and the evolutionary explanations have been overemphasized (Eastwick & Finkel, 2008a). Let's save this controversy for another myth (see Myth 21: Men are from Mars, Women are from Venus) and examine whether people's stated preferences actually line up with their behavior and satisfaction within their relationships.

Comparing stated preferences with implicit preferences

One of the best ways to tell whether a person's stated preferences match up with his or her actions is by looking at what people do in speed-dating situations. In a series of experiments, Paul Eastwick and Eli Finkel used speed-dating events to address a series of questions (for a description of their methods, see Eastwick & Finkel, 2008b; Finkel, Eastwick, & Matthews, 2007), including whether people's stated preferences match the preferences they demonstrate when they are in front of a real person. In speed-dating, people are paired up with another person for very short "dates" that last just a few minutes. At the end of that time, they have to decide whether or not they would be interested in meeting with that person again. It's a *forced-choice decision* because everyone must either say yes or no to the question. In their studies, they found that income did *not* make either gender more desirable to the other (all of their studies were at heterosexual speed-dating events). In addition, the gender difference for physical attraction seemed to vanish (Eastwick & Finkel, 2008a; Finkel & Eastwick, 2008; see also Kurzban & Weeden, 2005; cf. Fisman, Iyengar, Kamenica, & Simonson, 2006). In other words, there was quite a disconnect between what speed-daters were saying they preferred and what they actually preferred. Indeed, in one study, the correlations between speed-daters' stated preferences and their actual "yes" or "no" answer to the question of whether they wanted to spend more time with their dates ranged from zero to tiny (Iyengar, Simonson, Fisman, & Mogilner, 2005). These differences between stated preferences and exhibited preferences have been demonstrated across studies and paradigms (Feingold, 1990). The lack of gender differences in the associations between whether people wanted another date and the attractiveness as well as the earning potential of prospective partners has been replicated repeatedly, as has the lack of a correlation between stated partner preferences and actual partner preferences (e.g., Eastwick & Finkel, 2008a). In other words, what people say they want in an intimate partner is nearly worthless in predicting their actual preferences.

There are a few potential explanations for why we're so poor at gauging what we really want in a partner. The most likely explanation is that there are some aspects of how we think and feel that we simply cannot articulate. At best, we come up with an explanation for our behavior or decisions that is simply based on a guess or some theory that we've held for a long time. For example, if you find yourself attracted to someone and you ask yourself why, you might fall back on something like, "He reminds me of my friend from high school, which must be why I like him." Or, you might even fall back on a rudimentary belief, like "men prefer blondes." Either way, it's unlikely that you are capturing the complex nature of the cognitive and emotional processes at work. One of the most famous articles in psychology got at exactly this point. Nisbett and Wilson's (1977) seminal article explored how poorly we're able to report on our own mental processes. Based on this theory, Eastwick, Finkel and colleagues explored some of the ways in which the cognitive processes that are difficult to identify are at work when we make judgments about potential mates and why they seem to be so mismatched with our stated preferences. They are interesting and fun articles to read and – as always – I encourage you to read them and see what you think (Eastwick, Eagly, Finkel, & Johnson, 2011; Eastwick, Finkel, & Eagly, 2011; Reis, Maniaci, Caprariello, Eastwick, & Finkel, 2011).

Conclusion

We're not very good at predicting to whom we will actually be attracted. As I discuss in the next chapter, this is one of the downsides of online dating.

Note

1   The definitions I use here are distinct from the definitions proposed by Philip Cohen (2011), who suggested that "homogamy" should refer to same-sex marriage and "heterogamy" to opposite-sex marriage.

3 ONLINE DATING

The traditional off-line process of finding a suitable mate is inefficient and fraught with problems. This fact led Dan Ariely, a behavioral economist, to write that the process of finding a mate has been "one of the most egregious market failures in Western society" (Ariely, 2010, p. 215; for a discussion of the market metaphor for online dating, see Heino, Ellison, & Gibbs, 2010). Therefore, it's no surprise that online dating services are quickly becoming the most common way of meeting potential mates. About one-third of couples who got married between 2005 and 2012 met each other online, and 45% of those who met online used an online dating service (Cacioppo, Cacioppo, Gonzaga, Ogburn, & VanderWeele, 2013). The question of whether this trend is good or bad for relationships and the people using these sites is the subject of the three myths in this chapter.

Before getting into the myths of online dating, let's discuss what we know. First, married couples who met on- and off-line have similar levels of marital satisfaction and rates of divorce (with couples who met online having slightly higher marital satisfaction; Cacioppo et al., 2013). Thus, there is some evidence that there may be little impact of moving from off- to online dating. Second, off-line (analog?) dating is still the norm for college-age adults, who seem to eschew online dating. This reversal in the normally negative correlation between age and comfort in adopting new technology is a bit puzzling, but may have to do with the large number of potential mates in college. Third, people don't always tell the truth when they are online (shocking, I know). Online, women tend to be younger and lighter than they are in reality, and, online, men tend to be taller and wealthier than they are in reality (Ariely, 2010; Caspi & Gorsky, 2006). More serious deceptions have garnered attention in the media. For example, the documentary film titled *Catfish*

Great Myths of Intimate Relationships: Dating, Sex, and Marriage,
First Edition. Matthew D. Johnson.
© 2016 John Wiley & Sons, Inc. Published 2016 by John Wiley & Sons, Inc.

(Joost & Schulman, 2010; see also the subsequent eponymous MTV reality show, Dauw & Maroney, 2012) exposed an elaborate misrepresentation in one person's online dating experience. The question before us, however, is whether there are myths about online dating.

Specifically, there are aspects of online dating that many think of as beneficial that turn out to be detrimental. In their thorough review of the claims of online dating services, Eli Finkel, Paul Eastwick, Benjamin Karney, Harry Reis, and Susan Sprechter categorized the companies' proclaimed benefits as providing superior "access, communication, and matching" (2012, p. 3). Each of these claims is associated with a myth about online dating, which I address in order.

Myth #8 Having access to innumerable online profiles of potential partners increases the likelihood of finding Mr. or Ms. Right

One of the most frequent complaints one hears from single men and women is about their lack of access to potential partners. Watch nearly any episode of television shows like *Girls* or *Louie* and one can see the pervasiveness of this issue among singles. The lack of access to potential partners has been discussed by social scientists in the general context of the American decline in community-centered activities (e.g., Putnam, 2000) and in more specific contexts, such as the increased rates of incarceration and mortality of African American men (e.g., W. J. Wilson, 2009). So, it's easy to see the appeal of drastically increasing one's dating pool by using an online dating service. Or, as a friend once put it to me, "I don't go to church and I don't like going to bars, so I went online." It's also easy to understand that many would assume that having access to more potential partners should increase the likelihood of finding the right person. In their critique of online dating services, Finkel et al. (2012) describe three problems that come with the larger pool of prospective partners provided by online dating services.

People cannot use the information in online profiles to determine whether particular individuals will be a good match

With most online dating services, the first encounter one has with a potential mate is through an online profile, as opposed to conventional off-line ways of meeting people, which are typically face-to-face. To determine whether a person is a good match, clients of these services review the profiles looking for the qualities they deem important (some companies offer matching services, which I will discuss in Myth 10). Notice that the underlying assumptions here are that people can predict which qualities described in a profile are appealing and which qualities will make someone a compatible partner (see Myths 6 and 7).

The first assumption is straightforward and correct. There's a rich empirical literature that supports the notion that humans are quite good at assessing the qualities of an individual from a relatively brief exposure, even online. In one study, participants were shown pictures of other people's faces and asked to rate them for trustworthiness. In addition, the activity in the part of the brain known to be associated with emotion, the amygdala, was measured using functional magnetic resonance imaging (FMRI) as they viewed each face. Importantly, the activity in the amygdala had a stronger association with the consensus ratings of trustworthiness for each face than the participant's own rating (Engell, Haxby, & Todorov, 2007). This and other research (e.g., Rule & Ambady, 2010) clearly demonstrate that humans are capable of quickly discerning who is more and less appealing from brief exposures to relatively small amounts of data, such as online profiles.

That we're good at making judgments with "thin slices" of data turns out to be good and bad news. The good news is that, because people tend to be good at this, it decreases the likelihood of going out with a murderer (cf. Grossman, 2013). As Finkel et al. (2012) point out, the bad news is that, because most people are good at this, people with appealing profiles tend to be inundated with requests for contact. This problem is well known in the industry and has been described in the popular press. For example, one of the founders of OK Cupid, Christian Rudder, was quoted in *The New Yorker* describing how the problem is unique to online dating as follows:

> In a bar, it's self-correcting. You see ten guys standing around one woman, maybe you don't walk over and try to introduce yourself. Online, people have no idea how "surrounded" a person is. And that creates a shitty situation. Dudes don't get messages back. Some women get overwhelmed. (Paumgarten, 2011, p. 43)

Rudder is describing, albeit in colorful language, the problem that suitors are unable to determine whether to invest time and effort in pursuing someone online based on their competition. This is the downside of people being accurate assessors of profiles, which was the first assumption underlying the benefit of increasing the pool of potential mates.

The second assumption was that people understand which qualities will make someone a compatible partner. As with the first assumption (that people can accurately assess who is generally appealing), there's a large research literature on the second assumption; however, that literature consistently indicates that people aren't able to predict the characteristics of potential mates they will be compatible with. That people cannot make this prediction about potential partners should not be surprising because people lack insight into their rationale for most preferences and behaviors (as I discussed in the previous myth).

In summary, the fact that most online dating services utilize user profiles as the initial way of introducing potential partners leads to two problems. First, the fact that people tend to find the same things appealing means that there are too many people seeking out the most generically appealing profiles without providing a sense of how many people are virtually crowding around that profile. This leads to a problematic market in which "sellers" and "buyers" have trouble connecting. Second, the extent to which people have idiosyncratic preferences for an intimate relationship partner – these preferences are correlated with neither how much they will like that person when they meet face-to-face nor how much they will like them years down the road.

Comparing online profiles to other profiles appears to disrupt the development of satisfying intimate relationships

So far I have described how there's a great deal of research that suggests that the information contained in online profiles will not assist people in determining whether the person behind any particular profile will be a good match. However, if this problem is ignored and we assume that the information in the profiles is useful, Finkel et al. (2012) describe a second issue. In conventional (i.e., off-line) dating, potential partners are usually evaluated individually. Even in a crowded club in which most of the patrons are evaluating others as potential mates, once a conversation begins, the evaluation is done on an individual basis. This means the person is being evaluated against the evaluator's ideals and standards, not against someone else with whom the evaluator is speaking. Certainly, there are rare situations where one could imagine nearly simultaneous verbal evaluations (e.g., game shows), but generally speaking conventional dating involves a separate evaluation of each candidate and online dating involves comparative evaluations. Finkel et al. describe the problem as follows:

Browsing profiles places people into a *joint evaluation* mode in which they compare multiple potential partners nearly simultaneously, whereas pursuing a relationship with a particular partner places people into a *separate evaluation* mode in which they evaluate one specific partner in isolation. (p. 30)

The problem is that these two types of evaluations can lead to different outcomes.

Much of the research that has been done on the impact of evaluating something in a joint evaluation mode versus a separate evaluation mode has been done in the domain of products, because shopping often involves comparing products to each other side by side and then purchasing one and evaluating it later by itself. What researchers have consistently found is that the factors that were emphasized in the side-by-side comparison (i.e., in a joint evaluation mode) are different than the factors on which people report being satisfied with a product after the purchase (i.e., in a separate evaluation mode).

These differences have been studied and developed into a broader model (Hsee & Zhang, 2010), but for the purposes of online dating one can see how the differences between joint and separate evaluation modes could be especially problematic. A person browsing profiles may evaluate the profiles based on appearance, salary, and shared interests, then, upon meeting the potential partners face-to-face evaluates them based on sense of humor, freshness of breath, and how they treat waiters. In this situation, it's easy to imagine that the differences between the two types of evaluation could be completely different. Furthermore, as I noted in the previous myth, there's a strong possibility the people might not even be able to articulate why they did or didn't like a particular person (Nisbett & Wilson, 1977). In addition, Finkel et al. (2012) note that the joint and separate evaluation modes also differ in the degree to which they elicit critical evaluations (more in the joint mode) or attitudes that encourage fulfilling and pleasurable actions (more in the separate evaluation mode). One could argue about the wisdom of one mode over the other. In fact, the possibly apocryphal advice from Benjamin Franklin to "keep your eyes wide open before marriage, and half-shut afterwards" suggests that joint evaluations are better, but they don't seem to engender the development of deep and meaningful relationships.

Selecting someone from a large pool of potential partners may be problematic in four ways

One of the perceived benefits of online dating is that it greatly expands the number of people from whom one can select as a potential mate. People often cite access to more single people as the primary reason they use online dating services. Yet, it turns out that the sheer number of people from whom one can select is fraught with problems as described by Finkel et al. (2012).

First, there's a well-established principle called *choice overload*, which is when there are so many options that a person feels overwhelmed and simply avoids making any decision in lieu of making the effort to wade through the choices. Although this concept is somewhat controversial and there's been debate about it in the empirical literature (see Chernev, Böckenholt, & Goodman, 2010; Scheibehenne, Greifeneder, & Todd, 2010), data from intimate relationship researchers suggests that choice overload can be an issue when it comes to dating. Alison Lenton and her colleagues have done a series of experiments in which they manipulated the number of potential mates, both in online dating situations (Lenton, Fasolo, & Todd, 2008; Lenton & Stewart, 2008) and in speed-dating situations (Lenton & Francesconi, 2010). Across these studies, she and her colleagues found that increasing the pool didn't enhance the satisfaction of the participants, and it's possible that increasing the options from an experimentally reasonable number (e.g., 64) to the very large numbers available to online dating service customers may lead to further decreases in satisfaction or to paralysis (Finkel et al., 2012). Interestingly, Lenton and colleagues even compared the effects of having a large pool of potential mates across species and found that humans did worse and rodents did much better under these conditions (Lenton, Fasolo, & Todd, 2009).

Second, there's evidence that with more options people become lazier at evaluating the options. This is a relatively old concept. The idea being when there are more choices people go from careful analysis of all of the options, including the assessment and weighting of multiple aspects of each option, to only examining a few aspects of each option without carefully analyzing the conflicting information. This work by Amos Tversky (1972) and expanded upon with Daniel Kahneman (e.g., Tversky & Kahneman, 1974) led to Daniel Kahneman, a Psychologist at Princeton University, being awarded the Nobel Prize in Economics in 2002 (in all likelihood Tversky would have shared the award if he had been alive; Kahneman, 2003). Lenton and colleagues found that these principles applied to dating situations as well. For example, when there are more potential dates being evaluated, people evaluate them on more basic characteristics, like height, instead of doing more thorough and meaningful evaluations (Lenton et al., 2009; Lenton & Francesconi, 2010).

Third, there's compelling evidence that having a large pool of potential mates leads to the selection of a partner who is further from one's ideal partner than when selecting from a smaller pool (Wu & Chiou, 2009;

Yang & Chiou, 2010). This is important because relationship ideals represent the specific characteristics that would make the perfect relationship or person (whether that is an intimate partner, parent, child, etc.). Garth Fletcher and Jeffry Simpson (2001) developed a theoretical model that describes how ideals function in relationships and, along with their colleagues, have found – among other things – that the closer one's partner is to an ideal partner, the greater the relationship satisfaction (e.g., Fletcher, Simpson, & Thomas, 2000). Ironically, Yang and Chiou found that those who are most impacted by the problem of greater choice leading to partners that were further from their ideal were those people who put a greater emphasis on having the ideal partner. If we were to divide the world into "maximizers," people who seek to optimize any situation or get the ideal of any option, and "satisficers," people who will choose something that simply meets their needs, as Herbert Simon (1956) did, Yang and Chiou found that the maximizers kept going back to search for more potential partners instead of more thoroughly evaluating ones that were closer to their ideal. They theorized that maximizers feel a need to do an exhaustive search, which of course is impossible in the online dating world.

Fourth, large pools of potential partners lower the likelihood of a person being willing to commit to one person. There's a great deal of support for this, but it can be boiled down to the fairly simple principles in social exchange theory. The basic idea is that there are rewards and costs to being in a relationship and that we're more satisfied when the rewards outweigh the costs (Thibaut & Kelley, 1959). In addition to satisfaction, there is also dependence in a relationship. Dependence is greater when the rewards of the relationship are outweighed by the opportunity costs. In the case of online dating sites, making a commitment to someone means sacrificing the opportunity to seek other potentially better partners among the thousands who have posted their profiles. This can lead to lower levels of commitment because commitment is made up of both satisfaction and dependence (M. P. Johnson, 1973; for a more detailed discussion of the components of commitment, see Myth 18). In other words, the likelihood of staying in (i.e., committing to) a relationship is reduced in proportion to the number of viable and desirable alternatives that seem readily available (Levinger, 1976; for a review of what predicts relationship dissolution, see the meta-analysis by Le, Dove, Agnew, Korn, & Mutso, 2010). Thus, having so many potential partners at one's fingertips can highlight the opportunity cost of committing to one person and lower the likelihood of engaging in a deep meaningful relationship.

Conclusion

Although it seems perfectly reasonable to assume that having access to innumerable online profiles of potential partners increases the likelihood of finding Mr. or Ms. Right, there are three reasons that this increased access may be more detrimental than beneficial. First, the information in online profiles is not especially helpful in determining whether particular individuals will be a good match. Second, the act of comparing online profiles to other profiles appears to disrupt the development of satisfying intimate relationships. Third, the sheer number of profiles of potential partners can overwhelm people so that they become fatigued with evaluating profiles, use lazy methods of evaluation, move away from their ideals, and shy away from commitment. Therefore, despite the apparent benefits of having millions of profiles at our fingertips, these benefits are, in the words of Finkel et al. (2012), "mitigated somewhat by the widespread emphasis on introducing users to potential partners through profiles, which fail to capture the essence of a person" (p. 34).

Myth #9 Meeting potential partners electronically prior to meeting them in person decreases the chances of a successful relationship

Online dating services necessitate having electronic interactions, or as researchers call it computer-mediated communication (CMC). While one can imagine situations outside of online dating that would begin with CMC, it's an integral part of online dating. The question is whether this type of communication prior to in-person communication is helpful or detrimental to the development of a meaningful intimate relationship. To determine whether CMC is beneficial or harmful, I started by reading many articles about it in the popular newspapers and magazines. I came away from this exercise even more confused. A brief review of articles in the lay press suggests that there are some who believe that CMC prior to meeting potential partners enhances the likelihood of a fulfilling relationship (e.g., Orantia, 2013), more who believe the opposite (e.g., Loudon, 2013), and many more that focus on the potential danger of CMC (e.g., C. Jones, 2010). So, this myth could have easily been different; however, in speaking with the college students in my classes, I have found that they are dubious about CMC despite their nearly constant use of it. My students told me about the frequent misunderstandings and hurt feelings that seem – to them – more prevalent when communicating by text or other electronic means than when talking face-to-face.

What do relationship scientists have to say about it? To address this, I again turned to Finkel and colleagues' (2012) review. They addressed the following three questions about CMC prior to meeting a potential partner in person: Can couples develop intimacy using CMC? How best should couples transition from exclusively using CMC to face-to-face communication? And, can CMC be a reasonable substitute for face-to-face interactions? Let's answer each of these questions in turn.

Can couples develop intimacy using CMC?

Online communication in some form is now essentially ubiquitous. Only the truly hardcore Luddites still refuse to use computers to communicate in some capacity. This includes using CMC to socialize and build new and established relationships. We now take for granted that the widespread use of social media enables us to stay in touch with people we care about and to form new relationships. In fact, since 2009 those who don't use CMC for socializing are considered to be disengaged from the lives of their friends and family (Manjoo, 2009). Given the widespread use of CMC, it's important to remember that when chat rooms and other forms of CMC first came out the people who interacted using CMC were more task-oriented and disinhibited; therefore, CMC was initially thought to be a poor medium for socializing (for a review, see Baym, 2006). To be sure, it's easy to find places on the Internet that are still task-oriented, and it's easy to find people being disinhibited in all kinds of unsavory ways; however, for our purposes, I am primarily focused on the use of CMC to evaluate potential mates and to foster intimacy with others.

Finkel and colleagues describe two primary models for the ability of CMC to foster intimacy. The first model suggested that, compared to face-to-face interactions, CMC interactions would result in a reduction of intimacy. This would result from having fewer interpersonal cues during CMC. For example, in CMC it's difficult to tell when a text message or tweet that was meant as humor was actually perceived as humor. Therefore, in this model the comparatively low level of affective cues that are available during CMC is thought to diminish the likelihood of developing intimacy. This model was especially prevalent in the 1980s when CMC was in the early phases (e.g., Kiesler, Siegel, & McGuire, 1984; Rice & Love, 1987).

Like the telephone, people primarily thought of CMC as a business tool in the early years (Fischer & Carroll, 1988), and earlier theories reflected this belief. However, in the 1990s Joseph Walther began developing a new model of how people were utilizing CMC to develop their relationships. He suggested that instead of suppressing intimacy, CMC was leading people to become *hyperpersonal* by allowing them to share a lot of information and by modifying the more traditional cues and developing other cues specific to CMC (Walther, 1996). He and his colleagues conducted a meta-analysis of CMC studies and found that as long as there was no time limit on the discussions or relationships, which would be the case when it was being used in an online dating situation, CMC interactions were no different from face-to-face interactions (Walther, Anderson, & Park, 1994).

Since this finding, there's been research on the cues that people use to understand and interpret CMC (e.g., Gunraj, Drumm-Hewitt, Dashow, Upadhyay, & Klin, 2016). As I have spoken with my students, friends, and clients, I have heard about some of these cues. For example, my college students put a great deal of emphasis on the speed of responding to text messages. They earnestly spoke about their friends who would be upset if they didn't respond immediately to a text message, even if they were in class. The students felt that it only takes a few seconds, "so what does it mean if you aren't willing to give me a few seconds of your time?" Their anecdotal comments are supported by research indicating that quicker responses are associated with more support and care (Ledbetter, 2008). So, while people have developed ways of increasing the number of cues that are used in CMC (see also Derks, Bos, & von Grumbkow, 2007; Walther, Loh, & Granka, 2005), the question remains as to whether more recent research has also supported the ability of CMC to foster intimacy and, if so, how?

Since Walther and colleagues' (1994) meta-analysis, quite a few studies have examined the development of intimacy using CMC. There appears to be a robust and consistent effect that CMC fosters more intimacy. For example, in one study, researchers examined the strategies people use during CMC to reduce uncertainty and which of these lead to statements of affection. In this study, 81 opposite-sex participant couples were randomly assigned to each other and to one of the following three conditions: face-to-face, visual CMC supported by a webcam, or text-only CMC. Interestingly, text-only CMC couples made more statements of affection than face-to-face couples. In addition, couples in both CMC conditions made more intimate self-disclosures and asked more intimate questions than participants who were speaking face-to-face (Antheunis, Schouten, Valkenburg, & Peter, 2012). This study adds to a large empirical literature (e.g., Antheunis, Valkenburg, & Peter, 2007, 2010; Bargh, McKenna, & Fitzsimons, 2002) that provides additional support for the social information processing theory (Walther, 1992, 1995), which supports the fact that people will use different and more hyperpersonal strategies (Walther, 1996) when using CMC compared with face-to-face communication.

Now that it's clear that initiating a relationship using CMC can have a more positive effect, the question of why and how exactly this might work is still unclear. Finkel and colleagues (2012) address this question from two perspectives, the virtual "speaker" and the virtual "listener." Psychologists have theories that would inform both of these perspectives. First, let's discuss how hyperpersonalization may work with the speaker. One of the most appealing features of "speaking" to someone via text-based CMC is that it provides more control over the message. This is something that media and public relations consultants will often point out if you find yourself being asked difficult questions by reporters. So, often when a company or a person is on the hotseat in the press, they will "issue a statement" instead of speaking to reporters or answering questions directly because it gives them more control and allows them to parse their words more carefully. Similarly, text-based (and to a lesser extent video-based) CMC allows the speaker to be more strategic in his or her presentation to the other person in the CMC stage of online dating. Of course, the desire to present oneself in the best possible manner is certainly nothing new (Goffman, 1959); however, CMC enhances the ability to accentuate one's positive aspects and spin negative aspects (N. Ellison, Heino, & Gibbs, 2006; McKenna, Green, & Gleason, 2002). For example, people might write about a love of hiking when they mostly want to appear athletic, even if they rarely walk more than a block or two. In addition, the lack of cues as to how the "speaker's" message was received may lead to further disclosures to fill the void that nonverbal and other affective cues would fill, which would in turn foster further intimacy (Reis & Shaver, 1988).

Next, let's examine how hyperpersonalization may function in the mind of the virtual "listener." As I already discussed, CMC by its nature offers fewer cues than face-to-face communication, so the "listener" is left to fill in the negative space in these interactions. How humans interpret ambiguity and gaps in communication has been studied by social psychologists and others for many years. In modern psychology, this work started with Fritz Heider (1958), who wrote about the need to understand and control the world around us. This work turned into a fruitful line of theory and research (e.g., Kelley, 1971) that collectively can be referred to as attribution theory – as in to what am I attributing someone's behavior. Attribution theory forms the foundation of social cognition. To really understand how humans influence each other, I recommend reading up on attribution theory (for a good review, see Fiske & Taylor, 1991) and how attributions influence marital quality (e.g., Bradbury & Fincham, 1990; Karney & Bradbury, 2000). Returning to the increased ambiguity in CMC prior to meeting face-to-face, people in this situation are probably wanting to move "toward" (to borrow a phrase from Horney, 1945) potential mates. If people have expectations of a positive outcome, they will look to confirm their hopes for such an outcome by putting a positive spin on ambiguous or even negative information and behavior. So, they are more likely to interpret ambiguous information in the CMC more positively than they might in other situations. In other words, if someone wrote that he "loves animals," this statement might be interpreted as "Oh good, he'll be comfortable with the fact that I have three cats and two dogs," when in reality he meant that he liked to watch wildlife and visit zoos.

In addition to interpretations of specific messages, people also make attributions about ambiguous CMC actions. For example, if someone has not responded to a message in a timely manner, the other person might attribute it to situational factors that are beyond the control of the other person. Positive attributions regarding behavior and understanding of communications are likely to be more positive in the very early stages of a courtship when expectations are running high, regardless of whether the medium is a face-to-face conversation or a CMC. Still, the effect of the "listener's" perception of the communication on intimacy is stronger in CMC than in face-to-face conversations (Jiang, Bazarova, & Hancock, 2011). In addition, the same study found that this effect was driven by CMC "listeners" giving more weight to self-disclosures than listeners in face-to-face conversations.

In the end, it's clear that couples in the initial stages of courtship who use CMC, compared with face-to-face interactions, tend to be more careful in crafting their messages, to be more self-disclosing, and to make more positive attributions about ambiguous information. All of this makes CMC-using couples more likely to make statements of affection and to feel more attraction to each other, which leads to greater levels of intimacy.

Are the benefits of CMC maintained when couples transition from exclusively using CMC to including face-to-face communication?

Having established that the CMC that is inherent to online dating services allows greater levels of intimacy compared with the face-to-face communication that is inherent to off-line dating, most users want to transition to face-to-face interactions with potential partners they meet online. The question is whether the benefits of CMC are maintained when making the transition.

In their review, Finkel and colleagues (2012) described two possible answers to this question, one positive and one negative. One possibility is that the benefits aren't only maintained, but potentially even enhanced by making this transition. They noted that even brief CMC preceding a face-to-face encounter led to more self-disclosure and intimacy (Bargh et al., 2002) and that CMC appears to be especially helpful for socially anxious individuals (McKenna et al., 2002). Thus, the initial use of CMC could enhance closeness by facilitating disclosures that could enhance later interactions. Or, as Finkel et al. put it: "people's CMC-revealed inner beauty could outshine social deficits or unappealing physical qualities, thus permitting subsequent face-to-face interaction to promote relationship growth" (p. 36; see also Cooper & Sportolari, 1997). They also noted that the use of CMC followed by face-to-face interactions could have a negative effect because individuals may have formed overly positive or specific perceptions of the person they are meeting and could be disappointed when reality falls short of the person's imagination or the other person's deception (Caspi & Gorsky, 2006). This seems like a plausible hypothesis given research from off-line relationships on the effects of failing to live up to relationship ideals (Fletcher et al., 2000) and failing to meet specific expectations in interactions (Fincham, Harold, & Gano Phillips, 2000). So, does initial CMC enhance or devalue later face-to-face interactions?

While there's not a great deal of empirical literature on this, it appears that the data support the enhancement hypothesis. In a brief laboratory experiment, men and women were randomly assigned to each other and either interacted once via an online chat followed by a face-to-face interaction or via two face-to-face interactions. People in the CMC followed by a face-to-face interaction group liked each other more than the face-to-face only group (McKenna et al., 2002). Studies that followed this one examined the timing of making the switch and noticed something important. When the transition from CMC to face-to-face happened after three weeks the enhancement hypothesis was supported, meaning the face-to-face interactions following CMC resulted in more favorable impressions than face-to-face only interactions. However, when the transition took place after six weeks, the benefits of the initial CMC were lost (Ramirez & Wang, 2008; Ramirez & Zhang, 2007). So, how can people maintain the benefits of online communication as they transition to off-line communication? Make the transition within three weeks of the initial online contact. This should not be too difficult because – at least in one study – most participants transitioned to face-to-face meetings within a week of their initial online communication (Whitty & Carr, 2006).

And, can CMC be a reasonable substitute for face-to-face interactions?

No, but mixing the two can enhance relationships.

The affect we express through nonverbal cues and vocal cues beyond what is being said (e.g., tone of voice) are powerful tools for understanding social context. Importantly, these affective cues have small to moderate associations with relationship satisfaction (M. D. Johnson, 2002). In addition, there are ways in which face-to-face interactions allow communication skills to be more sophisticated and subtle. These types of skills, for example verbally indicating that you are listening by saying "uh-huh" as the other person speaks (which is called a verbal assent), can interact with couples' expressions of affect in ways that alter couples' marital satisfaction in the early years of marriage (M. D. Johnson et al., 2005). All of this is consistent with the idea that being in the presence of another person is the best way to experience the full "gestalt" (Asch, 1946) of the person, so that an impression may be formed.

Conclusion

Preceding face-to-face interactions with CMC is likely to enhance relationships. For those already in an intimate relationship, using CMC as an enhancement to face-to-face interactions appears to be worth the effort. This is true in both local and long-distance relationships as well as across types of media (Hampton, Sessions Goulet, Her, & Rainie, 2009; Rainie, Lenhart, Fox, Spooner, & Horrigan, 2000; Ramirez & Broneck, 2009). In other words, although the content of the CMC messages matters (Slatcher, Vazire, & Pennebaker, 2008), the use of CMC enhances intimacy overall. Of course, if all else fails, one can join the increasing ranks of those who use CMC to dissolve a relationship (e.g., "Its ovr b/n u n me" by Weisskirch & Delevi, 2012).

Couples who are "matched" by online dating services are more likely to have satisfying relationships

> Out of all the single people you will meet in your life, only a very few would make a great relationship partner for you. Some singles aren't attractive to you. Others aren't ready for a relationship. Of the rest, many are great people who you might enjoy chemistry with initially, but they aren't compatible with you in the important ways that make long-term dating and relationships work. That's where eHarmony comes in. By combining the best scientific research with detailed profiling of every member, we screen thousands of single men and single women to bring you only the ones that have the potential to be truly right for you. (eHarmony, 2012)

> The online dating process begins with the Chemistry Profile, which helps us to get to know you on a deeper personal level. Once we have your results, we use the latest research of world-renowned biological anthropologist, Dr. Helen Fisher, to predict which single men or women you'll have relationship and dating chemistry with. (Match.com LLC, 2012)

As the marketing information quoted above indicates, some online dating sites claim to have an algorithm or formula that can match you with someone with whom you will have a long-lasting and successful relationship. These companies describe their methods in scientific terms and often employ scientists as consultants. So, the question is: Do their algorithms work? As discussed in the introduction, the testing of one's hypotheses is the basis of science. Therefore, the most straightforward approach for any of these companies would be to make their algorithms public and test their effectiveness, and then allow the scientific community to review the findings in detail. This is what scientists do on a regular basis. However, as of the writing of this book (as far as I know), these companies have refused to disclose their algorithms or test them in a way that would lead other scientists to conclude that any one specific algorithm improved relationship outcomes over another algorithm or a control condition, such as allowing users to self-select their partners. This is not surprising because these companies have little incentive to open themselves up to this level of scrutiny.

Nevertheless, knowing neither the algorithms nor the internal research results of these companies, Finkel and colleagues (2012) set out to determine whether the matching could improve relationship outcomes. They did this by first looking at whether relationship outcomes can be predicted, which is something I discuss in Myths 14–20. Second, they examined whether personality characteristics predict relationship outcomes. Third, they looked at the literature on similarity and compatibility of personality in predicting relationship success. Following their lead, let's dig into the research on personality and compatibility to see if the bold claims of places like eHarmony are backed up by data.

Does an individual's personality predict relationship outcomes?

Most of the online dating services that claim to match people base this claim on personality measures as well as things like interests and demographic data. For the purposes of reviewing this myth, I am not considering the more silly exceptions, such as the company GenePartner, which claims that "the probability for successful and long-lasting romantic relationships is greatest in couples with high genetic compatibility" and offers a service that "determines the level of genetic compatibility" (GenePartner, 2013). If personality is the main basis of these claims, does an individual's personality predict relationship outcomes (setting aside the question of matching or complementing personalities for now)?

To put this question another way, do individuals vary in their ability to have meaningful and successful relationships, or what some might call *relationship aptitude* (Finkel et al., 2012). Most likely your intuitive answer is "yes; of course some people are better than others at intimate relationships!" If this was your reaction, you are correct. There are many theories that attempt to explain these differences, and there's a huge amount of research testing these theories. Some of the theories that are relevant to this question are ones that I touch on in discussions of other myths; however, when it comes to using personality variables to predict marital success, we can go back to some of the earliest models of marriage. For example, Lewis Terman (1938, p. 110) wrote the following: "Whether by nature or by nurture, there are persons so lacking in the qualities which make for compatibility that they would be incapable of finding happiness in any marriage ... and still others whose dispositions and outlooks upon life would preserve them from acute unhappiness however unfortunately they were mated." The personality traits that Terman and others found in those early years as being associated with marital satisfaction (i.e., marital happiness) over time have stood the test of time and – more importantly – the test of replication.

These days, most of the empirical work on personality as a predictor of relationship success uses the well-known five-factor model of personality (also known as the "Big Five"; McCrae & Costa, 1997), in which people are measured as having more or less of each of the following five personality traits: openness, conscientiousness, extraversion, agreeableness, and neuroticism. Each of these factors has been associated with relationship outcomes to some degree (for a meta-analysis, see Malouff, Thorsteinsson, Schutte, Bhullar, & Rooke, 2010). However, the factor that has far and away the strongest associations with relationship outcomes is neuroticism, which is also called negative affectivity. Think of neuroticism as David Watson and Lee Anna Clark (1984) defined it, "the disposition to experience aversive emotional states" (p. 465). In other words, people who are high on neuroticism have a propensity to see things negatively and to experience negative emotions more than most people, even when there's no apparent reason for negativity. You probably know somebody who is always complaining, nervous, or sad – even in the face of good news. People who are high on neuroticism are particularly likely to have poor intimate relationships. Neuroticism is a powerful predictor of relationship distress and dissolution. It has been demonstrated to be a key mechanism linking broader theories of relationship development to actual marital outcomes (Davila, Bradbury, & Fincham, 1998). Neuroticism appears to play a role in many of the other known predictors of marital dissatisfaction and divorce, including sexual satisfaction (Fisher & McNulty, 2008), how couples solve problems (Karney & Bradbury, 1997), how spouses support each other (Pasch et al., 1997), and how spouses think about their partner's behavior (Karney, Bradbury, Fincham, & Sullivan, 1994). Most impressively, compared to other personality traits, neuroticism was by far the strongest premarital predictor of marital dissatisfaction and divorce 45 years later (Kelly & Conley, 1987). Clearly, neuroticism packs a punch when it comes to relationship outcomes.

In addition to thinking of personality in terms of the "Big Five" factors, personality can also be thought of in terms of personality disorders. The *Diagnostic and Statistical Manual of Mental Disorders* (DSM; American Psychiatric Association, 2013) differentiates most mental disorders – like depression and anxiety – from *personality disorders*. As you might imagine, these are thought to be more pervasive and stable (although they are less stable than originally thought, e.g., Lenzenweger, Johnson, & Willett, 2004). The personality disorders in the DSM overlap with aspects of the Five Factor Model, but they are considered disorders because they lead to significant impairment in people's lives. Several personality disorders are associated with marital distress and dissolution (as are most mental health problems). For example, people with high levels of psychopathic traits, such as an inability to have empathy, end up hurting (or worse) those around them (see Myth 22). Another personality disorder that predicts distress and divorce is Borderline Personality Disorder (Bouchard, Sabourin, Lussier, & Villeneuve, 2009), which is defined in part on a person's having volatile personal relationships. As such, avoiding relationships with people with Borderline Personality Disorder makes sense, unless you are looking for a lot of drama (although, it should be noted that there are quite effective treatments for Borderline Personality Disorder; Clarkin, Levy, Lenzenweger, & Kernberg, 2007). Other personality disorders are also associated with relationship distress (S. C. South, Turkheimer, & Oltmanns, 2008). In the end, personality does appear to impact intimate relationships.

Having established that individual personality characteristics and disorders predict relationship outcomes, the next question is whether online dating services that collect personality data screen out those with a low likelihood of having successful relationships. Again, it's difficult to know the answer to this without knowing the specific algorithms they use. However, it seems likely that at least some are doing just this. For example, eHarmony has indicated that the following are the three primary reasons that they reject potential customers: they are married, they are under the minimum age requirements, or they give inconsistent answers (E. McCarthy, 2009). However, they also screen out people based on personality traits (Kornblum, 2005). Therefore, to the extent they are removing people who are neurotic or have more serious mental health disorders, online dating services are likely providing a valuable service to their customers who make the cut and are allowed to use the service. Of course, the true test would be for these companies to open their data to allow scientists to examine whether their screening mechanisms are indeed screening out people with poor aptitudes for relationships.

Does the similarity and complementarity of personality of a couple predict relationship success?

While screening out people who are less able or willing to demonstrate strong relationship aptitude is likely to be a valuable service, this is not what most of these companies are claiming. Rather they are claiming that they will match people based on their characteristics – or, as Finkel and colleagues (2012) put it, they've adopted the *compatibility perspective*. Again, without being able to directly test the benefits of these companies' matching algorithms, let's examine the science behind the claim that relationships will benefit when couples have high degrees of similarity in their personalities or high degrees of complementarity in their personalities. This is the crux of the argument for many of the online dating websites: similarity or complementarity is predictive of better outcomes for your relationship (e.g., E. McCarthy, 2009).

First, let me be clear that these companies aren't claiming to match on race or religion, which people tend to do on their own anyway. Nevertheless, these happen to be two variables on which there are some complementary effects. Couples who marry within their race or ethnicity are 10% less likely to divorce after 10 years than people who marry someone of a different race or ethnicity (Bramlett & Mosher, 2002). In addition, people from the same religious organizations have better relationship outcomes (Heaton & Pratt, 1990). Again, matching on race and religion is not what these companies are offering and happens most of the time anyway. What these companies are offering is to match based on the similarity or complementarity of personality variables. So, what do the data look like?

As I reviewed in Myth 6, researchers have conducted many studies to determine whether personality similarity or complementarity is beneficial. There are some reports that similarity is beneficial, but other studies found that, when controlling for the effects of the individual personalities, the effects vanished or became very small. The definitive study of personality similarity found that, after controlling for individual effects, similarity accounted for 0.5% of the success of the relationships (Dyrenforth et al., 2010). In terms of complementarity, the idea that certain personality traits will be particularly well suited for other personality traits, the data simply don't support such a claim. For example, there's no evidence that introverts and extraverts are attracted to one another more than to people more similar to themselves on that dimension (Hendrick & Brown, 1971). As Finkel and colleagues described the empirical literature on complementarity, it "has been reviewed repeatedly, and in every case the idea that complementary personalities might provide a basis for compatibility in romantic relationships has been dismissed" (2012, p. 47).

Conclusion

In summary, it seems that the claims of online dating services that there's value in matching couples based on the personality variables and other data that they collect are dubious. To the extent that they are providing any benefit in collecting personal data, it's that they may well be screening out people with whom you would rather not have a relationship. Of course, their success at being the personality gate-keeper – screening out the people who are unlikely to have successful relationships and including people who are likely to be solid partners – is something we're unlikely to know unless the companies release their data.

4 SAME-SEX RELATIONSHIPS

Research on sexual-minority individuals and families has increased rapidly in the last decade. This rise has coincided with greater acceptance of sexual minority families in the United States. Unfortunately, the greater acceptance in the United States and elsewhere has been countered with terrible repression in other countries, including in Uganda where the repression appears to have been fomented by American expatriates. A broad discussion of the historical, political, and cultural dynamics of sexual minorities and same-sex relationships is beyond the scope of this book and my expertise. However, I raise the issue because it's with this backdrop that I review three myths about same-sex relationships.

Let me begin by noting my use of the terms "same-sex relationship" and "sexual-minority" to describe gay/lesbian/bisexual individuals. In doing so, I am intending to use the terms most often used in the research literature. More importantly, I am trying to avoid terms that the majority of individuals with some same-sex attractions use, such as lesbian, gay, or bisexual (Laumann, Gagnon, Michael, & Michaels, 1994; Mosher, Chandra, & Jones, 2005; Wichstrøm & Hegna, 2003). As Rith and Diamond (2013) put it, the use of the term "sexual minority" reflects the universal experience of those who are sexually attracted to people of the same sex in "that their same-sex relationships place them squarely outside conventional norms prescribing uniform heterosexuality" and "that these ties are pursued in a society that posits only other-sex romantic ties as healthy, normative, and desirable" (p. 123).

It's also worth acknowledging the strong feelings that research on sexual minorities and same-sex relationships can engender. When I speak

Great Myths of Intimate Relationships: Dating, Sex, and Marriage,
First Edition. Matthew D. Johnson.
© 2016 John Wiley & Sons, Inc. Published 2016 by John Wiley & Sons, Inc.

about the issues that I will describe here – whether in large venues or small groups – there are often strong feelings. People share beliefs and feelings that are highly variable, but quite often strongly felt. The responses I've heard range from simple-minded to metaphysical. I have encountered people who described sexual relations outside of the context of a man and woman as a sin. As well as people who have questioned the very premise of sexuality, describing it as a social construct and nothing more. Finally, I have known psychologists who focus on the differences between same- and other-sex relationships and psychologists who focus on the similarities. In my experience, most of these folks are well meaning (I don't hang out with people who are filled with hate). The point is that in all likelihood I will describe research findings that may be described or manipulated in ways that embolden those who seek to repress sexual minorities and that may challenge the beliefs of some who work hard to support their friends and family who are in same-sex relationships.

As with the rest of this book, I have endeavored to write about the research as I have read it, with the assumption that those with extreme points of view may not find the data convincing. Any finding as it relates to sexual minorities is observed through the looking-glass of our social and political context; thus it's important to read the following myths within the historical context of the repression of sexual minorities that continues today. Neither I, as your guide through the data, nor you, as the consumer of research, are able to avoid the distortions of our cultural perspectives.

With these caveats in mind, I will discuss the following three myths about same-sex relationships. The first myth of this chapter is really two myths. If you believe that the gender to which people are attracted is stable, you are wrong. If you believe that the gender to which people are attracted is fluid, you are also wrong. In this myth, I explain how this can be. The second myth discusses the differences (and similarities) between same- and other-sex relationships. Finally, the third myth covers some of the faulty science that was presented as evidence in the media and in U.S. courts that children raised by other-sex couples are better off than children raised by same-sex couples. Although courts and public opinion to date haven't been swayed by those peddling this bad science, calling out those who would usurp relationship science to support their social and religious convictions is part of myth-busting.

The gender to which people are attracted is stable (or: the gender to which people are attracted is fluid)

You'll notice that this is the only myth in this book that I describe in two opposing ways. Some people believe that the gender to which people are attracted is stable. Others believe it can vary. This divide is found among cultural commentators, including among those who strongly advocate for sexual minorities, with some (e.g., Urquhart, 2014) arguing for stability and others (e.g., Ambrosino, 2014) arguing for fluidity. In fact, the division among those who have considered the issue professionally reflects the split among Americans who are evenly divided on the issue of whether sexual orientation is malleable (Pew Research Center, 2003, 2013).

I have heard and read both perspectives. You may be wondering, well if one is a myth, in the sense that it's widely believed but not true, then why not list that one as the myth? The answer, of course, is that life is complicated. Nowhere is this heuristic more true than when it comes to sexuality. Nevertheless, I will not be taking a middle of the road approach, like "well it really is something between fluidity and stability," or "everyone has times when they are more fluid and more stable." It's not that I will describe research that suggests both are true for everyone. As it turns out, I list both sexual stability and sexual fluidity as myths because one appears to be true for one sex and the other true for the other sex. There are multiple studies that suggest that the gender to which men are attracted is mostly stable and the gender to which women are attracted is more fluid.

Definitions and cultural context

Before going any further, it makes sense to talk about the language and vocabulary I will be using. Specifically, I'll define and distinguish the following concepts: sexual orientation, sexual identity, sexual fluidity, and sexual arousal. Note that these definitions reflect how I will be using these terms; however, there are more sophisticated definitions available elsewhere.

Sexual orientation. This is the predisposition for same-sex or other-sex intimate relationships. The key feature of sexual orientation is the desire for a same- or other-sex relationship, as opposed to attraction or behavior.

As I will discuss, relationship scientists are mostly in agreement that there are people with homosexual orientations who have never been in a same-sex relationship, and there are – albeit fewer – people with a heterosexual orientation who have mostly engaged in same-sex relationships. I didn't use the term "sexual orientation" in the title of this myth because I am not suggesting that the research supports the idea that sexual orientation is fluid for men or women, rather this myth deals with whether sexual attraction is fluid or stable. Indeed, most scientists consider sexual orientation to be consistent across the lifespan (Diamond, 2008b).

Sexual identity is related to sexual orientation, but specifically refers to the label someone uses to describe his or her sexuality. For example, people may describe themselves as "gay," "lesbian," "straight," or "bisexual." These labels tend to have social, political, and cultural meaning. In addition, the label may or may not reflect the person's behavior. For example, the late Rev. Peter Gomes, the Plummer Professor of Christian morals at the Harvard School of Divinity and the Pusey Minister of Memorial Church at Harvard University, described himself as "gay" but also noted that he had remained celibate (McFadden, 2011). Sexual identity labels may express more than orientation – for example, "questioning" or "queer." Finally, it should be noted that some would prefer to not use labels at all. No matter what identity – if any – people use to describe themselves, it should be considered a self-description.

Sexual fluidity. Having described sexual orientation and sexual identity, I will turn to the main point of this myth. Sexual fluidity is the ability to find people of both genders sexually arousing, which has also been referred to as *erotic plasticity* (Baumeister, 2000). Of course, being sexually aroused by someone doesn't mean that the person is necessarily open to a having an intimate relationship with the person who is arousing him or her, or even with others of that person's gender.

Sexual arousal. As I described in Myth 1, by and large there are two ways that scientists measure, or *operationally define*, sexual arousal. The first way is self-reports of sexual arousal. For example, a participant in a study may be given a dial that is turned to reflect the participant's feelings of arousal at any given point during the study; perhaps, while watching an erotic video. The second method is through the use of a plethysmograph, which is a medical device that measures the volume of blood flow. The two types of plethysmography used in this research are penile and vaginal, depending on the anatomy of the participant. A penile plethysmograph measures the blood flow and the resulting swelling of the penis as an indication of arousal. A vaginal plethysmograph measures blood flowing to the vaginal walls, which is a precursor to increases in secretions of moisture in the vaginal canal and an indicator of sexual arousal.

In most of the studies I will discuss, the most interesting findings come from either plethysmography or the difference between self-report ratings and plethysmography readings. As with any behavioral research, it's best to use multiple methods to assess the variables of interest (Campbell & Fiske, 1959). Happily, quite a few studies have used both self-report ratings and plethysmography readings to assess sexual arousal, so we can examine the degree to which these two methods correspond. In a meta-analysis of 132 studies, the correlation between self-report and genital measures of sexual arousal was strong for men ($r = .66$) and small to medium for women ($r = .26$). This means that men's self-report was quite similar to their penile plethysmography readings, whereas, women's self-reports were substantially different from their vaginal plethysmography readings (Chivers et al., 2010). I discussed some of the implications of this research in Myth 1, in which I compare women's and men's libidos. Nevertheless, for now, you should know that I focus most of my discussion on the plethysmography results, with the assumption that these are more reflective of arousal than self-reports (see the Chivers et al. article mentioned above for an analysis of this assumption and the moderators of the gender difference).

Cultural and political considerations

As I mentioned in the introduction of this chapter, it's important to note that data related to sexuality is viewed through our own cultural lens. So, let me qualify some of the results we will discuss at the outset. Lisa Diamond's book on sexual fluidity (2008b) outlines a number of questions that are *not* addressed by the data on sexual fluidity. Sexual fluidity is not a proxy for sexual orientation (i.e., sexual fluidity is not an indicator of being "bisexual"). In addition, the presence of sexual fluidity in women means neither that sexual orientation is an artificial construct nor that sexual orientation can be changed. Finally, there are a number of theories about same-sex sexuality that range from reasonable to ridiculous. As I will discuss, some of the research on sexual fluidity provides marginal insight into some of these, but there's a long and unfortunate tradition of overinterpreting the findings on sexual fluidity in an effort to support or refute certain theories. For interesting perspectives on the linking of biological, psychological, sociological, and political treatments of desire, see the work of Anne Fausto-Sterling (2007), Sarah Radtke (2013), and Lisa Diamond (2006a).

The studies of Meredith Chivers and colleagues

As I described in Myth 1, Meredith Chivers, Gerulf Rieger, Elizabeth Latty, and J. Michael Bailey (2004) set out to determine whether men and women had similar levels of sexual fluidity. To do this, they recruited men and women who were attracted to either men or women nearly exclusively. In other words, they excluded people who reported sexually fantasizing about both men and women. They gave the participants a dial that they turned to indicate how sexually aroused they were feeling at any given moment and they asked the participants to fit themselves with a plethysmograph to measure blood flow to their genitalia. With the participants all hooked up and seated in a recliner in a dimly lit room, they showed the participants an 11-minute film depicting sexually neutral scenes, like landscapes, and playing relaxing music. This allowed the participants to get used to their setting and to being hooked up to the plethysmography equipment. This also allowed the researchers to determine the baseline levels of blood flow and self-reported arousal. Then, the participants watched a series of six 2-minute erotic videos. Three of the six video clips depicted oral sex. The oral sex was between two men in one clip, between two women in another, and between a man and a woman (cunnilingus) in the third. The other three clips depicted penetrative sex, again between two men (anal penetration), between two women (vaginal penetration with a strap-on sex toy/dildo), and between a man and a woman (vaginal penetration). The order of the clips was randomized across participants and there was an interval between clips that allowed for a return to baseline arousal. As with other studies, the correlation between self-report ratings and genital readings of arousal were much (5 standard deviations) lower for women compared to men, so I will focus on genital blood flow readings.

What did men find sexually arousing? Men who indicated a preference for women found erotic videos depicting two women the most arousing, followed by videos depicting a man and a woman, followed by videos depicting two men. Men who preferred men found the videos with two men the most arousing followed by the videos with a man and a woman, followed by the videos with two women. All of the differences for men were statistically substantial differences. In other words, men were aroused by what they said would arouse them and not aroused by what they didn't think would arouse them.

What did women find sexually arousing? Women who preferred men found all of the erotic videos similarly arousing (as measured by blood flow to the vaginal walls) and at rates that were comparable to the heterosexual men who were watching heterosexual sex (see Myth 1 for a discussion of gender similarities and differences in libidos). Women who preferred women found the video clips depicting two women the most arousing followed closely by the other two types, which yielded similar levels of arousal. Therefore, it seems that women are much more fluid than men when it comes to what is sexually arousing.

At this point, you may be wondering whether sexual fluidity is something that is learned or whether it's innate. Could it be that men are conditioned to only find one gender attractive, whereas women are conditioned to be more open to both genders? After all, there are gender differences in what is acceptable and appropriate when it comes to affection and other matters related to sexuality. In an effort to address this question, Chivers and colleagues (2004) included a group of participants who were male-to-female transsexuals (participants who were born with male genitalia and transitioned to the female gender, including hormonally and surgically). This is an important group to include because they are genetically male but their gender is female. Their inclusion goes some distance in addressing the question of whether the difference in sexual fluidity is a result of "nature or nurture." If the male-to-female transsexuals were to respond like the other women in the study, this would support (but not prove) that arousal specificity (or lack thereof) is learned (i.e., nurture). If the male-to-female transsexuals were to respond like the men in the study, this would support (but again not prove) that arousal specificity is innate (i.e., nature).

Before I tell you what happened, you may be wondering about whether plethysmography works in people with surgically constructed vaginas. The answer is yes. Although there are different ways of constructing what is referred to as a neovagina, the lining is highly sensitive and vascular (Schroder & Carroll, 1999). Therefore, barring complications, the vaginal plethysmograph would work similarly well in a vagina and a neovagina.

So, what did male-to-female transsexual participants find arousing? Transsexual women who preferred men responded with the same pattern of arousal as men who prefer men, with male–male sex being most arousing followed by male–female sex, followed by female–female. Transsexual women who preferred women were more similar to men who prefer women than to the other women in the study. Like men who prefer women, transsexuals who prefer women found the video clips with two men the least arousing, but they found the clips of two women and a woman and man similarly arousing (see Figure 6, which is the graph from Chivers et al., 2004, p. 740). Therefore, it seems that transsexual women demonstrate sexual arousal specificity that is similar to men. This supports the

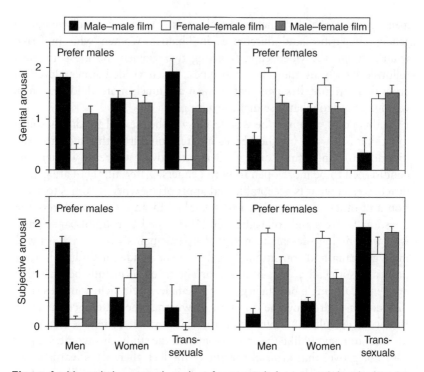

Figure 6 Mean plethysmograph readings from genitals (upper graphs) and subjective ratings (lower graphs) of arousal while watching male–male, female–female, and male–female sexual stimuli (relative to arousal while watching neutral videos), for men, women, and male-to-female transsexuals, as a function of self-reported preferred sexual attraction. Units are within-subjects standard deviations. Error bars show standard errors of the mean. (Reproduced from Chivers et al., 2004, p. 740).

possibility that the sex difference in sexual fluidity is genetically determined rather than learned (Chivers et al., 2004; A. A. Lawrence, Latty, Chivers, & Bailey, 2005).

The results in Chivers and colleagues' 2004 study have been further developed and replicated in subsequent studies (e.g., Chivers, 2005, 2006, 2010; Chivers et al., 2007; Chivers & Timmers, 2012). For example, it appears that men who identify as bisexual have genital arousal patterns similar to gay men (although a few were similar to straight men) as opposed to patterns that would reflect sexual fluidity (Rieger, Chivers, & Bailey, 2005). In addition, Lisa Diamond conducted a 10-year study of women that describes in great detail the sexual fluidity of women (Diamond, 2008a). Therefore, it seems that the data on sexual fluidity are reasonably consistent and suggest that women are more sexually fluid than men.

Given the consistent findings that women are more sexually fluid than men, what might explain this? Barry Kuhle and Sarah Radtke (2013) argue that there's an evolutionary advantage for women to have sexual attraction to other women because of the advantages of having another woman to assist in raising their children. Specifically, they note that mothers may find themselves in a situation in which the fathers of their children are unable or unwilling to assist in parenting. However, if mothers get assistance from other non-parental adults (this is called allo-parenting; for a discussion of this phenomenon, see Sarah Blaffer Hrdy, 2008), their offspring are more likely to grow up and procreate.

Others have proposed alternate explanations for female sexual fluidity, including that it's a byproduct of the decoupling of female arousal and proceptivity (Diamond, 2006b) or that women have a reduced, thus more malleable, sexual drive that allows them to engage in this behavior as a reaction to misogyny and male power (Baumeister, 2000). Whether or not any of these theories are valid, the data seem clear: women are more sexually fluid than men.

Finally, there's the conundrum that if men's sexual attraction is not fluid and apparently not tied to cultural influences, is the gender to which they are attracted genetically determined? And, if so, how can these genes replicate over generations? It appears that the answer to the first question is yes. There's evidence that there's a genetic component to men's sexual orientation and that it comes from the mother's genetic contribution, which would explain the way in which such a characteristic can be transmitted across generations when such genes would appear to have a disadvantage in terms of procreation. Although there are several caveats to these results, there's a growing consensus among scientists regarding the genetic component to sexual attraction in men (e.g., Camperio-Ciani, Corna, & Capiluppi, 2004; Hamer, Hu, Magnuson, Hu, & Pattatucci, 1993).

Conclusion

To summarize, I quote directly from Chivers and colleagues (2004, p. 741):

> A self-identified heterosexual woman would be mistaken to question her sexual identity because she became aroused watching female–female erotica; most heterosexual women experience such arousal. A self-identified heterosexual man who experienced substantial arousal to male–male erotica, however, would be statistically justified in reconsidering his sexual identity.

Myth #12

There are no differences between same-sex relationships and heterosexual relationships

When the conversation among relationship scientists or people who are simply interested in relationships turns to comparisons of same-sex relationships and other-sex relationships there's often a sense that – at their heart – the two types of relationships are essentially similar. After all, two people in love experience many of the same highs and lows whether they are in love with someone of the same gender or a different gender. Indeed, this attitude has been reflected in polling data (Pew Research Center, 2013) and in media coverage of the same-sex marriage debate (Hitlin, Jurkowitz, & Mitchell, 2013). It has also been my experience in working with couples in my private practice. Over the years, I have worked with both same- and other-sex couples. By and large, the issues were quite similar whether the couples were two women, two men, or a man and a woman. So, my anecdotal sense was that the similarities outweighed the differences.

It turns out that my clinical impressions were consistent with the research literature: other-sex couples and same-sex couples are clearly more similar than they are different. In fact, the data are strong enough that I considered wording this myth in the other direction; however, changing attitudes and increasing rates of acceptance of sexual minorities (Lipka, 2014; Pew Research Center, 2013) led me to focus on the differences instead of the similarities because the differences are also worthy of consideration.

Similarities between same-sex and other-sex couples

Before getting into the differences, let's review some of the many ways in which couples are similar regardless of gender composition. The similarities begin even before people enter into a relationship. The qualities that people find attractive in a potential mate are similar regardless of their sexual orientation. Most people agree that they are seeking partners who are affectionate, dependable, and compatible. To the extent that there are gender differences in mate preferences (see Myths 7 and 21), the differences remain the same despite the gender to which people are attracted. In other words, men are slightly more likely to emphasize the physical attractiveness in a potential partner regardless of whether that partner is a man or woman. Women, on the other hand, are slightly more likely to emphasize the personality of a potential partner regardless of whether that partner is a man or woman (e.g., Bailey, Gaulin, Agyei, & Gladue, 1994). Finally, sexual minority and majority individuals report meeting potential partners in the same ways, through mutual friends, at work, in bars, at social events, and on the Internet (e.g., Bryant & Demian, 1994; Elze, 2002).

Lawrence Kurdek conducted extensive research on the similarities and differences in the relationship quality and the predictors of relationship quality across different types of couples. In terms of relationship satisfaction, same- and other-sex couples are fairly similar (Kurdek, 1994, 1998b, 2008). In addition, the predictors of changes in relationship satisfaction are also very similar across same- and other-sex couples (e.g., Kurdek, 2004). For example, all three types of couples (i.e., male–male, female–female, and female–male) argue about similar matters, such as money (e.g., Kurdek, 2006), and have similar levels of problem-solving skills (e.g., Schreurs & Buunk, 1996). Finally, when it comes to the end of a relationship, there are no differences in the reason for or the impact of relationship dissolution across relationships between two men, two women, or a man and a woman (Kurdek, 1997). Therefore, in the end, there are more similarities than there are differences (for reviews, see Kurdek, 2005; Peplau & Fingerhut, 2007; Rith & Diamond, 2013). Still, there are some differences.

Differences between same-sex and other-sex couples

To the extent that there are differences between same-sex and other-sex couples, there are two broad explanations for such differences. The first explanation is based on what scientists refer to as either *stigmatization* (e.g., Diamond, 2006c) or *context* (Bradbury & Karney, 2014), and it focuses on the stressors that are typically faced by people in same-sex couples due to their sexual-minority status. The second explanation is often called *gender-related dynamics* or *gender-role theory* (e.g., Rith & Diamond, 2013), which focuses on the differences that may result in combinations of two men versus two women versus a man and a woman. In describing some of the differences between same- and other-sex couples, both of these perspectives may offer explanations.

Stress and support
In the United States there's a clear trend toward greater acceptance of sexual minorities (Gallup, 2014; Savin-Williams, 2008). For example, the rapidly shifting laws on same-sex marriage have given legal legitimacy to

many families that didn't enjoy the same legal benefits and protections of marriage (see Myth 13) as other-sex couples. Perhaps more importantly, U.S. politicians and voters have shifted from repeatedly voting to ban same-sex marriage to repeatedly voting to allow it. These changes have led to improved well-being for many people considered sexual minorities (e.g., Savin-Williams, 2005). Despite these advances, 38% of Americans still consider same-sex relationships to be morally wrong (Newport & Himelfarb, 2013). Thus, the burden of social stigmatization and homophobia is still present in the lives of sexual minorities and still presents challenges for same-sex couples that aren't faced by other-sex couples. Approximately 20% of sexual minorities in a national probability sample indicated that they experienced a crime based on their perceived sexual orientation (Herek, 2009). In another study, around a third of the sample reported being a victim of violence (Henry J. Kaiser Family Foundation, 2001). The stress of prejudice and discrimination is well documented and associated with mental and physical problems (e.g., Balsam, Beauchaine, Mickey, & Rothblum, 2005; Cochran & Mays, 2009; Feinstein, Goldfried, & Davila, 2012). Beyond the direct effects of discrimination, sexual minorities often experience diminished support from their families of origin (Oswald, 2002). This stressor is in addition to perceived discrimination from businesses (e.g., Walters & Curran, 1996), such as when renting a hotel room (D. A. Jones, 1996), and governments (United States v. Windsor, 2012). The net effect of the stigma endured by sexual minorities is to create more stress and fewer sources of social support that enhance relationships.

Sexual activity and satisfaction

As discussed in Myth 1, the difference in the sex drive of men and women is not as great as most people assume, especially when measuring physiological responses instead of stated preference or behavior. That said, it's still the case that some differences in the sexual beliefs and behavior of men and women appear to lead to differences in the sexual activity and satisfaction of couples with two women, two men, and a man and a woman. As for sexual activity, same-sex couples with two men report greater sexual activity than other-sex couples (cf. Blumstein & Schwartz, 1983), and same-sex couples with two women report less sexual activity than other-sex couples (for review see, Peplau, Fingerhut, & Beals, 2004).

The latter difference is persistent enough that it has led to a debate among scholars regarding the reasons for the lower frequency of sexual activity among lesbian couples. Some have argued that women have a broader conceptualization of what is considered "sexual" (e.g., cuddling, fondling, and hugging; Frye, 1990). This would be consistent with evidence that there are widespread differences in what people think it means "to have sex" (e.g., S. A. Sanders & Reinisch, 1999). Others have speculated that this difference in frequency of activity could be the result of women being socialized not to initiate sex or be seen as particularly sexual (see also Myth 1; Nichols, 1987, 1988). It's also notable that women in same-sex relationships report greater frequency of orgasms than women in other-sex relationships (e.g., Kinsey, 1953; Peplau, Cochran, Rook, & Padesky, 1978), which helps explain why, despite the differences in sexual frequency, lesbians don't report being less happy with their sex lives than others (Kurdek, 1991). A final difference is that men in same-sex relationships are more likely to be accepting of and to engage in sexual activity outside of their primary relationship. Although this finding has been documented in multiple surveys, before and during the AIDS epidemic (e.g., Blumstein & Schwartz, 1983; Bryant & Demian, 1994; Solomon, Rothblum, & Balsam, 2005), it's also clear that non-monogamy is less threatening to men in same-sex relationships than to lesbians and other-sex couples (Bringle, 1995).

In summary, sexual activity and satisfaction are ways in which male and female same-sex couples differ from each other and from other-sex couples. Yet there's still much to be learned about whether these differences are social constructions and whether they will persist as more same-sex couples get married and as other generational changes take hold (for reviews, see Diamond, 2006c; Peplau et al., 2004; Rith & Diamond, 2013).

Relationship dissolution

The third broad way in which other- and same-sex couples differ is in their rates of relationship dissolution. Despite having similar rates and patterns of relationship satisfaction (Kurdek, 1998b, 2001; Roisman, Clausell, Holland, Fortuna, & Elieff, 2008), some researchers have found that same-sex couples have higher rates of dissolution compared with married couples, especially married couples with children (Kurdek, 2004). This may be accounted for in part by the stigmatization and lack of support offered by the government and society more generally, as described above. However, even in countries in which there have been long-standing laws protecting the legal and parental rights of same-sex couples, the differences in relationship dissolution rates persist. Specifically, in a study of couples in one such country (Sweden), researchers found that 13% of other-sex couples dissolved their relationship within five years, compared to 20% of male same-sex couples and 30% of female same-sex couples. This finding held even after controlling for other variables known to be associated with relationship dissolution (Andersson, Noack, Seierstad, & Weedon-Fekjær, 2006).

So, what is going on to explain these results? Tom Bradbury and Ben Karney (2014) think it may be one of three possibilities. First, even though same-sex couples in Sweden enjoy more rights and greater acceptance than in other countries, like the United States, there's still less societal pressure for same-sex couples to maintain their relationships than for other-sex couples (e.g., Henry J. Kaiser Family Foundation, 2001). Second, women may be more likely to make a clean break from relationships that are unfulfilling because they tend to value exclusivity more than gay men (Bringle, 1995). Third, same-sex couples may have higher standards, especially with regard to equality within the relationship (e.g., Kurdek, 2004), than other-sex couples and, if these standards aren't met, same- and other-sex couples often consider ending the relationship (see Overall, Fletcher, & Simpson, 2006).

Similarities revisited

It's important to return to where I started this chapter. Despite a focus on the differences between same- and other-sex couples, it's worth reminding ourselves that there are more similarities than there are differences. One especially noteworthy way in which there's similarity across couples is in the potential for violence within the couple. A review of the research literature on interpersonal violence in female and male same-sex couples by Leslie Burke and Diane Follingstad (1999) found no reliable indications of differences in the rates of interpersonal violence across the types of couples. This finding surprises many people (see Myth 22) and seems inconsistent with what we know about men being more violent than women (Moffitt, 2001). I've highlighted the similarity of the problem of interpersonal violence because it warrants more attention (e.g., Tesch, Bekerian, English, & Harrington, 2010) and because it demonstrates that same- and other-sex couples are similar even in ways that are counterintuitive.

Conclusion

To summarize, the research provides more evidence of similarities than differences between same-sex and other-sex relationships. I am cognizant that the differences (and similarities) I've described are considered in the context of societal and political influences, after all homosexuality itself was once considered a mental illness by the American Psychiatric Association (for current thinking on the mental health of sexual minorities, see Kitzinger, 1987; Savin-Williams, 2008). Nevertheless, I think it's safe to conclude that although same- and other-sex couples are more similar than different, there are reliable differences.

Myth #13 Children raised by other-sex couples are better off than children raised by same-sex couples

In the United States, the issue of same-sex marriage is changing rapidly. In the span of a few short years, there have been large swings in public opinion and in the legal status of such unions. Michael J. Klarman (2013) presents the history of the push for and against same-sex marriage, so I will retell neither the history nor the current status of the same-sex marriage debate. Rather, I will focus on one particular myth that has come out of this debate.

The idea that children raised by other-sex married couples are better off than children raised by same-sex married couples has been discussed around kitchen tables, in academic journals, and in courtrooms. Where did this myth come from? According to *The New York Times*, it came from "opponents of same-sex marriage" who used the argument "to play one of their most emotional and, they hoped, potent cards: the claim that having parents of the same sex is bad for children" (Eckholm, 2014b, p. A16). They played this card in a trial in federal court challenging Michigan's ban on same-sex marriages (Deboer v. Snyder, 2014). The trial came about because, in 2012, April DeBoer and Jayne Rowse sued to overturn a Michigan law that prevented them from co-adopting their three children. The two women are nurses who separately adopted children born with special needs. They wanted to protect each other's parenting rights and the rights of their children in the event that one of them was to die. The trial judge suggested expanding their suit to challenge Michigan's ban on same-sex marriage. During the two-week trial in federal court, sociologist Mark Regnerus testified that the Michigan ban on same-sex marriage should be upheld because allowing same-sex marriage puts children in these families at a disadvantage (Eckholm, 2014a).

A flawed study (Regnerus, 2012a)

The basis for his testimony stemmed from a study that that was initially designed and funded by the Witherspoon Institute, a conservative organization that describes itself as supporting "scholarly research and teaching that enhance understanding of the crucial function that marriage and family serve in fostering a society capable of democratic self-governance" (Witherspoon Institute, 2012), as well as the Bradley Foundation, which describes its programs as supporting "limited, competent government; a dynamic marketplace for economic, intellectual, and cultural activity; and a vigorous defense, at home and abroad, of American ideas and institutions" (Bradley Foundation, 2006). Their efforts to design and fund this study were spearheaded by W. Bradford Wilcox, an associate professor of sociology at the University of Virginia with ties to several socially conservative foundations and organizations. It appears that Wilcox and the head of the Witherspoon Institute set out to find a reputable academic institution to conduct the study they had envisioned. They found the study director and institution they were looking for in Mark Regnerus, an associate professor of sociology at the University of Texas at Austin and a research associate of the university's Population Research Center. Such recruitment of a researcher is an unusual process because usually social scientists design their own studies and bring proposals of such studies to funding agencies. It appears that process was reversed in this case, despite claims to the contrary (Regnerus, 2012b). Shortly after data collection began, it appears that Regenerus, Wilcox, Scott Stanley (see Myths 14, 15, & 18), and a staff member from Focus on the Family (a conservative Christian organization founded by James Dobson) met to discuss how to publicize the results in time for the court cases on same-sex marriage that were widely expected (P. N. Cohen, 2013).

In addition to misrepresenting the origin of the study and the author's relationship with the funders, there are other irregularities about the study that should cause concern even before examining the data. For example, the timeline of this study as outlined in Philip Cohen's blog, Family Inequality (P. N. Cohen, 2012), shows the following impossibilities:

- Paper received by *Social Science Research* (the journal that published the article): February 1, 2012
- Data collection ended: February 21, 2012
- File "containing the collected data" delivered to University of Texas: February 24, 2012
- Revised paper received by *Social Science Research*: February 29, 2012

So, of course this means that the manuscript was submitted to the journal prior to the end of data collection, after which the author would need to clean the data, conduct the statistical analyses, and write up the results. Speculation of collusion between the editorial staff of the journal and the author of the study led to a full review of the process. With regard to timeline, it seems that Regnerus submitted his manuscript prior to the completion of data collection without mentioning this in the manuscript or to the editor (Sherkat, 2012).

In addition to the timeline irregularities, it turns out that two of the paid consultants on the study were also reviewers of the manuscript on behalf of *Social Science Research* (Bartlett, 2012), including – apparently – Wilcox (Rose, 2012) who seems to have been involved since the inception of the study. This is problematic and irregular. It's kind of like asking the coach of a football team to be one of the referees during a big game. It should be noted that the editor of *Social Science Research*, James D. Wright, has indicated that he knew that two of the reviewers were involved with the study, but that he trusted them to "check their ideological guns at the referee's door" (Wright, 2012, p. 1342). Yet, it seems they didn't. An independent inquiry into the review process of this and a review paper appearing in the same issue (Marks, 2012) found that there were multiple problems with the review procedure. The author of the inquiry concludes that the failure of the review process led to the publishing of two articles that have "serious flaws and distortions that were not simply ignored, but lauded in the reviews" (Sherkat, 2012, p. 1347).

The methodological problems with the study

There are enough problems with the Regnerus (2012a) study that a complete recounting of the issues is beyond the scope of this myth, but let's begin with the question that he set out to answer: "Do the children of gay and lesbian parents look comparable to those of their heterosexual counterparts?" (p. 755). To answer this question he classified the types of families in which children were raised into eight types of household settings. The following are the verbatim descriptions of the groups (with acronyms spelled out and followed by number of participants in each group:

1. Intact biological family: Lived in intact biological family (with mother and father) from 0 to 18, and parents are still married at present ($N = 919$).
2. Lesbian mother: Participant reported participant's mother had a same-sex romantic (lesbian) relationship with a woman, regardless of any other household transitions ($N = 163$).
3. Gay father: Participant reported participant's father had a same-sex romantic (gay) relationship with a man, regardless of any other household transitions ($N = 73$).
4. Adopted: Participant was adopted by one or two strangers at birth or before age 2 ($N = 101$).
5. Divorced later or had joint custody: Participant reported living with biological mother and father from birth to age 18, but parents are not married at present ($N = 116$).
6. Stepfamily: Biological parents were either never married or else divorced, and participant's primary custodial parent was married to someone else before participant turned 18 ($N = 394$).
7. Single parent: Biological parents were either never married or else divorced, and participant's primary custodial parent did not marry (or remarry) before participant turned 18 ($N = 816$).
8. All others: Includes all other family structure/event combinations, such as participants with a deceased parent ($N = 406$).

Did you catch that? Reread categories 2 and 3 and notice how they don't match what Regnerus set out to study. Given that his conclusions were used in lawsuits about same-sex couples getting married and adopting children, one would think that those two groups would have been children raised in same-sex headed families. In fact, most of the children in those two groups were raised in families in which their parents had an other-sex relationship that ended. In other words, Regnerus was essentially comparing children raised in families that experienced divorce or other types of disruption (possibly due to one parent coming out as a sexual minority) to families in which two biological parents raised the child and remained married. It's not surprising then that he found effects. It's well known that family stability is associated with the well-being of children (see Myth 25). At no point did he report the outcomes of children who were raised in same-sex headed households.

As I mentioned before, there are other problems with this study. These include sampling issues (Sherkat, 2012); the fact that he used the adult child's report of whether one of their parents engaged in same-sex relationships without any further substantiation, which is considered an invalid method of assessing sexual orientation (Gates et al., 2012); and fact that he conflated the rejection of the hypothesis that there are no group differences with support for the hypothesis that same-sex headed households are "uniquely problematic for child development" (p. 766; although his study lacks evidence to support either hypothesis; Perrin, Cohen, & Caren, 2013). In summary, Regnerus (2012a) claims that his study demonstrated that children raised in same-sex headed households have different outcomes than other children, when in fact the major flaws in the design and insufficient numbers of the very couples he claims to be studying render his conclusions unsupportable.

The consensus of the social scientists

Not only are the claims regarding the Regnerus study out of line with the data from the same study, but claims that children of same-sex parents fare worse than children of other-sex parents are at odds with the scholarly consensus. Indeed, the 13,000-member American Sociological Association (ASA) presented the consensus research findings of sociologists on this issue to the federal courts in an *amicus* (i.e., a friend of the court) brief (American Sociological Association, 2012). In the brief, the ASA wrote that "when the social science evidence is exhaustively examined – which the ASA has done – the facts demonstrate that children fare just as well when raised by same-sex parents. Unsubstantiated fears regarding same-sex child rearing do not overcome these facts and do not justify upholding" bans on same-sex marriage (p. 5). They go on to cite convincing research that there are no differences between same- and other-sex parents in terms of children's academic achievement (e.g., Potter, 2012), even when the children of same-sex parents have higher levels of biological and environmental risk factors prior to adoptive placement (e.g., Lavner, Waterman, & Peplau, 2012). There are also no differences when it comes to social development (e.g., Wainright & Patterson, 2008), mental health (e.g., Gartrell & Bos, 2010), sexual behavior (e.g., Patterson & Wainright, 2012), or substance abuse (e.g.,

Wainright & Patterson, 2006). In other words, there is essentially no evidence that same-sex couples are worse parents than other-sex couples.

Why it matters

As of this writing, the federal judge in Detroit who heard the case challenging Michigan's ban on same-sex marriages (Deboer v. Snyder, 2014) ruled that the law was unconstitutional. However, Regnerus testified that the ban should be upheld and pointed to his flawed study as evidence that same-sex marriage may be harmful to children. Despite the obvious problems with this study, it continues to be cited as valid (e.g., Johnson et al., 2012) and supportive of legal efforts to ban same-sex marriage and to ostracize families headed by same-sex couples (e.g., Ablow, 2012). In the Michigan case, Federal Judge Bernard A. Friedman dismissed the study and those who supported it, concluding "the Court finds Regnerus's testimony entirely unbelievable and not worthy of serious consideration" (Deboer v. Snyder, 2014, p. 13). Indeed, the judge went further in his decision, noting that taking the position of Regnerus, Wilcox, and others arguing against same-sex marriage "to its logical conclusion, the empirical evidence at hand should require that only rich, educated, suburban-dwelling, married Asians may marry, to the exclusion of all other heterosexual couples" (p. 22). Thus, while this judge noticed that this study was flawed and that Regnerus and those testifying in a similar manner were part of a dubious element of social science, others may not notice. More importantly, continuing to cite profoundly flawed studies like this gives a cloak of scientific integrity to what is essentially discrimination.

Conclusion

Regnerus (2012a) purported to test whether children raised by sexual-minority parents were dissimilar in their adult well-being to other children. The fallout from the publication of his flawed study was swift and loud. It received a great deal of press and shook up politicians, activists, and academics. In the end, the fallout was not as great as it might have been because the judge in the trial at which it was discussed unequivocally dismissed the study and its author. Nevertheless, those who are against same-sex marriage continue to cite this study, despite it being essentially uninformative in terms of addressing the parenting qualities of same-sex couples, while ignoring the overwhelming research indicating that same-sex couples are as good as other-sex parents. In conclusion, the Regnerus study doesn't demonstrate any problems with children raised in same-sex headed households because he didn't have "children raised in same-sex headed households" as a group in his study. Therefore, the scientific literature is where it was before his study: without any evidence that children from same-sex families are at a disadvantage compared to children from other types of families (Perrin et al., 2013).

5 PREDICTING SUCCESS AND FAILURE IN RELATIONSHIPS

Predicting human behavior is tricky business. I remember hearing a story about a famous financier who received a letter from a man who wrote that he was very impressed with the financier's ability to amass a large fortune by predicting the direction of the markets, and he wondered if he would share his thoughts about what the markets would do in the coming year. He went on to write that he had enclosed a self-addressed and stamped envelope for his response. The financier read the letter and turned to his secretary and said, "For the price of a stamp, this man wants to know what I would give my entire fortune to know." And yet, we frequently hear of people claiming to know the future. Whether it's financial advisers, business consultants, psychics, or clergy, many people think they can see the future and want to tell us about it – usually for a price. Not to be outdone, psychologists also try to predict human behavior and those studying intimate relationships (like me) are right in the thick of it.

This chapter describes seven myths that purport to help you predict the outcome of relationships, especially marriages. In discussing each of these myths, I focus on the studies in which relationship scientists measured some aspect of the couple, often behaviors but also personalities, stress, or treatments, and then follow those couples into the future. These types of studies are called longitudinal or prospective studies. Considered the gold standard for determining the causal direction of an effect when we cannot manipulate a variable or randomly assign participants to conditions (e.g., we cannot randomly assign some participants to violent relationships and others to nonviolent relationships), longitudinal studies allow scientists to

Great Myths of Intimate Relationships: Dating, Sex, and Marriage,
First Edition. Matthew D. Johnson.
© 2016 John Wiley & Sons, Inc. Published 2016 by John Wiley & Sons, Inc.

assess variables over time to see which changes precede other changes. For example, intimate partner violence is correlated with relationship dissatisfaction (Stith, Green, Smith, & Ward, 2008), but does violence precede relationship dissatisfaction or does relationship dissatisfaction precede violence? Longitudinal studies have allowed scientists to develop models for how relationships develop over time and to explain why some marriages remain mostly happy, some marriages become unhappy, and some marriages end in divorce.

The catch here is that we're not as good at doing this as some researchers have claimed and as has been portrayed in the media. In a series of studies that observed married couples having disagreements and followed them over time, some researchers made surprisingly strong claims about their ability to predict marital outcomes. In particular, a few scientists claim to be able to predict marital outcomes with over 90% accuracy (Buehlman, Gottman, & Katz, 1992; Gottman & Levenson, 1999; C. T. Hill & Peplau, 1998; other studies describe accuracy rates above 80%, such as Gottman, 1994; Larsen & Olson, 1989). Prediction rates this high need to be examined carefully, not only because they are so impressive, but also because they've received widespread attention in the media.

Indeed, other scientists have reviewed these data carefully and found that there are several reasons to doubt such high levels of predictive accuracy (Bradbury & Karney, 2014; Heyman & Slep, 2001). Of the many issues with these claims, one is worth considering as you read the discussion of the myths in this chapter. As I described before, to predict marital outcomes, scientists follow couples over time. At the end of the study, they use statistics to determine which combination of variables from the beginning of the study best predict the outcomes that they found at the end of the study. In a way, you could call this "*post*diction" instead of *pre*diction. Imagine at the end of a chess match, going back and finding the combination of moves that led one player to beat the other. This is a perfectly reasonable and worthy thing to do (and I have done it both in my research and in my amateurish chess matches); however, it would be unreasonable to then make claims that your postmortem analysis can be applied to other chess matches with the same degree of accuracy. To be able to make that claim, one would need to do what scientists call *cross-validation*, which is when you take the results of one group of subjects and use them to make predictions about another group of subjects. For example, if I were to describe a study in which I found that spouses who display a certain combination of contempt and defensiveness in their disagreements accounted for 90% of the divorces in my study, I would then need to collect data from a new set of subjects in a separate study and determine whether the same combination of contempt and defensiveness in disagreements found in the first study still accurately predicts divorce in the second study. No such study predicting marital outcomes using cross-validation has been done to my knowledge. Therefore, as you read the findings that I describe in the following myths, remember that the effects haven't been cross-validated, so we cannot be certain whether they would be predictive in other studies, much less in the case of a particular relationship.

Enough with the caveats – let's examine what we think we know about what does and doesn't predict relationship quality. First, I begin the chapter by addressing the fact that the rate of conjugal cohabitation has risen sharply in recent years. Part of the increase is explained by the fact that couples believe living together will help determine their readiness for marriage generally and to their current partner specifically, but I will make the case that this is a myth. Second, I examine whether premarital counseling or relationship education programs prevent discord and divorce. In the third and fourth myths of the chapter, I discuss the role of communication and problem-solving skills in intimate relationships. Fifth, I examine the impact of having children on the relationships of parents. In the sixth and seventh myths, I describe how stress and supporting your partner in times of stress change relationship and personal satisfaction. By the end of the chapter, I hope to have dispelled some myths regarding the prediction of relationship outcomes.

Myth #14 Living together before marriage is a good way to determine whether you're with the right person

As of 2013, there were around 8.1 million other-sex couples living together without being married in the United States (U.S. Census Bureau, 2013a). This represents a 16-fold increase from 1970, when cohabitation was relatively rare (S. L. Brown, 2004). As nonmarital cohabitation has increased, it has gone from 10% of the relationships of women aged 19–44 in the United States to 23% of these relationships. In addition, roughly two-thirds of all first marriages are preceded by cohabitation, up from 11% in 1970 (Manning, 2013). This change has coincided with changes in attitudes about the acceptability of premarital cohabitation. It's now considered a normal and even beneficial stage of the relationship, whereas it was thought of as improper and even shameful a couple of generations ago (Thornton & Young-DeMarco, 2001). In fact, it's still illegal for a man and woman to cohabit without being married in Florida (under the Lewd and Lascivious Behavior statute, 1868), Michigan (under the Lewd and Lascivious Cohabitation and Gross Lewdness act, 1931), and Mississippi (under the Adultery and Fornication; Unlawful Cohabitation code, 1848). Legality aside, nonmarital cohabitation has clearly become normative and acceptable in the United States.

The data I have reviewed thus far focus on the United States, but the prevalence and acceptability of nonmarital cohabitation varies greatly by country (Hiekel & Castro-Martín, 2014). In Europe alone, there are countries like Sweden, with a cohabitation prevalence rate of 53% among young adults and an approval rating of 4.5 (out of 5); and like Ukraine, with only 3% of young adults cohabiting and an approval rating of 2.5 on a 5-point scale (Liefbroer & Dourleijn, 2006). Beyond differences by country, there are also ethnic differences (although these appear to be diminishing); age differences, with younger couples being more likely to cohabit; and educational differences, with less-educated couples being more likely to cohabit (Manning, 2013). Regardless of these differences, one thing remains clear: premarital and nonmarital cohabitation is on the rise.

In 2011, 70% of high school seniors agreed or mostly agreed with the statement "It's usually a good idea for a couple to live together before getting married in order to find out whether they really get along" (Johnston, Bachman, & O'Malley, 2013). This was consistent with the rates of young adults who agreed with this statement (Popenoe & Whitehead, 2001). However, it's becoming clear that for many young adults cohabitation is not an alternative to marriage, but rather an alternative to being single. When interviewed, many couples talked about cohabitation as something to do as a relationship progressed, but none of them talked about it as an alternative to marriage (Manning & Smock, 2005). Thus, most Americans believe that cohabitation is a natural step in the progression toward a healthy and happy marriage.

The effects of premarital cohabitation

It makes logical sense that it should be beneficial to test-drive a potential spouse by living together before committing to marriage. The catch is there's no support that cohabitation before marriage improves the quality of marriage or decreases the chance of divorce. In fact, the opposite seems to be true. Catherine Cohan reviewed "over 100 studies with American samples spanning 25 years" and found "that not one shows any evidence that marriage preceded by cohabitation is superior in any way to direct entry into marriage" (2013, p. 106). In fact, the negative impact of premarital cohabitation is now so well known among relationship scientists that we simply call it "the cohabitation effect."

The effect of cohabitation on dissolution
In Cohan's review (2013; see also Jose, O'Leary, & Moyer, 2010), there was a clear effect of cohabitation: couples who cohabited before they married were more likely to dissolve their marriage. This effect was consistent across generations and methods. The one caveat to this finding is that the negative effects disappear if neither spouse has been married before and the couple is already engaged when they cohabit (Stanley, Rhoades, Amato, Markman, & Johnson, 2010); however, there's still no indication that couples benefit from cohabitation. It's possible that, as cohabitation becomes more acceptable (Soons & Kalmijn, 2009) and seen as sign of commitment similar to engagement, the negative effects of cohabitation may diminish (for further discussion of this theory, see Manning & Cohen, 2012). Even with these caveats, the finding is robust: Many studies have found that premarital cohabitation predicts divorce and certainly doesn't appear to prevent divorce.

The effect of cohabitation on relationship quality
Even if there is a correlation between premarital cohabitation and divorce, is it possible that cohabitation could lead to better marriages? Again, the answer is emphatically "no" (Cohan, 2013; Jose et al., 2010). In the past 20 years, during which researchers conducted multiple studies that examined couples who lived together before they married and couples who didn't live together prior to marriage, those who lived together before marriage reported lower marital satisfaction (e.g., Tach & Halpern-Meekin, 2009), worse communication skills (e.g., Cohan & Kleinbaum, 2002), increased likelihood of aggression (Kline et al., 2004), lower commitment (Stanley, Whitton, & Markman, 2004), and greater neuroticism (a strong correlate of marital quality; Stafford, Kline, & Rankin, 2004).

The effect of cohabitation on children

In addition to being correlated with aspects of marriage, cohabitation is correlated with child outcomes as well. About 41% of children born in the United States are born to unmarried mothers (J. A. Martin, Hamilton, Osterman, Curtin, & Mathews, 2013), and about 18% are born to mothers who are unmarried but cohabiting with the child's biological father (Martinez, Chandra, Abma, Jones, & Mosher, 2006; for more details on these trends, see Gibson-Davis & Rackin, 2014). There's an inter-generational transmission effect as well, with the children who live with cohabiting parents being more likely to cohabit outside of marriage when they're adults (Sassler, Cunningham, & Lichter, 2009). In terms of the association between nonmarital cohabitation and child well-being, children who live with cohabiting parents experience poorer health compared with those living with married parents (e.g., Schmeer, 2011).

Further evidence of the dissimilarity of cohabitation and marriage on child outcomes comes from research on what happens when these relationships end. The data regarding the impact of divorce on children are well known (see a discussion in Myth 25), but the termination of a cohabiting relationship is not as impactful on children (e.g., Fagan, 2013) and is no different than when the child's parents cohabit cyclically (Nepomnyaschy & Teitler, 2013). In other words, it appears that better child outcomes are associated with the strength of the commitment of parents to each other. Or, put more simply, children tend to thrive better with married parents than with cohabiting parents (see also Myth 13).

Understanding the cohabitation effect

To understand the potential reasons that cohabitation before or instead of marriage appears to be associated with negative effects let's examine four hypotheses. For a longer discussion of each of these theoretical perspectives see the review by Cohan (2013).

Weeding hypothesis

The weeding hypothesis is the idea that people will learn more about the problems and benefits of a particular person by living with a potential spouse. In doing so, people can then "weed" out partners who aren't well suited for marriage (Becker, Landes, & Michael, 1977). Relationship scientists have largely abandoned this hypothesis in light of the data that the cohabitation effect seems to be negative; however, the weeding hypothesis remains popular among the public (as noted previously), despite the robust findings that support the exact opposite of this hypothesis.

Selection hypothesis

The selection hypothesis maintains that the people who are more likely to cohabit are also more likely to possess other characteristics that tend to predict worse outcomes for marriage. For example, people whose parents divorced, who have lower incomes, or who are pregnant or had a child without being married are all more likely to cohabit and more likely to get a divorce (e.g., Bennett, Blanc, & Bloom, 1988; Bumpass & Sweet, 1989). More than demographics, many point to beliefs and attitudes that might influence both the decision to cohabit and the likelihood of getting a divorce. Indeed, people who chose not to cohabit before marriage are also less likely to consider divorce an acceptable option (e.g., Stanley et al., 2004). The fact that this is the case has led many researchers to examine the association of premarital cohabitation and later divorce while controlling for other variables like religiosity. Generally, the cohabitation effect remains even when controlling for these other variables (e.g., Cohan & Kleinbaum, 2002).

However, as the study of the cohabitation effect has become more sophisticated, some aspects of the selection hypothesis have been supported. For example, in one study the effect disappeared when the authors excluded women who didn't have a child before being married (Tach & Halpern-Meekin, 2009). In other words, couples who had a child when they were not married were more likely to cohabit before marriage and more likely to have discordant marriages. This outcome didn't hold for couples without children. In the end, it appears that the selection hypothesis is part of the story but can't fully explain the cohabitation effect.

Causality hypothesis

As I noted in introducing this chapter, causality is difficult to determine when studying intimate relationships. Ethically, we cannot randomly assign couples to cohabit before marriage. So, to infer causality when we can't use random assignment, scientists tend to turn to longitudinal studies that follow the same subjects over time. This kind of work is expensive and time consuming, so few researchers do this. Here is what we know: Using data from a 23-year longitudinal study in which participants were assessed seven times, researchers found that people tend to become more accepting of divorce and less religious following nonmarital cohabitation (Axinn & Thornton, 1992; Thornton, Axinn, & Hill, 1992). As cohabitation continued, subjects became less interested in marriage and children (Axinn & Barber, 1997; M. Cunningham & Thornton, 2005; McGinnis, 2003). Thus, it seems that the initiation and maintenance of nonmarital cohabitation leads to changes in attitudes that are associated with the likelihood of both marriage and divorce in ways that impede long-term marriage.

Inertia hypothesis

The inertia hypothesis is that couples don't see cohabitation as an alternative – or even a step toward – marriage (Manning & Smock, 2005); rather, they view finances, housing, and convenience as the primary reasons for cohabitation (Sassler, 2004). Couples who cohabit for these reasons often make these decisions quickly compared to couples who decide to marry (Casper & Bianchi, 2002). As an extreme example, Catherine Cohan (2013) described a couple she met who moved in together the day they met because he was losing his housing. More commonly, couples often describe how one or the other was spending two or three nights a week at the other's home, so they eventually decided not to pay two rents or to move some of their things to the other's place. As cohabitation continues, couples invest more and more in their relationship and their home. These investments (i.e., sunk costs) serve to constrain the couple in the relationship. This inertia, coupled with societal and familial pressure to marry, may then lead to marriage for couples who otherwise would not get married if they weren't living together. Scott Stanley and his colleagues refer to this as "sliding versus deciding," meaning that couples slide into marriage instead of deciding to get married (Owen, Rhoades, & Stanley, 2013; Stanley, Rhoades, & Markman, 2006).

Considerable evidence supports this hypothesis. The most compelling evidence is that couples who cohabit after they get engaged appear to be immune from the negative consequences of premarital cohabitation. Galena Kline Rhodes and her colleagues (including Stanley) have demonstrated this effect in three different studies (Kline et al., 2004; Rhoades, Stanley, & Markman, 2009; Stanley, Rhoades, et al., 2010). Therefore, deciding to marry before moving in together seems to set in motion some of the relationship benefits of making a formal commitment, whereas deciding to move in together before deciding to marry appears to diminish some of the benefits of making a commitment to marry.

Conclusion

In the end, there's overwhelming support for not cohabiting with an intimate partner prior to marriage. Or, as Catherine Cohan (2013, p. 118) put it:

> The American research evidence over the last 25 years shows no benefits of cohabitation in terms of the key outcomes that social scientists measure – personal well-being and relationship adjustment, satisfaction, and stability. Contrary to the notion that cohabitation is beneficial to a relationship, it may undermine the success of a future marriage, particularly when it occurs before engagement, involves multiple cohabitation experiences with different partners, or results in the birth of a child prior to marriage.

Certainly, there are caveats to this conclusion and the changing demographics of marriage and intimate relationships in the United States may end up changing this picture in the future (cf. Jose et al., 2010); but, for now, the answer to the question of whether cohabiting with a partner might be beneficial to the relationship is an emphatic no!

Myth #15   Premarital counseling or relationship education programs prevent discord and divorce

A couple wanting to get married will often find that, if they want to be wed by a member of the clergy, they need to attend premarital counseling or relationship education classes. These can vary widely from meeting with the person who will perform their ceremony for an hour to more formal programs lasting around 18 hours. The assumption behind all of these programs is that couples should know what they're getting into and that they should consider this decision carefully. Then, if they decide to get married, they should be given some skills and insights that help them prevent discord and dysfunction from developing. These two aspects – the "Are you sure you want to do this?" and the "Here are some things you should know about marriage" – are both emphasized to varying degrees by different faiths and different programs. For example, the Catholic Church puts a strong emphasis on carefully evaluating whether the two members of a couple are a good match, especially when it comes to their thoughts on having and raising children. This emphasis is based on the Catholic belief that "marriage and conjugal love are by their nature ordained toward the procreation and education of children" (Second Vatican Council, 1966). Other programs emphasize the information and skills that are thought to help married couples have fulfilling relationships.

The history of premarital counseling and relationship education programs is about as old as marriage, with older generations teaching younger generations about marriage. An extreme version of this was practiced by the Oneida Community in the middle of the 19th century. In their community, virgins were taught about sex and marriage by the oldest members through a practice they called "ascending fellowship" (see inset for more details; Hillebrand, 2008).

Marriage and relationship education in the Oneida Community

The Oneida Community was one of many 19th-century utopian communities. It was founded by John Humphrey Noyes, who was very critical of the institution of marriage. Shortly after Noyes established the community, the members adopted the practices of "Complex Marriage" and "Male Continence."

In Complex Marriage, all of the adults were married to all of the adults of the other gender. There were two rules of Complex Marriage. First, any man and woman who wanted to cohabit had to obtain each other's consent through a third party. Remember that in the 19th century (and currently in some cultures) women were often married without their consent. Second, exclusive relationships were forbidden. Couples found to be monogamous were separated for a period of time.

The practice of Male Continence was a form of contraception in which men and women would have intercourse, but the man was never to ejaculate, including during sex and after withdrawal. This practice was consistent with the religious teaching that men should not "spill their seed," and Noyes felt that an unwanted pregnancy was another case of spilled seed – or wasted semen. As you can imagine, young men were less practiced at this than the older men. This led to the related practice of "Ascending Fellowship."

In Ascending Fellowship, Central Members of the community, who tended to be oldest, introduced virgins to Complex Marriage. The older members selected the virgins with whom they would partner for the process of guiding them through the introduction

---

to the sexual and spiritual aspects of Complex Marriage. The virgins were obligated to accept the offer because the Central Members were of a higher rank. There were many reasons for this practice. It was felt that the virgins were less likely to fall in love with the oldest members, and thus less likely to want to be in a monogamous relationship with them. In addition, the older men were more practiced at male continence, thus less likely to impregnate young women. The older women were past menopause, so they could teach the young men "Male Continence" without fear of becoming pregnant.

As you might imagine, these practices were difficult for many outside the community to accept. Yet, despite external opposition, the community practiced these principles from 1849 to 1879. For more information on the Oneida Community, read the works of Carden (1969), Ericson & Robertson (1973), Foster (1981), Klaw (1993), or Robertson (1970).

To get a sense of some of the more common teachings offered to young couples, it's worth going through some old books on the subject. For example, a book that was directed toward men – most of these types of writings were specifically written for either men or women – was called *Manhood and Marriage* (Macfadden, 1916). In the preface, the author boasts that the "book is literally crammed with plain information" and reassures readers that they will not be offended by the material because the author "asked a prominent Sunday School official in one of the largest states in the union to go over the book carefully and change any statement therein that could possibly offend even the most fastidious reader" (p. xii). But, enough with the preface, here is what the men of 1916 were taught (from the opening lines of Chapter 1, "The Importance of Virility"):

> No one can estimate the value of strong manhood. It is a physical asset that is beyond valuation, and beyond price. Vigorous manhood may come to one naturally through inheritance, and in the first flush of youth one may enjoy the turbulent exaltation that comes with the supreme force of superb virility without giving any special thought to the matter; but you can rest assured that if this splendid possession is retained even to middle age, you must have adhered, at least to a reasonable degree, to the laws that govern the retention of manly powers.

The advantage of being a perfect man – vigorous, resourceful, fearless! Who can describe it? Can we attempt to define this glorious possession in mere words? No! Manhood is the crowning glory of a masculine career.

And, it goes on like this for 364 pages covering all manner of subjects related to marriage, from determining whether you are a "complete man" to "selecting a wife" to "love-making and its dangers" to the issue of whether husband and wife should share a bed to "a man's duty toward a pregnant wife" to "the erring wife" to "quarreling and making up" to "the truth about masturbation" to "seminal losses" to several chapters on "how to build virility" and a few more on the "diseases of men." The book is a wild ride. Other books of this era written for women are equally cringe-inducing.

Happily, the cultural and intellectual revolutions of the last century led to changes in how couples were educated. The work of B. F. Skinner and the principles of behaviorism led to changes in how marriage and intimate relationships more generally were conceived. Following the lead of behaviorism, John W. Thibaut and Harold H. Kelley set out to see how behavioral and cognitive processes could be applied to group behavior and decided to start with the smallest group, two people. In their landmark book, they described how behavioral principles operated interpersonally (Thibaut & Kelley, 1959). Out of this work and that of other luminaries (e.g., Bandura, 1969, 1977), behavioral marital therapy was born (Jacobson & Margolin, 1979; Stuart, 1969, 1980). This type of therapy was designed to treat couples already having problems, which I will discuss in greater detail in Myth 23 (Marital therapy doesn't work). And, out of this grew behavior-based *preventive interventions* (these are sometimes called *primary interventions*; see the inset) for marriage.

Definitions of three types of interventions

Primary interventions are meant to prevent a problem or illness and are targeted toward an entire population without regard for risk (e.g., anti-drug commercials on television). Secondary interventions are targeted toward people who are at-risk for the problem or illness, but who don't yet have the problem (e.g., people at risk for heart attacks who take aspirin daily). Tertiary interventions are those in which people are treated for a problem they already have (e.g., an appendectomy on a patient with appendicitis).

The best-known of the behaviorally based programs to prevent marital discord and divorce is the Prevention and Relationship Enhancement Program, more commonly known by its acronym PREP. Howard Markman first started by thinking about how behavioral principles could be applied to predict which marriages would succeed and which would fail (Markman, 1979). From there, he wondered about how he might use this knowledge to prevent marital problems from developing in the first place (Markman & Floyd, 1980). So, he developed a program to prevent discord and divorce and he set about seeing if it would work. The PREP approach, which he developed with the help of colleagues, teaches couples communication, conflict management, and problem-solving skills in addition to highlighting aspects of marriage that are thought to be protective against discord and divorce, such as friendship, commitment, and shared activities.

The initial results from research to determine whether PREP was working were quite promising and suggested that the program had lasting effects (Markman, Floyd, Stanley, & Storaasli, 1988; Markman, Renick, Floyd, Stanley, & Clements, 1993). The catch was that more than half of the couples who were randomly assigned to the treatment group declined to participate in the treatment, so couples receiving PREP were more motivated than couples in the control group. Therefore, it was unclear whether any differences between the two groups were due to the couples in the experimental group (1) receiving PREP, (2) being more motivated, or (3) being different in some other way that was associated with volunteering for a relationship education course. In other words, the initial study was effectively a *quasi-experimental* design (i.e., not truly experimental). Since these initial studies, there have been many more studies that were quasi-experimental, with similarly promising results (e.g., Hahlweg, Markman, Thurmaier, Engl, & Eckert, 1998; Stanley et al., 2005; Stanley et al., 2001). However, the effectiveness of PREP in preventing discord and divorce became murkier when looking only at studies that used random assignment (i.e., truly experimental). I counted nine of these studies. There was either no effect or mixed effects on discord and dissolution in five studies (Allen, Rhoades, Stanley, Loew, & Markman, 2012; Halford, Sanders, & Behrens, 2001; Laurenceau, Stanley, Olmos-Gallo, Baucom, & Markman, 2004; Markman, Rhoades, Stanley, & Peterson, 2013; Trillingsgaard, Baucom, Heyman, & Elklit, 2012), there were slightly negative effects in two studies (Rogge, Cobb, Lawrence, Johnson, & Bradbury, 2013; van Widenfelt, Hosman, Schaap, & van der Staak, 1996), and there were positive effects in two studies (Kaiser, Hahlweg, Fehm-Wolfsdorf, & Groth, 1998; Stanley, Allen, Markman, Rhoades, & Prentice, 2010). Thus, there appears to be a discrepancy in the results, with quasi-experimental studies of PREP appearing to have better outcomes than studies using random assignment.

The widespread adoption of premarital counseling or relationship education programs prevent discord and divorce

As I described above, the initial results from PREP and other marriage and relationship education programs held great promise. Indeed meta-analytic findings on these programs suggested that there were small (J. Cohen, 1988) positive effects across studies (Hawkins, Blanchard, Baldwin, & Fawcett, 2008). In the late 1990s and early 2000s, policy analysts and politicians also began noticing that poor people were less likely to be married, but no less likely to have children (e.g., J. Q. Wilson, 2002). This was about the same time some of the promising studies about marriage and relationship education programs began getting media attention. The increasing visibility of the correlation between single parenthood and poverty as well as the increasing awareness of relationship education programs got the attention of politicians. Many began to see marriage as a key part of the solution to poverty. As momentum for the marriage solution built, there was a call to encourage marriage among people in poverty and to provide relationship education programs to bolster this effort. While the initial push for increasing rates of marriage and decreasing rates of divorce came from social conservatives (e.g., Blankenhorn, 1995; Waite & Gallagher, 2000; Whitehead, 1997), the effort drew bipartisan support, including from then-Senator Barack Obama (2006). This momentum culminated in the United States Congress and President George W. Bush taking approximately $100 million annually from the Temporary Assistance for Needy Families (TANF; i.e., federal welfare) budget and designating that it be used to promote values that are marriage-friendly or to teach relationship skills (Deficit Reduction Act of 2005, 2006). With some modifications, more recent Congresses and President Obama have continued diverting these funds, now reduced to about $80 million, from TANF to programs to change the values and skills of the poor so as to increase the number of children living with two parents (for an interesting review of the federal effort to promote values and skills conducive to marriage, see Avishai, Heath, & Randles, 2012; Heath, 2012).

What has been the impact of the federal government spending $100 million a year on average since 2007 on marriage and relationship education efforts? In a review I wrote on the federal effort (M. D. Johnson, 2012), I argued that it hasn't worked out very well. There were four large studies that were conducted to evaluate the federal efforts. The first study randomly assigned 5,102 unmarried couples to either the intervention or a control group. The interventions varied across eight cities. Across all of the locations, there was no effect of the interventions on couples' relationship quality, partner support, communication skills, infidelity, likelihood of still being together, likelihood of being married, and a host of other variables. When looking at the data by location, one site had a small positive outcome for family stability (but no positive outcome for relationship status or quality) and another site had stronger negative effects for relationship status, father involvement and family stability. Therefore, it appears that these programs had no effect on the relationships of unmarried couples and possibly some negative effects (Wood, Moore, Clarkwest, & Killewald, 2014; Wood, Moore, Clarkwest, Killewald, & Monahan, 2012) despite couples reporting that they liked the intervention (Randles, 2014).

The second study was similar to the first, but the sample was 5,395 married couples. It was also conducted at eight locations around the country. The 12-month data from this study showed that there was no difference in terms of who was still married. However, overall, there were several very small positive effects of the intervention (Hsueh et al., 2012) that appear to be maintained through 30 months (Lundquist et al., 2014).

In a third study, 187,844 couples who went through marriage and relationship education programs sponsored by the federal government, but administered through community agencies and churches, were examined to assess the impact on their relationship quality and likelihood of being married. There were no effects either overall or broken down by city for the likelihood of still being in the relationship or being married. There were also no effects for indicators of marital quality (there were a couple of negative effects in particular cities). So, despite a very large sample, the community-administered programs seem to not work at all (Bir et al., 2012).

Finally, in a fourth study, Alan Hawkins, Paul Amato, and Andrea Kinghorn (2013) examined whether the money that the federal government has been putting into these programs had an impact on the number of marriages and divorces across the country and in a state-level analysis.

To do this, they examined the correlation between federal spending and demographic changes since the federal spending started on a state level. They found that there was no effect if District of Columbia was not included (it's an outlier presumably because a large chunk of federal money was spent there; M. D. Johnson, 2014a; cf. Hawkins, 2014).

Despite all of the data suggesting that these programs are having essentially no effect, there are still strong advocates for maintaining this funding (e.g., Hawkins, Stanley, et al., 2013). In contrast, I have argued that the dismal findings of these outcome studies mean that continuing to divert money from TANF that poor families might use to buy food, clothes, and other essential items is a disservice to the poor and should be stopped (M. D. Johnson, 2013, 2014b).

But, teaching couples skills can't hurt, right?

Even if marriage and relationship education programs aren't working for poor couples, and even if the data are a little sketchy about whether they work for middle-class couples, surely it won't hurt me to learn some skills that will help my marriage. That's what my colleagues and I thought. In addition, we thought that we could improve on the PREP results. So, we developed another premarital intervention designed to prevent discord and divorce. We based it on data indicating that acceptance is an important skill in a marriage (see also Jacobson & Christensen, 1996) and that it's a skill that we could build, much like PREP emphasizes skills associated with communication and problem-solving (Markman, Stanley, & Blumberg, 1994). Therefore, we developed a primary intervention that emphasized acceptance of one's partner and encouraged displaying empathy and positive regard toward one's partner. We called our intervention CARE (Rogge, Cobb, Johnson, Lawrence, & Bradbury, 2002), and we tested it against PREP, which I was trained on when I was a student with Howard Markman at the University of Denver. However, we felt that we needed to test both of these against both active and inactive control groups. For the active control group, we decided to make the couple think about their relationship. For this group, we brought them to campus just like the PREP and CARE couples, and we told them about the importance of thinking about their relationship and how to maintain it, but we didn't teach them any skills as we were doing with the PREP and CARE groups. We called this the Relationship Awareness (RA) group. Then, after our little lecture on relationship awareness, we had them watch a widely available commercial film that depicts a couple talking about their marriage, including the good times and the difficulties. After they watched this film, *Two for the Road* (Donen, 1967), they engaged in a 50–60 minute semi-structured discussion of the film and used it as a vehicle for reflecting on their own relationship. When they left, their homework was to watch one movie per week for four weeks, from a list of relationship-oriented films we provided, and to discuss the film and their relationship using a list of open-ended questions we provided. There was also a group of couples who didn't want to participate in any relationship classes and we used them as an inactive control (No Tx) group; however, this group, being self-selected, should be interpreted with caution. We then followed all of the couples every six months for three years.

After three years, 24% of the couples who were in the self-selected inactive control group (No Tx) dissolved their relationships compared to 11% in each of the other three groups (PREP, CARE, & RA). However, there were no relationship satisfaction differences among any of the groups. While this was not what we had predicted, even more surprising was the fact that PREP and CARE seemed to have unintended consequences. Women in the PREP group, which emphasized communication skills and problem-solving skills, exhibited more hostile conflict than the CARE or RA groups. This finding was odd because these were the type of skills that PREP should have addressed. Similarly, women in the CARE group displayed less emotional support over time compared to the PREP and RA groups, which was also the opposite of our expectations, because the CARE training emphasized being supportive. So, in the end, it seems like watching a movie and discussing its relevance to your own relationship is not only as good as, but it seems better than, attending a marriage and relationship education class because the classes may have unintended negative effects (Rogge, Cobb, Lawrence, Johnson, & Bradbury, 2013, p. 958; see also Williamson et al., 2015).

Conclusion

Despite the allure of marriage and relationship education programs, they appear to have little if any effect on relationship outcomes, and they may even have deleterious effects. This appears to be true whether they are delivered to middle-class couples or poor couples and whether they are delivered by professionals or community members. In the end, perhaps the best thing to do is rent a romantic comedy and talk with your partner about it for about an hour.

Good communication is the key to a happy relationship

> A conceptualization of "the husband is unhappy because he doesn't communicate well" is about as useful a conceptualization as "the patient died because his heart stopped beating."
>
> (Heyman, 2001, p. 6)

This quote by Richard Heyman captures part of the problem when couples and therapists focus on communication issues to resolve problems in the relationship, and yet they do. In fact, communication is the most common issue that couples (especially wives) want to address when they seek marital therapy (Doss, Simpson, & Christensen, 2004). Even couples not seeking therapy, when surveyed, noted that improved communication (as well as more money and better sex) was something that they wanted for their marriage (Kaslow & Robison, 1996).

Communication problems are certainly associated with relationship distress; however, relationship scientists have had difficulty understanding whether communication problems follow other problems in the relationship or whether communication problems precede relationship distress. Furthermore, if communications deficits do precede relationship dissolution, are they simply one of the final steps in the long walk toward divorce – as suggested in quote above – or did the communications deficits occur before other relationship problems surfaced? Behavioral scientists refer to these as "proximal" versus "distal" causes (see inset on the next page).

The question of the role of communication in intimate relationships is long-standing and difficult to understand, so let's start where the field started: social learning theory.

Social learning theory

Social learning theory (Bandura, 1977) was born from behaviorism (Skinner, 1974). The foundation of social learning theory is that we learn to interact with others through reinforcement of some behaviors and punishment of other behaviors. In applying the theory to intimate relationships, two members of a couple learn from (and provide training to) each other. Ideally, interpersonal behaviors that are positive or adaptive are reinforced, and those that are negative or dysfunctional behaviors are ignored or punished. This situation would lead to the maintenance of

Proximal versus distal predictor variables

In general, *proximal* predictors or determinants are considered direct predictors of an outcome. For example, cancer is a proximal predictor of death. *Distal* predictors are indirect. For example, smoking is a distal predictor because it causes cancer, which leads to death. In relationship science, proximal and distal variables are often described in models about the development of marital discord. For example, the proximal context of a couple having a discussion would include the thoughts and feelings of the two partners prior to beginning the discussion, whereas the distal context would be the more stable aspects of the couple, like the personality or mental health of the two partners (e.g., Bradbury & Fincham, 1987, 1988). Considering both proximal and distal causes of behavior leads to more comprehensive models of human behavior. As basic as this may seem, many models of human behavior focus on one or the other for the sake of parsimony and simplicity. Weighing the benefits of pared-down models versus more comprehensive models is inherent to many scholarly disciplines, including relationship science.

relationship satisfaction for both members of the couple. In contrast, the theory predicts the deterioration of relationship satisfaction when negative or dysfunctional interpersonal behaviors are reinforced and positive or adaptive behaviors are ignored or punished. The theory is as simple as that (cf. the somewhat broader focus of social exchange theory; Thibaut & Kelley, 1959).

Social learning theory meets all of the criteria of a strong theory: it's causal, observable, simple, and testable (Platt, 1964; Popper, 1959). Therefore, relationship scientists adopted the approach and applied it to what they were observing in marriages (e.g., Stuart, 1969; Weiss, Hops, & Patterson, 1973). The appeal of the theory had a lot to do with the focus on how couples communicated when there was a problem to be solved or during disagreements. The first scientific studies supported the theory. Couples satisfied with their marriage displayed different behaviors during problem-solving discussions than unsatisfied couples (Raush, Barry, Hertel, & Swain, 1974).

In particular, John Gottman (1979) conducted a series of studies in which he examined how satisfied and unsatisfied couples differed when discussing problems. First, he found that unsatisfied couples displayed fewer positive behaviors and more negative behaviors. Although this is not particularly surprising, the degree to which dissatisfied couples used negative affect (*affect* is expression of emotion, e.g., tone of voice or dismissive facial expressions) compared with satisfied couples was higher than expected and the most consistent discriminator of the two types of couples. Second, Gottman found the opposite of Tolstoy's famous opening sentence of *Anna Karenina*: "All happy families are alike; each unhappy family is unhappy in its own way." Rather Gottman found that dissatisfied couples' conversations were more predictable than those of satisfied couples. Finally, he found that dissatisfied couples responded to negative affect with more negative affect more often and for longer than satisfied couples.

Gottman's empirical testing of the application of social learning theory to couples became the foundation for behavioral interventions designed to prevent (Markman, 1979, 1981; Markman & Floyd, 1980) and treat (Jacobson & Margolin, 1979; Stuart, 1980) marital distress (see Myths 15 and 23, respectively). In addition, it led other relationship scientists to try to determine whether communication during conflict could not only discriminate between satisfied and dissatisfied couples, but also could predict which couples would be satisfied, dissatisfied, and divorced. To do this, relationship scientists followed couples over time to see if their communication predicted changes in their relationship satisfaction. The longitudinal effects of couple communication during problem-solving discussions on relationship satisfaction have varied to a much greater degree than would be expected based on social learning theory and the early results from the discrimination studies (for a review of these findings, see Weiss & Heyman, 1990).

Here is what we know: On average, relationship satisfaction decreases over the course of a marriage (e.g., Kurdek, 1999). Negative affect (e.g., displays of anger and contempt), communication skill deficits (e.g., making global rather than specific complaints about one's partner), and reciprocation of negativity tend to predict lower satisfaction longitudinally (and as negativity moves to aggression, the effects are even stronger, e.g., Rogge & Bradbury, 1999), whereas positive behaviors, such as expressing affection and carefully listening to one's partner, predict more stable levels of satisfaction over time (e.g., E. Lawrence, Pederson, et al., 2008; Mattson, Frame, & Johnson, 2011; Smith, Vivian, & O'Leary, 1990). The catch is that the variation in the direction and magnitude of the effects reported in the literature has been greater than expected, including some studies with counterintuitive findings. For example, Karney and Bradbury (1997) noted that wives' negative behavior predicted stability in husbands' and wives' satisfaction over time. Similarly, Heavey, Layne, and

Christensen (1993) found that husbands' negativity and demandingness predicted more stable relationship satisfaction in wives (cf. Caughlin, 2002). Thus, it seems that the role of communication during conflict may be more complicated than expected based on the social learning theory (Kenny, Mohr, & Levesque, 2001). This possibility is evident in three different findings. First, the longitudinal effect of communication quality appears to change based on contextual stressors (e.g., being unemployed or having an ill parent; McNulty & Russell, 2010). Second, in a study of newlyweds, my colleagues and I found that the use of good communication skills, even in expressing negative affect, still predicts more stable satisfaction (see next myth; M. D. Johnson et al., 2005; Kim, Capaldi, & Crosby, 2007). Third, in a different sample of newlyweds, Tom Bradbury and I found that satisfaction is more stable over time if spouses are able to respond to the changes in a conversation so that they display similar communication patterns over the course of a conversation (M. D. Johnson & Bradbury, 1999). These complicated findings have led some relationship scientists (including me) to the conclusion that focusing exclusively on communication during conflict as a predictor of changes in relationship satisfaction misses too many other potential predictors of relationship discord and divorce (e.g., Heyman, 2001).

Expanding on the role of communication in intimate relationships

Models of intimate relationships and the interventions used to treat relationship discord that were initially based on social learning theory have expanded in the last two decades. This expansion beyond social learning theory mirrors similar expansions beyond behavioral explanations for behavior in other domains of psychology. Strictly behavioral forms of psychotherapy have become relatively rare, with most "behavioral" interventions now incorporating cognition (e.g., thoughts, beliefs, perceptions), mindfulness, or psychodynamic components. In etiological models of marriage, for example, the cognitive components of marriage have been studied for some time (Bradbury & Fincham, 1990; Fincham & Bradbury, 1987a; Fletcher & Fincham, 1991; Fletcher & Kerr, 2010). However, there's far less research linking communication and the partners' cognition in the development of relationship development and discord (e.g., Osterhout, Frame, & Johnson, 2011). Therefore Tom Bradbury and I have argued for expanding social learning theory to better understand intimate relationships in the following ways (M.D. Johnson & Bradbury, 2015).

Focus on aspects of communication strongly associated with dysfunction

Some forms of communication are obviously destructive. For example, using physical aggression (see Myth 22) in relationships predicts relationship dissolution (e.g., Rogge & Bradbury, 1999); the data are unequivocal on this point (e.g., A. Langer, Lawrence, & Barry, 2008; O'Leary, Slep, & O'Leary, 2007). The field has carefully studied ways in which more subtle or complicated communication variables predict relationship outcomes. The results of these studies haven't always replicated or have been deemed statistical artifacts (e.g., Woody & Costanzo, 1990). Therefore, it may be time to shift the focus from trying to instill communication skills, which have relatively small predictive effects (M. D. Johnson, 2012, 2014a), to preventing aggression (Del Vecchio & O'Leary, 2004; O'Leary & Slep, 2012).

Linking enduring vulnerabilities with communication

As I have described elsewhere, there are more comprehensive models of relationship development than those based exclusively on social learning theory. One such model is the vulnerability–stress–adaptation model of marriage (Karney & Bradbury, 1995), which begins with the construct of enduring vulnerabilities. The influence of enduring vulnerabilities on communication is a potentially fruitful avenue for more research. For example, there are links between attachment styles and communication skills (e.g., Cobb, Davila, & Bradbury, 2001). In addition, recent work on the role of genetics on communication in marriage has described the association between enduring vulnerabilities within our DNA and our patterns of communication (Haase et al., 2013; Schoebi, Way, Karney, & Bradbury, 2012). Making the connection between enduring vulnerabilities and communication might allow the development of screening procedures that could identify couples who would benefit from communication skills training.

Linking context and communication

Communication doesn't happen in a vacuum. Context matters. The influence of context is especially important when it comes to how we communicate with our loved ones. Context, broadly defined, includes work issues (e.g., Repetti, 1989), parenting stress (e.g., Kluwer & Johnson, 2007), and discrimination (Murry, Brown, Brody, Cutrona, & Simons, 2001) to name just a few aspects of context. The context of relationships is often what couples emphasize when they first show up for therapy. For example, a couple might tell me about an autistic son or that one of them was just laid off. The couples in my practice seem to feel it's important that I know this, and they're right. It's worth listening to how couples think context has influenced how they communicate with each other.

Conclusion

Communication is clearly an important part of intimate relationships. To say otherwise would be absurd, but it's likely that counselors and couples alike who focus on communication exclusively are missing out on other important aspects of the relationship. Communication and the social learning theory more generally have helped relationship scientists understand the proximal causes of relationship distress and dissolution. The outcome research from counseling programs to prevent and treat relationship distress discord is clear: Focusing intensely on training couples to improve their communication skills is not paying off and doesn't appear to be the key to a successful relationship.

Myth #17   The key to a good relationship is knowing how to solve your problems

In the previous myth, I wrote about how communication predicts some relationship outcomes, but not as much as relationship scientists originally expected, and, in Myth 15, I wrote about how teaching couples communication skills seems to have little or no impact on preventing relationship problems from developing. Perhaps, then, the thing to do is to simply solve the problems within the relationship. If your spouse is complaining that you're doing too little of the housework, then you might be tempted to hire a housekeeper. Or, if your spouse is concerned that you're too hard on your children, then you might decide to relent more often. (Ice cream for supper? Sure.) Take the following example:

ELEANOR: "You know we haven't had a vacation that didn't involve your parents or my sister in years. I would really like to get away, just us and the kids."
EZRA: "You know this is the busy season at the office, but maybe after the year-end deadlines."
ELEANOR: "It would be fun to do that, to just get away – just the four of us."

Ezra gets up and walks out of the room. Eleanor is surprised, but she doesn't think much more about it and goes back to reading the newspaper.

About 15 minutes later Ezra returns to the breakfast table and declares, with a grin, "It's all taken care of I just booked us four airline tickets and a week at Disney World starting June 3rd." He then sits down and awaits the praise that he's certain he deserves.

"You did what?!" Eleanor exclaims.

"Look here is the confirmation number of the flights. Here's the hotel reservation. And, here's a seven-day pass to all of the parks at Disney World!" He then passes her several sheets of paper fresh from their home printer confirming the online reservations.

Eleanor's shock turns to anger. "Why did you do this? Why didn't you ask me? What were you thinking?"

Ezra is confused and surprised. "You just said … I mean 15 minutes ago you said you wanted to take a trip. I just made it easy for you."

Eleanor yells "I was two rooms away! The kids are upstairs! Why would you do all of this without even talking to us?"

"I wanted it to be a surprise and to make it easy for you," Ezra, now getting angry himself, continues, "but, I can see that – as usual – I screwed it up. I'll go cancel everything and see if I can get our money back." He then storms off to the computer to cancel everything.

In situations like the one with Ezra and Eleanor, one member of the couple puts problem-solving ahead of understanding.

As with individuals, all couples have problems. This includes happy couples. In fact, even happy couples have problems that persist throughout their relationships. They remain happy because their problems aren't overwhelming and because they are able to manage their conflict around these problems. In other words, they don't let their problems come to define their relationship. Many of the couples I counsel can't see past their problems and want to solve them right way. This makes sense. In fact, couples who were surveyed about what changes they'd like in their marriage ranked problem-solving right after more money, better sex, and improved communication (Kaslow & Robison, 1996). This finding is consistent with my experience with couples in my private practice who often propose solutions to their problems in the first session (If she would just quit her job … If he would just make dinner once in awhile …). I find this is especially true when someone is accustomed to making quick decisions and operating at a fast and efficient pace at work. It's difficult to turn that off when coming home.

I've even found that my doctoral students who are learning how to do couple therapy make this mistake regularly. For example, a novice therapist might say, "Alright, so you both seem to be upset about the house being messy. So how about we divide up the cleaning chores between the two of you? Nurhan, which rooms would you like to clean?"

What makes this a rookie mistake, whether you're the therapist or a member of the couple, is that it doesn't lead to understanding. Even if Nurhan started cleaning the bathrooms every week, that wouldn't help him understand the impact of his prior behaviors and, more importantly, he will have missed an opportunity to better understand his wife and his marriage. As Howard Markman, Scott Stanley, and Susan Blumberg put it in their well-known book, *Fighting for your Marriage* (1994, p. 153): "Understanding one another is more important for maintaining respect and connection than is solving every problem that life throws your way."

Evidence that problem-solving is not the key to a happy marriage

Along with several colleagues, I conducted a study to determine the relative impact of problem-solving skills versus affective expressions (as you'll recall, affect is the expression of emotion) as predictors of change in marital satisfaction (M. D. Johnson et al., 2005). To examine this, we sent letters to every couple who got a marriage license in Los Angeles County in a nine-month window. To make certain that none of the newlyweds had carry-over effects from previous marriages, we only recruited couples in which neither spouse had been married previously and neither had any children. We then invited them to come into our lab to participate in our study for money. We ended up with 172 newlywed couples.

When they first came into the lab, we had them complete forms that included measures of marital satisfaction and questionnaires asking about the problems in their marriage. They completed these forms separately, and while they were still apart we asked each of them to select the biggest problem in their marriage and whether they were willing to discuss it with their spouse. When they came back together, we flipped a coin to determine whose topic would be discussed first, the husband's or the wife's. We asked the couple to discuss each topic for 10 minutes without interruption. We then left them alone and filmed them from the next room. We then watched the video of the newlyweds discussing the two problems in their relationship – one selected by the husband and one selected by the wife.

To assess the problem-solving skills the couples displayed, a team of students coded the video tapes for 27 different skills (Hahlweg et al., 1984). We grouped the skill codes into positive skills, such as being direct (for an excellent study on the benefits of being direct, see Overall, Fletcher, Simpson, & Sibley, 2009), offering constructive solutions, accepting responsibility, and negative skills, such as devaluing the other person, denying responsibility, and making "yes, but" statements, etc. (Hills & Johnson, 2000). To assess the affect expressed in the discussions, a different team of students coded the videos for eight different types of affect. We also grouped affect into positive affect, which included humor, affection, and interest, as well as negative affect, which included only anger and contempt (for a detailed discussion of these groupings, see M. D. Johnson, 2002). In the end, we had rated wives' and husbands' use of positive and negative skills as well as expressions of positive and negative affect in discussions of wife-selected and husband-selected problems. After all this, we followed the couples for four years, assessing their marital satisfaction every six months.

Affective expressions as predictors of change in relationship satisfaction

The use of positive affect (i.e., humor, affection, and interest) by both husbands and wives during discussions of problems that wives raised helped to maintain relationship satisfaction for wives. Similarly, wives who displayed positive affect in the discussions of issues that husbands raised led to the maintenance of husbands' relationship satisfaction. On the other side of this coin, husbands and wives experienced steeper declines in relationship satisfaction the more wives were angry and con-temptuous during the discussion of husbands' topics. In the end, there was support for the idea that maintaining a good attitude, even when discussing problems in the relationship (at least when discussing issues that wives see as problems), helps wives stay happy in the relationship, and wives who are angry and dismissive of husbands' concerns are likely to be in marriages in which both spouses are unhappy.

Problem-solving skills as predictors of change in relationship satisfaction

We then examined problem-solving skills without considering affect. There were neither benefits to having good problem-solving skills nor detriments to having poor problem-solving skills during discussions of wives' problems. However, when discussing issues raised by husbands, skills did matter. Husbands who demonstrated good problem-solving skills when discussing their own issues were more likely to maintain their relationship satisfaction and more likely to have wives who maintained theirs. So it seems that problem-solving skills have essentially no influence on either spouse when discussing wives' topics but do matter for husbands discussing their own issues in the marriage. This was a surprise, so we then looked at the interaction between problem-solving skills and affective expressions.

The interaction of problem-solving skills and affective expressions as predictors of change in relationship satisfaction

First, some housekeeping is in order: by "interaction" I mean the extent to which one variable moderates the impact of another variable on the outcome variable. In this case, we wanted to know whether the impact of problem-solving skills on changes in relationship satisfaction differed depending on the affect that spouses displayed during their discussions. We found that when discussing either spouses' topics, couples who rarely displayed poor problem-solving skills (e.g., devaluing the other person, denying responsibility, making "yes, but" statements) maintained their relationship satisfaction regardless of the amount of positive affect expressed by either spouse. However, for couples who frequently displayed poor problem-solving skills, the amount of positive affect they displayed mattered. Couples who frequently displayed poor problem-solving skills but also expressed a lot of positive affect were able to maintain their relationship satisfaction. Only the couples who displayed poor problem-solving skills *and* low levels of positive affect had their relationship satisfaction decline more sharply than other couples (see Figure 7). For more details on the specifics of this study, see our original write-up of the study (M. D. Johnson et al., 2005).

When I talk about this study, many people get understandably frustrated, especially when I review the data in Figure 7. To many, it seems preposterous that in the heat of an argument people are to maintain positive affect. This task is difficult for sure and requires a great deal of self-restraint and the ability to maintain a focus on the ultimate goal of growing closer not further apart. To illustrate this, let me tell you about a couple I watched as part of our research. The young couple was having a very difficult argument. They were using poor communication and problem-solving skills. She was quite pregnant and quite upset. As the argument went on, my prognosis for the couple grew worse. Then, as

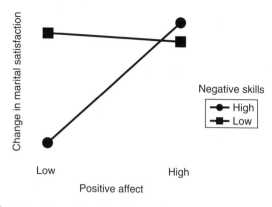

Figure 7 The interaction of positive affect and negative skills on changes in marital satisfaction. Adapted from Johnson et al. (2005, p. 23).

the argument was escalating, she got up and walked over to her husband. This alarmed the research assistants watching from the next room because they worried she would become physically aggressive. But, their concerns and my prognosis melted when she sat on his lap and placed his hand on her swollen belly. Her husband also melted. He calmed down and started rubbing her belly. This act of affection in the middle of a heated argument reminded both of them what was important and what was at stake. After this, I no longer worried about this couple's ability to weather what the world and their unborn child was going to throw at them.

So, then, what is one to do if not to try to solve relationship problems?

In the previous Myth, I tried to make the case that communication skills aren't necessarily the answer to relationship problems, and I tried to make the case that problem-solving skills aren't the only answer either. So, then what can someone do to improve her or his relationship? The first thing to remember is that you can change your relationship simply by examining your own thoughts about it. Even those relationship scientists who emphasize communication and problem-solving skills write about the importance of monitoring your own thoughts as a way to stay in control of your emotions (e.g., Markman et al., 1994). Indeed, our thoughts strongly influence our relationships, as demonstrated in a series of elegant studies conducted by Frank Fincham and Tom Bradbury. They showed that when people come up with a rationale to explain a partner's behavior, the quality of this rationale (which is described in terms of attributions – as in "to what do you attribute this person's behavior") has a powerful effect on current relationship functioning and future changes in relationship satisfaction (Fincham & Bradbury, 1987a, 1987b, 1988, 1989, 1993).

To illustrate this point, consider Mae and Nadav, an unmarried couple living together. If Mae is late, her husband Nadav might think one of the following possible things: (a) Mae must have been caught in traffic; (b) Mae is always running late, even though she knows it upsets me; or (c) Mae is just trying to make me angry by being late. Notice how the last two attributions might lead to a big fight when Mae comes home. We don't know why Mae is late, but by thinking one of the last two thoughts Nadav is already getting upset. These kinds of thoughts tend to escalate conflict and derail relationships. There are many different ways of handling the thoughts that make us miserable and that lead to depression, anxiety, and relationship distress. To do some work on your thoughts, check out the books by Byron Katie (Katie & Katz, 2005; Katie & Mitchell, 2002), who writes eloquently about how our thoughts can cause problems for us. Alternatively, if you are a counselor, check out Don Baucom and Norman Epstein's writings on Cognitive-Behavioral Couple Therapy (Baucom & Epstein, 1990; Epstein & Baucom, 2002) or Andy Christensen and Neil Jacobson's (2000) work on acceptance within relationships. In the end, I am suggesting that you start with the *intra*-personal work of understanding your relationship before developing the *inter*-personal skills of communication and problem-solving (for more on this distinction, see M. D. Johnson, 2015).

The research I described in this myth (M. D. Johnson et al., 2005) along with other studies (e.g., Huston & Chorost, 1994; E. Lawrence, Pederson, et al., 2008; Overall et al., 2009; Smith et al., 1990), make it clear that there are some benefits to monitoring your affect and speaking with your partner skillfully about difficult issues in your relationship (or when your partner is having a difficult time outside of your relationship, see Myth 20). To get a sense of these skills, I recommend reading Markman, Stanley, and Blumberg's (1994) book titled *Fighting for Your Marriage*, which details communication skills, such as complaining about your partner in ways that aren't as threatening, and listening to your partner in ways that demonstrate that you heard and understood what was being said. In summary, making both *intra*- and *inter*-personal changes may help you improve your relationship on your own or with a counselor (see Myth 23).

Conclusion

Problem-solving skills can be useful, but trying to solve a problem before fully understanding the issue or the deeper point being made by the other person is a common mistake. Markman and colleagues (1994) argue convincingly that many problems don't even need to be resolved if couples are simply able to discuss the problems in a meaningful and compassionate way. Still, there are data to support the fact that problem-solving skills predict changes in relationship satisfaction and dissolution. It's just that these have had smaller effects than many relationship scientists expected, leading to a resurgence in thinking about the need to focus on *intra*-personal aspects of relationships, including the power of monitoring one's thoughts, recognizing maladaptive thoughts as they come into your head, and interrupting those thoughts. By doing this, discussions about problems in relationships may include more affection, humor, and interest rather than anger, contempt, and defensiveness. This matters, because it turns out that the negative impact of poor problem-solving skills can be ameliorated by expressing positive affect during discussions about difficult issues.

Myth #18   Having children brings couples closer

> Matt and Kristi sitting in a tree,
> K-I-S-S-I-N-G.
> First comes love, then comes marriage,
> then comes baby in a baby carriage!

I remember being the object of this taunt with my first "girlfriend," Kristi, who asked me via note to "go with her" in the 2nd grade. I received the note at the beginning of art class. Despite having no idea what it meant, I replied "yes" immediately and was probably grinning from ear to ear (I liked being liked). Alas, I was too eager. Our romance ended by the end of art class – again via note – without us ever having said a word to each other while we were "going together." Later we rekindled the excitement of those 30 minutes by "going together" for a couple days that included silently sitting next to each other on the playground, which is when I heard the ditty above chanted with, what I would later decide, was equal parts derision and envy. As with much of life, the children on the playground were mostly right. Most married couples go on to have children (Kristi and I, however, never made it beyond our 48-hour anniversary).

Given the likelihood of having children, the question is, does having children bring couples closer together? Research indicates that many couples think that this is the case (e.g., Edin & Kefalas, 2005) and many others think that having a baby will not change their relationship much (e.g., Belsky, 1985). However, in reality, the answer is clearly and emphatically *no*!

The effect of having children on marital satisfaction

Let's begin with what happens in the archetypal families in which – as the playground song indicates – marriage precedes having children. The first thing to note, as I've mentioned previously, is that – on average – marital satisfaction declines following the wedding and continues to decline for the first few years. Some have argued that satisfaction follows a U-shaped curve over time with satisfaction increasing later (Kurdek, 1998a, 1999). However, others have demonstrated that the decline is more likely a straight path (Karney & Frye, 2002; VanLaningham, Johnson, & Amato, 2001). So, the question is does having children ease the decline in marital satisfaction or does having children hasten the decline?

To answer this question, Erika Lawrence and her colleagues (E. Lawrence, Rothman, Cobb, Rothman, & Bradbury, 2008) assessed the marital satisfaction of 156 newlywed and childless couples. They followed these couples for four years, collecting marital satisfaction scores and other measures every six months. By doing this, she and her colleagues were able to reach several conclusions. The first thing they found was that the happier couples were at the beginning of their marriage, the more likely they were to have a child within the first five years of marriage. This finding was consistent with other research that demonstrated that the married couples who are the happiest tend to have children the quickest (e.g., Carlson, McLanahan, & England, 2004; Shapiro, Gottman, & Carrére, 2000). Second, the researchers examined the impact of having a child on the decline in marital satisfaction. They found that couples having a child led wives' and husbands' marital satisfaction to decline more rapidly than that of couples who didn't have a child. In fact, over the course of the four years, the rate of declining marital satisfaction was nearly double for parents than for non-parents. Importantly, the researchers controlled for the initial levels of marital satisfaction, because happier couples were more likely to have a child. This provided an opportunity to rule out the possibility that the marital satisfaction of couples with children was declining more rapidly simply because their satisfaction was higher to begin with. Thus, it seems that becoming a parent is hard on a marriage.

One could argue that this is just one study; however, this finding is consistent with other studies. Brian Doss and his colleagues conducted a similar study but followed more couples for twice as long. The researchers found that the transition to parenthood had a negative impact on marital satisfaction as well as other aspects of marriage. They also noted that the "effects tended to be sudden and persist over time" (Doss, Rhoades, Stanley, & Markman, 2009, p. 617). Findings like these are consistent with other large studies of the effects of having children on marital functioning (e.g., Belsky & Hsieh, 1998; Don & Mickelson, 2014; Kurdek, 1999; K. M. Sanders, 2010) and the outcomes are even worse if the birth was unplanned (E. Lawrence, Rothman, et al., 2008). To learn more about the fact that having children reduces marital satisfaction, I suggest reading more detailed reviews of this research (e.g., Belsky & Pensky, 1988; Twenge, Campbell, & Foster, 2003).

The effect of having children on divorce

Knowing that having children reduces marital satisfaction and knowing that declines in marital satisfaction usually precede divorce (for reviews, see Huston, Caughlin, Houts, Smith, & George, 2001; Karney & Bradbury, 1995), it would follow that having children also increases the likelihood of getting a divorce – except that it does the opposite. The transition to parenthood is one of the few experiences that lowers marital satisfaction while raising the likelihood that the couple will remained married. Couples with children are less likely to get a divorce than those without children (L. K. White & Booth, 1985). This finding suggests that children become a powerful force that keeps couples together even when they might otherwise dissolve their relationships. Michael Johnson (1973) and others (e.g., Rusbult, 1980; Stanley & Markman, 1992) have written about the factors that make it difficult for couples to dissolve their relationship as "constraints," which form part of commitment, but are distinct from "dedication." In other words, dedication refers to the parts of a relationship that make you want to stay together and constraints are the parts of a relationship that make it difficult to break up. These factors appear to come into play strongly when a couple has children.

When children leave the nest

If the presence of children constrains a couple from divorcing and lowers relationship satisfaction, what happens when children leave home? Some couples experience an increase in relationship satisfaction once their children move out (L. K. White & Edwards, 1990); however, the financial independence of children removes the constraint of some dissatisfied couples and allows them to divorce (Heidemann, Suhomlinova, & O'Rand, 1998). These data should be interpreted cautiously because the most recent generation (so-called "Millennials") are more likely to live with their parents for longer and more likely to return to their parents' home after leaving (Fry, 2013). However, it appears that parents' marital satisfaction and time spent together aren't impacted when adult children move back in or out of their home (Ward & Spitze, 2004).

The effect of having children on couples who aren't married

There are many reasons why couples have children when they're not married. As of this writing, there are still countries that ban same-sex couples from getting married, and some of these couples want to have children. Cultural differences between middle-class and working-class couples lead more working-class couples to view marriage as something that would come after having children (Edin & Reed, 2005). In addition, more recent generations are delaying marriage, which in turn is leading to more unmarried couples having children (Pew Research Center, 2014).

It appears that having children is still hard on most relationships regardless of the circumstances. There are no differences between lesbian, gay, and other-sex couples in terms of relationship satisfaction across the transition to adoptive parenthood (Goldberg, Smith, & Kashy, 2010). Researchers have examined the relationships of committed same-sex male couples who adopt and found that, as with other types of couples, the strain of the transition to parenthood leads to stress and frustration; however, it appeared to reinforce the commitment of couples in ways that lowered the amount of extra-relational sex, despite reducing sexual satisfaction of the couples (Huebner, Mandic, Mackaronis, Beougher, & Hoff, 2012). With regard to class differences, there's certainly no evidence that the stresses of having a child are easier for working-class couples (e.g., Carlson, Pilkauskas, McLanahan, & Brooks-Gunn, 2011; Mazelis & Mykyta, 2011; Osborne, Manning, & Smock, 2007; Ryan, Tolani, & Brooks-Gunn, 2009) and having a child appears to be more stressful for working-class parents who are unmarried (Carlson & VanOrman, 2007). Thus, on average, the transition to parenting is hard on relationships across cultures and family structures.

Causes of the transition-to-parenthood effect

Even with careful planning, bringing a new child into a family is a sudden and jarring experience that will permanently change the dynamics of a relationship. Even in the 1950s, it was viewed as a "crisis" (Dyer, 1963; LeMasters, 1957) in that a couple must now reorganize their lives and their relationship to accommodate the child. The fundamental nature of this shift can be seen in how people view themselves. The arrival of a child means that couples are less likely to view themselves as lovers or spouses and more likely to view themselves as parents (Cowan et al., 1985; Cowan, Cowan, Heming, & Miller, 1991).

Coinciding with the change in identities is a change in behavior. For example, the arrival of a child leads couples to reduce the amount of pleasurable things that they say and do for each other (McHale & Huston, 1984), and these patterns of behavior don't recover as the children age (MacDermid, Huston, & McHale, 1990). Other aspects of the relationship begin to change as well. Couples who thought of their relationship as egalitarian begin to notice that they are falling into more traditional gender roles when it comes to housework and child-rearing (A. Claxton & Perry-Jenkins, 2008). These more gendered roles are just the beginning of some of the gender differences within the transition to parenthood.

Gender differences in the transition-to-parenthood effect

While the impact of having a child appears to affect the marital or relationship satisfaction of both mothers and fathers, there are some differences in the impact. First and foremost, women tend to take on more of the childcare and housework responsibilities. This occurs even when both spouses continue to work outside the home (Cowan, 1996) and in couples with highly egalitarian relationships before becoming parents (Nomaguchi & Milkie, 2003). This means that the roles of men and women tend to shift. Women often work less outside the home and men become more responsible for ensuring the family's income and security (Cowan & Cowan, 1992), which can lead men to spend less time with their child and give rise to feelings of indifference, guilt, or stress (e.g., Belsky & Kelly, 1994).

As much as the relationship changes for both partners, the effects of these changes are felt more strongly by women. The typical pattern of the mother reducing or eliminating her hours spent in outside work can lead to increased parenting expectations being placed on new mothers compared with new fathers. For example, it frequently becomes assumed that she will be the "on-call" parent with little or no "time off" from this role (Cowan, 1996). By spending more time at home, women also end up taking on more of the household chores that are typical of gender-based stereotypes, such as laundry and cleaning. New mothers also tend to have reduced social contacts and a narrowing of experiences. All of this tends to affect new mothers much more than new fathers in terms of their well-being. Indeed, on almost any measure of well-being, mothers are doing worse than fathers, including being more fatigued, depressed, anxious, and dissatisfied (Belsky & Kelly, 1994; Cowan & Cowan, 1992; Cox, Owen, Lewis, & Henderson, 1989; Nomaguchi, Milkie, & Bianchi, 2005; Twenge et al., 2003).

Conclusion

Unfortunately, the news here is not good: the transition to parenthood is hard on couples. When I talk about this finding, I often find myself ending up in a broader discussion about the societal and political dimensions of parenting. Clearly, parenting has become a lightning rod in American politics (although the transition-to-parenthood effect appears in other countries as well, e.g., Kluwer & Johnson, 2007) – the book *It Takes a Village* (Clinton, 1996) led to a firestorm of debate and acrimony, not to mention the publication of a competing book titled *It Takes a Family* (Santorum, 2005). Yet, whatever your political leanings, the fact is that most Americans expect to have children (Pew Research Center, 2014), and this will be hard on the relationships of those who make the choice to become parents. The stresses of parenthood on relationships may partially explain the dropping fertility rate, both in the United States (see Figure 8) and around the world (see Figure 9), as well as the increasing age of becoming a parent (Hayford, Guzzo, & Smock, 2014). It also may be no accident that as parents have become older and the fertility rate has dropped, the role of children has become more central to the lives of

American adults. Thirty years ago children were considered a peripheral part of the family but are now the center of the family (Senior, 2014), which gives me little hope that the relationship strain caused by becoming a parent will lessen in the near future.

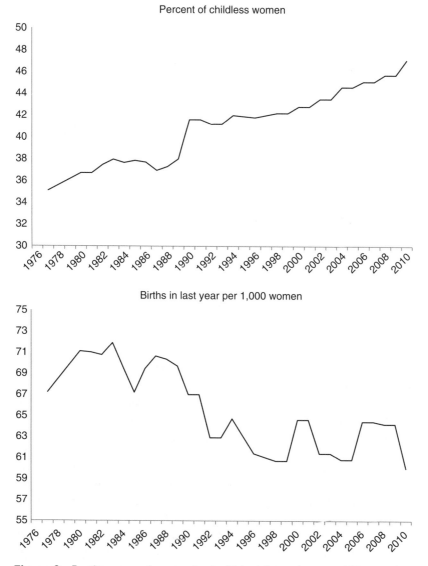

Percent of childless women

Births in last year per 1,000 women

Figure 8 Fertility rates of women in the United States between 1976 and 2010 (adapted from the U.S. Census Bureau, 2013b).

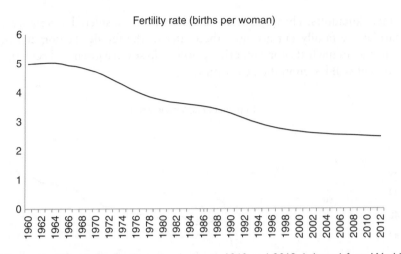

Figure 9 Worldwide fertility rates between 1960 and 2012 (adapted from World Bank, 2014).

Myth #19

Stress is bad for relationships

What could be more intuitive than the idea that stress leads to relationship problems? Indeed, when couples are asked whether they are concerned about the effects of stress on their relationships, they overwhelmingly say yes. This is true of couples in the military (e.g., Karney & Crown, 2007; see also Zoroya, 2013), couples caring for a loved one (e.g., Matthiessen, 2008), and couples experiencing financial hardships (e.g., Washburn & Christensen, 2008). But it turns out that the impact of stress on intimate relationships is more complicated than the simple idea that stress is bad for relationships.

Reuben Hill (1949) developed one of the first models of how adverse events affect families. His model included the stressful event, the family's tangible resources, and the family's definition of the event. Others adjusted Hill's model to include the impact of ongoing stress, such that a family's definition of the event and their resources may change as stressful events continue, which may in turn influence later events (McCubbin & Patterson, 1982). Most people assume that stressful events will impact everyone at some point, so this model has been viewed as particularly valuable to relationship scientists in predicting marital outcomes. Causal models of the impact of stress have been supported by retrospective (e.g., Cohan, Cole, & Davila, 2005) and prospective (e.g., Cohan & Bradbury, 1997; Cohan & Cole, 2002) research. Although there are a large number of potential stressors that may impact relationship satisfaction and status, I will briefly review the effects of stress associated with work, financial hardship, and parenting.

Effects of work

The stress of work (or school) on intimate relationships is well documented. For example, Rena Repetti studied men who were employed as air traffic controllers – a job that is among the most stressful – and found that they were more likely to withdraw from or be angry with their wives after more demanding days on the job (Repetti, 1989, 1994). Researchers have replicated the finding that job stress is associated with increased withdrawal and anger in marriage in other samples and across genders (e.g., Perry-Jenkins, Goldberg, Pierce, & Sayer, 2007; Story & Repetti, 2006). Additionally, levels of cortisol – the hormone most associated with stress – remain elevated well after most people are home from work and interacting with their spouses and children (Saxbe, Repetti, & Nishina, 2008). While these results may not be especially surprising, it's notable that withdrawal and time spent alone after a stressful work day may serve to reduce stress and decrease the potential for angry marital interactions. The flip side of this is that if spouses aren't able to withdraw, for example if their spouses are trying to be supportive and encouraging a discussion of the stressful events, this could lead to more angry and irritable responses (Repetti, Wang, & Saxbe, 2009). Indeed, angry interactions between spouses are more common following stressful days at work (Schulz, Cowan, Cowan, & Brennan, 2004). These results, and the fact that fathers tend to have fewer parental responsibilities, explain why many husbands and fathers can often be found alone and apart from their families in the evenings after work (Campos, Graesch, Repetti, Bradbury, & Ochs, 2009). Thus, it seems clear that stress at work impacts intimate relationships.

Effects of financial hardship

The association between financial hardship and relationship satisfaction is complex. It seems clear that underemployment and poverty are hard on marriage (e.g., Howe, Levy, & Caplan, 2004; Williamson, Karney, & Bradbury, 2013), but the effects need clarification (for reviews, see Schneider, 2011; Seccombe, 2000) because the picture is less clear when financial variables are considered above poverty levels or in conjunction with ethnic considerations. Looking at middle-class couples, higher salaries for husbands are correlated with lower rates of separation and divorce, but wives' income is positively associated with divorce (e.g., Chung, Tucker, & Takeuchi, 2008). It's unclear if wives' financial independence is lowering their level of relationship satisfaction or simply providing the means to dissolve an already unhappy marriage.

Sociologists have been trying to tease apart the marital and family effects of poverty and racial discrimination for some time. Poverty received a great deal of attention as an explanatory factor for the changes in African American family structure in the 1980s. William Julius Wilson (1987; for an update of his argument, see W. J. Wilson, 2009) considered the potential causal directions of the association between rising rates of unemployment and declining rates of marriage among African Americans. Following Wilson's original work on this association, some researchers described data that supported his claims (e.g., Fossett & Kiecolt, 1993; Lichter, McLaughlin, & Ribar, 1997), whereas other researchers didn't find an association between higher rates of unemployment and lower rates of marriage (e.g., S. J. South & Lloyd, 1992; Testa, Astone, Krogh, & Neckerman, 1993), and still other researchers found that the marriage rate was declining mostly for employed African American men (Ellwood & Crane, 1990; Jencks, 1992). Further analysis of these data revealed that unemployment and poverty certainly play a role in the structure of families of color; however, there are other important variables to consider (for a review, see McLoyd, Cauce, Takeuchi, & Wilson, 2000). For example, despite the lower rates of marriage and higher rates of divorce among some ethnic groups and low-income couples, marriage is valued similarly across cultures (Edin & Kefalas, 2005) and incomes (Trail & Karney, 2012). Of course, any discussion of ethnicity or race in conjunction with marital outcomes requires a reminder of the corrosive effects of discrimination, including on marriages (Trail, Goff, Bradbury, & Karney, 2012).

Effects of parenting stress

As with financial stress, the effect of parenting stress on marriage is also complex. The literature on the marital effects of the transition to parenthood epitomizes this complexity. Although parenting stress occurs whenever there's parenting, the transition to parenthood brings the onset of this stress into sharp relief. As discussed in Myth 18, the effects of the transition-to-parenthood on marriage are clear: Having children reduces relationship satisfaction in ways that are sudden and persistent (Belsky & Rovine, 1990; A. Claxton & Perry-Jenkins, 2008; Cox, Paley, Burchinal, & Payne, 1999; Mitnick, Heyman, & Smith Slep, 2009) but also decreases the likelihood of a couple dissolving their relationship (L. K. White & Booth, 1985). Of course parenting doesn't end in the child's infancy, nor does it happen in a vacuum. Many aspects of parenting can diminish or increase the impact of parenting on the relationships between parents. For example, children with physical health problems can be particularly challenging for maintaining marital satisfaction (e.g., Hoekstra-Weebers, Jaspers, Kamps, & Klip, 1998), as can children with autism and other developmental disabilities (Bluth, Roberson, Billen, & Sams, 2013).

In summary, parenting stress clearly impacts relationship satisfaction; however, the reverse may also be true, that greater relationship satisfaction reduces parental stress. Researchers who have examined a large sample of married and unmarried couples having a child and deemed to be "fragile" (i.e., at or near the poverty line) found that, among poor families, parental relationship quality and parenting quality are correlated (Carlson et al., 2011). In addition, they found that the parenting of non-biological fathers is better when they're married to the mothers (Berger, Carlson, Bzostek, & Osborne, 2008) and that married parents experience less stress than unmarried parents (Carlson & VanOrman, 2007). In conclusion, parenting stress appears to impact relationship satisfaction and relationship quality can impact parenting quality (e.g., Carlson et al., 2011); thus it seems that the association between parent–child and parent–parent interactions is probably bi-directional.

How can stress be good for intimate relationships?

So far, I have written about all of the ways in which stress is bad for relationships. However, stress can bring some couples closer together as surely as it tears some couples apart. As noted before (Myths 16 and 17), relationship scientists have focused considerable effort on studying how communication and problem-solving skills impact relationship outcomes. Therefore, it's not a surprise that how couples interact is the most frequently studied link between stressful events and relationship satisfaction and stability (Cohan & Cole, 2002). When one partner is feeling a lot of stress and the other partner tries to help, relationship scientists think of this as "support" or "social support" (see the next myth). This can mean helping a partner to feel better about the stressor, by offering emotional support, or by helping the partner deal with the stressor in pragmatic ways, by offering instrumental support. Of course, this is easier said than done when both partners in a couple are stressed (e.g., Bolger, Foster, Vinokur, & Ng, 1996). Nevertheless, partner support is one way to mitigate the impact of stress on a relationship.

Dyadic behavior (e.g., communication) can link stressors to relationship satisfaction through what scientists call mediation or moderation. In mediation the variables are chained together with each relying on the preceding variable, in the same way that pressing on a car's accelerator increases engine revolutions, which, in turn, increases the car's speed. In the mediated model of stress, behavior, and satisfaction, the stressful events impact dyadic behaviors, which impact relationship satisfaction. In other words, some aspect of dyadic behavior must be present for stress to impact relationship satisfaction. I could find no longitudinal studies that supported a mediating model even among those that specifically tested for it (e.g., Cohan & Bradbury, 1997).

In moderation, a third variable alters the association between two other variables. For example, bleach and ammonia each smell bad, but when combined the smell goes from bad to toxic. With regard to dyadic behavior moderating the association between stress and relationship satisfaction, two models have been tested: the stress-buffering model (S. Cohen & Wills, 1985) and the personal growth model (Caplan, 1964; Holahan & Moos, 1990; Schaefer & Moos, 1992). The stress-buffering model predicts that how couples interact – whether they are trying to solve problems or trying to be supportive – will reduce the negative effects of the stressor and that relationship satisfaction will remain stable. The stress-buffering model provided the basis for some forms of couple therapy (e.g., Jacobson & Margolin, 1979; see Myth 23) and programs for preventing marital discord (e.g., Markman et al., 1993; see Myth 15). In contrast, the personal growth model suggests that the impact of stressful events may be moderated in a way that actually improves relationship satisfaction. This model is the basis of some more recent models of treating and preventing relationship distress that use stressful events to improve the relationship (e.g., Christensen et al., 2004; Rogge et al., 2002). Cathy Cohan and Tom Bradbury (1997) tested both of these models in newlywed couples and found support for the personal growth model. Specifically, they found that wives who were constructive in what they said, even though they were expressing anger, experienced increases in marital satisfaction as a result of the stressors, whereas wives who only expressed anger (without being constructive) during the conversations were more likely to experience declines in marital satisfaction as a result of stressful life events.

The finding that stress can have both positive and negative effects on newlywed couples, depending on how couples interact, has been replicated in subsequent research. In one example from a natural experiment, Cohan and Steven Cole (2002) compared the county records of counties that were strongly impacted by a major hurricane to those of similar counties that were not impacted. They found that the divorce rate in the impacted counties spiked in the year following the hurricane. However, they found that the marriage rates also spiked in the affected counties compared to the unaffected counties. The fact that a catastrophic hurricane has the same impact on relationships as it does on trees – knocking down the weak ones and watering the strong ones – suggests that not all stress is necessarily bad for relationships.

Conclusion

Although stress is associated with many problematic outcomes, it can also lead a couple to grow closer together. This is no different than the stressors we experience as individuals. Some stressors overwhelm us, leading to problems like illness or getting fired, and other stressors make us stronger. If I asked you to name the accomplishment about which you are most proud, you would probably name one that involved great difficulty and stress. This can be true in relationships as well – some of the most stressful events in a relationship may be the events that bring couples closer together (for reviews of stress in intimate relationships, see Randall & Bodenmann, 2009; Story & Bradbury, 2004).

Myth #20 Supporting your partner will improve your relationship

Everyone experiences tough times at some point. The first of the Four Noble Truths in Buddhism acknowledges that if you're alive you will suffer. Recognizing this truth leads to the hope that others will love and support us, which is among the most fundamental of human desires. Social support in times of need can be instrumental, such as sharing information, loaning money, or helping with a task. Social support can also be emotional, such as the communication of care, concern, and validation (Cutrona, 1996). Having a strong network of social support appears to have many benefits, including improved mortality (Berkman, 1985). Although having a deep bench of social support is important, there are reasons to think that one's partner is the quarterback of the social support team (Coyne & DeLongis, 1986).

Showing support for a partner is one way of developing stronger relationships. This "fact of life" is consistent with the model described in the preceding myth, which described stress as having a potentially beneficial effect on relationships. Indeed, many couples recognize intuitively that support is important to a successful marriage. In one survey, respondents ranked mutual support the fourth most essential ingredient in a successful marriage, only topped by love, trust, and respect (that is some tough competition; Kaslow & Robison, 1996). Anecdotal evidence that people place great importance on receiving social support from a partner comes from how couples describe their courtship. As part of my research and clinical work, I've asked hundreds of couples how they met, fell in love, and decided to marry. One of the more common themes of these stories involves one of the partners going through a difficult time and describing the other person as having been especially supportive. Others talk about the fact that their partner seemed like a stable person who they could count on. Descriptions like these tell me that many look for partners who will be a support to them (and others seek out someone to whom they can be supportive).

It seems obvious then that supporting your partner during difficult times is the right thing to do. It should help your spouse and it should help your marriage. After all, the opposite is clearly true. Celebrating your partner's successes is good for your partner and good for you. Relationship scientists call this capitalization, because when something good happens to one person, the other partner can capitalize on the success by enthusiastically celebrating the success. This in turn improves the relationship and makes both partners feel even better about themselves (Gable, Gonzaga, & Strachman, 2006). So, it stands to reason that when one member of a couple is struggling with something, the other partner can try to be supportive. This support should help the person who is struggling and help the relationship. Yet, it turns out that the research on the benefits of support is surprisingly mixed.

Evidence that being supportive of your partner is good

Let's begin with what seems intuitive. The impact of believing that support is available in case the need should arise is fairly clear. If people believe that high-quality support is available (meaning that others will be there for them during times of stress), they are healthier and report greater well-being (S. Cohen & Wills, 1985; Sarason, Sarason, & Gurung, 1997; Uchino, Cacioppo, & Kiecolt-Glaser, 1996). We'll come back to how to give your partner the sense that you will be there in times of need, but the data are clear that the perceived availability of support is beneficial.

When it comes to the actual delivery of support, being highly responsive to a partner's disclosure of distress is associated with improved partner well-being (Gable, Gosnell, Maisel, & Strachman, 2012), improved relationship satisfaction (e.g., Pasch & Bradbury, 1998; Sullivan, Pasch, Johnson, & Bradbury, 2010), and improved functioning in other aspects of the relationship (Gardner & Cutrona, 2004). For example, support delivered by intimate partners observed in lab settings has been shown to build feelings of closeness and support, boost positive mood and self-esteem, and foster greater goal achievement across time (e.g., N. L. Collins & Feeney, 2000; B. C. Feeney & Collins, 2003; J. A. Feeney, 2004; Overall, Fletcher, & Simpson, 2010). Others have found that support is particularly important, even compared to other ways in which couples might interact (Hilpert, Bodenmann, Nussbeck, & Bradbury, 2013). In short, support is beneficial.

Research that suggests that being supportive of your partner is bad

Despite studies that have verified the popular idea that social support is beneficial, there's a surprisingly robust literature that describes the problems with social support. Let's say something bad happens to Jack that has nothing to do with his marriage to Jill. If Jack comes home and talks about the bad thing that happened, he's likely to have more anxiety, a lower sense of well-being, and reduced relationship satisfaction than on days that he didn't disclose a negative event to Jill. Furthermore, Jill's responsiveness can help, but it will not get Jack back to where he would be if he didn't talk about any negative events from his day (Gable et al., 2012). The explanation for this finding is complicated, so let's try to understand it.

John Pearce, Michael LeBow, and Janet Orchard (1981) conducted a study that perfectly captures this complexity. They randomly assigned married women who were trying to lose weight to one of three conditions in which the women engaged in a weight loss program and were followed for 12 months (there were also two other control groups). In the first group, husbands accompanied their wives to the weight-loss classes and were asked to be an active part of the treatment, including the reinforcement and modeling of new eating habits. For example, if wives "were asked to chew and swallow each bite before picking up cutlery, spouses were instructed to do the same while in their wives' presence" (p. 238). In the second group, husbands were never contacted by the researchers. In the third group, the husbands received a letter from the researchers explicitly asking them not to participate in their wives weight-loss program. The letter emphasized the need for self-reliance in this program. The husbands were asked not to sabotage the program, but to essentially ignore any changes in their wives' eating habits or appearance. The wives whose husbands were part of the treatment lost more weight than the wives whose husbands were never contacted; however, there was no statistical difference between the group with husbands who helped a lot and the group with husbands who were told to avoid helping (see Figure 10). So, it seems that husbands who are supportive have essentially the same impact as husbands who make a point of doing nothing. This outcome is consistent with findings that receiving support from a spouse actually slows down the recovery from a heart

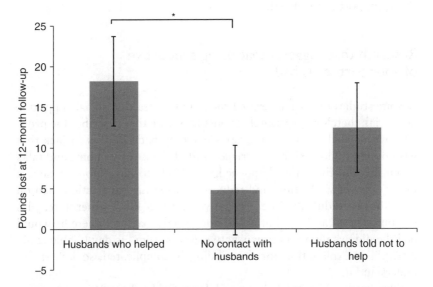

Figure 10 The amount of weight lost by wives who received the same weight-loss program, but whose husbands either participated and assisted in the program, were not contacted at all, or were instructed to do nothing to help their wives. Note that there were 12 women in each group and that the only statistical difference was between the group with husbands who helped and the group with husbands who were not contacted, $^*t$ (22) = 3.21, p = .004 (two-tailed). (Adapted from J. W. Pearce et al., 1981. Reproduced with permission of the APA.)

attack (Helgeson, 1993). What explains why receiving social support from a partner may be detrimental?

In their book on social support within relationships, Kieran Sullivan and Joanne Davila (2010) discuss the importance of matching the support that is provided with the support that is needed or wanted. Matching in this way can be difficult and requires the provider of support to know his or her partner well enough to be able to understand a particular situation and the type of support that might be needed. A person disclosing a difficult problem may simply be wanting to vent and looking for an empathic ear. In this case, support may simply involve tolerating the emotions of the partner and validating concerns expressed. In other cases, the person might be seeking a very specific type of support. For example, if one member of a couple is trying to lose weight, a supportive act would be skipping dessert in solidarity with the partner. These kinds of supportive behaviors may not even be noticed by the person seeking support, and it turns out that might be a good thing!

Niall Bolger, Adam Zuckerman, and Ronald Kessler (2000) examined 99 couples in which one member of the couple was preparing to take the New York Bar Exam. These are the exams that lawyers take at the end of law school so they can practice in a particular jurisdiction (in this case the State of New York). These preparations are incredibly stressful experiences, and prior studies had demonstrated that the last week before a major exam is the most stressful period (Bolger & Eckenrode, 1991), so Bolger and his colleagues used daily diaries of the period right before the bar exam to assess the amount of support that the examinees reported receiving from their partners and the amount of support that the partners reported providing to the examinees. They looked at data from each day and noted whether the couple fell into one of the following four categories:

- Examinee reported receiving support and the partner reported giving support.
- Examinee reported receiving support and the partner reported giving no support.
- Examinee reported receiving no support and the partner reported giving support.
- Examinee reported receiving no support and the partner reported giving no support.

They found that the benefits of partner support were the greatest when the examinees reported receiving no support and the partners of the examinees reported providing support, or what the researchers called *invisible support.* For example, couples in this situation were the only couples whose symptoms of depression decreased as the test got closer. Couples in the other three groups reported increases in their symptoms of depression (there were similar results for anxiety). Thus, an awareness of receiving support from one's partner actually resulted in worse outcomes over time. This counterintuitive finding about the benefits of invisible support has been replicated in subsequent studies and has led to a great deal of interest in finding ways to explain and ameliorate the negative effects of "visible" support.

In subsequent studies, researchers described the negative effects of receiving support as having diminished in proportion to the amount of support between spouses (a) having approached equity (Gleason, Iida, Bolger, & Shrout, 2003); (b) being provided in response to the specific need for support (see prior discussion of "matching" support; Bar-Kalifa & Rafaeli, 2013; Maisel & Gable, 2009); (c) being provided in response to higher levels of distress (Girme, Overall, & Simpson, 2013); and (d), for unmarried couples only, being seen as promoting relationship goals rather than preventing relationship problems (Molden, Lucas, Finkel, Kumashiro, & Rusbult, 2009). The surprising conclusion seems to be that providing support to a partner can have negative effects on the person in need of support and on the relationship unless that support goes unnoticed.

Capitalization

Although providing support to one's partner when they're in need can have a negative effect, there are times when providing support is clearly the right thing to do. As I mentioned previously, capitalizing on positive events is good for individuals and for couples.

Before discussing the benefits of supporting your partner when things go well, here's a little background on the research on positive events for individuals. Let's begin with the idea that happiness is not simply the absence of suffering (cf. Epicurus; Bergsma, Poot, & Liefbroer, 2008), but that happiness stems from the positive events in our lives and our ability to notice these events. For a long time, psychology has accepted that our well-being is largely dependent on our interpretation of events in our lives. When it comes to the positive aspects of life, those who can accentuate and expand the positive components of life are able to lead more pleasurable and fulfilling lives. Barbara Fredrickson (2001) wrote about expanding one's ability to "tolerate" positive emotions. Thinking more specifically about positive events, people who possess the ability to notice positive events and to invest in them as a way of enhancing the impact of the events tend to be more satisfied with life and to experience less depression. The capitalization of positive events can happen in several ways; for example, thinking about what you did to put yourself in the situation where the positive event happened is one way. If your boss liked your work on a project, you can think about how hard you worked on that project. If you found money on the ground, you can think about how you were paying attention to your surroundings. More in line with the myth about social support, another thing you can do is tell others about the positive event. Christopher Langston (1994) demonstrated that celebrating positive events and talking about them with other people can enhance the effect of the positive event on one's mood and – importantly – on one's well-being going forward. Notice that this response is the opposite of what people with depression tend to do. Depression creates a filter that makes it more difficult to see the positive aspects of one's life (S. E. Taylor & Brown, 1988). So, by all means, when something goes well in your life celebrate it! You will be better for having done so.

Just as there are benefits to capitalizing on positive events in our own lives, there are benefits to capitalizing on the positive events that happen to the people we care about. Suppose your partner comes home and announces the following:

"Guess what!"
"What?" you say looking up from the book you were reading.
"Tarah walked in my office right as I was packing up to come home and asked me to sit down so that we could talk for a few minutes. As you can imagine I was terrified because she looked so serious. I thought I was about to be laid off!"
Noticing the opening you say, "Well I have been reading about lay-offs everyday it seems."
"But, she started talking about what a good job I've been doing and that upper management noticed the quality of my work. She even went through that report I wrote last month and talked about how much of a difference it made in their thinking about the Midy account. Then, she said that they want me to be the regional account manager for our area. She said that I would be getting a $10,000 raise and that I will start in June. Can you believe it?"

What should you say now? Shelly Gable and her colleagues have made this a multiple choice question by breaking down your potential responses along two dimensions: active versus passive, and constructive versus destructive (Gable, Reis, Impett, & Asher, 2004). So, here are your options for reacting to your partner's good news:

- Active-constructive: Getting up from your chair and embracing your partner you yell "That is fantastic! I am so proud of you! I am so pleased that your bosses see how hard you work and how smart you are! You're really going to knock their socks off in the new position! We need to get some champagne to celebrate! But, first tell me all of the details. What exactly did she say about the report you wrote?"
- Passive-constructive: Staying seated, you say in a steady voice "That is great news. What will be included in your new responsibilities?"
- Active-destructive: With a shocked look on your face, you say "Really? I'm surprised they didn't give that position to Lauren, she seems so much more qualified than you. Do you really think you're up to the task?"
- Passive destructive: Staying seated, you say "Well, I'll never be promoted. I wish my boss wasn't such a jerk. Let me just finish this chapter, and we can talk about it some more."

In multiple samples, Gable and her colleagues found that couples who mostly respond to disclosures of positive events using active-constructive techniques had more intimacy and better relationship satisfaction (Gable et al., 2006; Gable et al., 2004). The responses to positive events seems even more critical to well-being and relationship quality than responses to negative events (Gable et al., 2012).

Perceived availability of potential support versus the actual receipt of support

As I mentioned toward the beginning of this myth, the perception that support will be available when things go wrong seems to have more of an impact on personal and relationship functioning than the actual quality of the support people receive. But this leads to the question, how do we determine whether our partner will be there for us in times of need? If we don't always benefit from received support during stressful times, and if the best response to negative events is invisible support, how will we know if our partners have our backs? It turns out, not surprisingly, that the perceived quality of partner-provided support in the past predicts the perceived quality and availability of support in the future. In addition, the day-to-day ability to capitalize on the positive events experienced by one's partner predicts the perceived quality and availability of support in the future just as well as previous support. However, the day-to-day partner support for negative events has no effect on the perceived quality and availability of support in the future (Gable et al., 2012). In other words, the amount of support we think we'll get in times of stress matters.

What influences how much support we think we'll receive, other than our personality characteristics (see Davila & Kashy, 2009; Simpson, Rholes, & Nelligan, 1992)? It turns out that the quality of the support we received during previous bad times and our partners' responses to ongoing positive events (but not their responses to ongoing bad events) predict whether we feel that our partner will be there for us when things go wrong.

Conclusion

One of the benefits of being in an intimate relationship is having someone there to support us when things go wrong. It seems obvious that giving your partner support in times of need is beneficial to your partner, to you, and to the relationship; however, it's not that clear. It's more important to be supportive of your partner when things go well. In the event that things go badly for your partner, the best kind of support you can provide is the kind that your partner doesn't even know about. So, perhaps if your partner has had a bad day, it may be best to leave him or her alone and quietly do things that help. On the other hand, if she or he has had a good day, make sure you're cheering loudly. Your partner will benefit, and your relationship will be stronger.

6 DIFFERENCES, DISCORD, AND DISSOLUTION

"Marriage is one long conversation, checkered by disputes."
(Stevenson, 1908, p. 189)

The Robert Louis Stevenson quote above captures the fact that all marriages and long-term relationships go through difficult times. One of the beliefs I have to counter with some couples is that disagreement is dysfunctional. Once people think about it rationally, they recognize that of course partners will disagree simply because they're different people. How boring would relationships be if there were no disagreements? Think for a moment about one of your favorite teachers. I would guess that your favorite teacher was one who challenged you. You're probably picturing a teacher who didn't simply give you a good grade, but one who let you know that you could do better and inspired you to improve. Now think about your intimate partners, parents, children, and other important people in your life as teachers. The relationships that mean a lot to you are also your most challenging relationships, in part, because they matter and, in part, because you're learning from them. So, I often begin my work with couples by noting that they're teaching each other and that part of that teaching will lead to disagreements. And, that's OK.

In this chapter, I explore five myths about some of the more disagreeable aspects of intimate relationships. First, I explore the myth that men and women are fundamentally different in how they approach intimate relationships. Perhaps no myth in this book is so pervasive and

Great Myths of Intimate Relationships: Dating, Sex, and Marriage,
First Edition. Matthew D. Johnson.

dysfunctional. By telling ourselves – even in jest – that the other gender is nothing like our gender, we put them in the category of the "other." Social scientists have long known that by emphasizing "otherness," the differences between our group and the "other" group, we make it easier to mistreat them. Why do this, when it only serves to makes us less understanding and compassionate toward each other? This myth will also explore aspects of masculinity and femininity within relationships, including sex-role characteristics to look for in a partner.

The second myth in this chapter is that only men perpetrate violence in intimate relationships. Relationship scientists like K. Daniel O'Leary and Amy Slep (2012) have made a compelling case that we do women no favors by ignoring the role that they may be playing in perpetuating some aggressive or abusive relationships. I end this myth by discussing what we know works to prevent and treat violence in intimate relationships. Most importantly, I make three points crystal clear. To those who are perpetrators of violence: what you are doing is more likely to result in the dissolution of your relationship than the continuation of it. To those who are victims of intimate partner violence: the best way to protect yourself is to be unavailable to your pursuer. To everyone else: whether or not you're aware of it, you know someone who has been touched by intimate partner violence. To help them and others, support your local domestic violence agency.

Third, I discuss the myth that marital therapy (i.e., couples counseling) doesn't work. While there's room for improvement, on average marital therapy can help improve relationship functioning when it's done by a competent and well-trained therapist. I also discuss some caveats and other considerations when contemplating couples counseling.

Finally, in the fourth and fifth myths of the chapter, I discuss the dissolution of relationships. In the fourth myth, I address whether the "first cut is the deepest." Borrowing a line from Cat Stevens' famous song, I examine whether the first heartbreak we experience leaves an indelible mark that stains the rest of our relationships. In the fifth myth, I write about divorce and the idea that getting a divorce makes people happier.

Myth #21 Men are from Mars, women are from Venus

A man finds a lantern on a beach. While brushing it off a genie pops out and grants him three wishes. After the first two wishes have been granted, the man says that he always wanted to visit Hawaii, but he's afraid to travel by plane or boat.

So, he says, "I want you to build a bridge from Los Angeles to Honolulu." The Genie replies: "That's absurd! The engineering for such a bridge is completely impossible. The ocean is too deep to sink supports. For any kind of bridge like this you'd have to consider the weather and the strong ocean currents. Plus, it would have to be high enough for ships to pass under it. It's impossible. I simply can't do it. Come up with something else."

"OK." And, after thinking it over, the man asks "Can you explain women to me?"

The genie pauses for a moment, and asks "So, do you want this bridge to have two lanes or four lanes?"

Or, how about this one:

Q: What's the difference between men and government bonds?
A: Bonds mature.

Jokes like these remind us that the gender wars are alive and well. But, are men and women really that different? A lot of people certainly seem to think so, including comedians like Jodi Miller who says men are like cats because they're aloof and emotionally unavailable and women are like dogs because they need to be groomed and like shoes (J. Miller, 2013). In addition to spawning thousands of jokes, the belief that men and women are fundamentally different has led to self-help books with titles such as *Men Are from Mars, Women Are from Venus* (Gray, 1992); *He Says, She Says: Closing the Communications Gap Between the Sexes* (Glass, 1992); or *You Just Don't Understand: Women and Men in Conversation* (Tannen, 1990). Then, there's the genius of Steve Harvey, a comedian who wrote a relationship book titled *Act Like a Lady, Think Like a Man* (2009). His book spent two years on the best seller list, including 23 weeks as the #1 advice book (Reddicliffe, 2010), and was made into a movie that was #1 on its opening weekend. So, it would seem that emphasizing the differences between men and women resonates with, well, men and women.

Whether women and men are really that different can be scientifically described by two basic hypotheses: the gender differences hypothesis and the gender similarities hypothesis. As you might expect, this debate is not new and certainly not new to psychology. As far back as 1914, eminent psychologists, such as E. L. Thorndike, were debating whether the differences between the genders were as strong as people had assumed. In fact, as Hyde (2005) pointed out, one of Thorndike's contemporaries wrote the following about declarations of psychological differences between men and women: "the truest thing to be said at present is that scientific evidence plays very little part in producing convictions" (Woolley, 1914,

p. 372). The sad truth is that Helen Thompson Woolley could have written those words today (over 100 years later!) and they would be no less true. Taking our cue from Woolley, let's look at the data on gender differences.

On measuring differences between populations or groups

It's best to begin with what we mean by differences between two groups or populations. This necessitates explaining a couple of statistical principles. Wait, don't skip ahead! The statistical concepts are simple (I promise) but essential for understanding claims of gender differences.

At the most basic level, two groups can be said to differ on a variable of interest if the scores on the variable are more different between the groups than they are within the groups. In other words, is the between-group variability greater than the within-group variability? This can be tested with a simple ratio of between-group differences over within-group differences, which is essentially the definition of a t-test. Once the value of this ratio is determined (for example, once the t-test has been calculated), the probability that the two groups are different based on random chance is determined. Part of scientific dogma is that two groups aren't considered to be statistically different unless the likelihood of the difference being due to random chance is less than 5% (i.e., $p < .05$). If it's not (i.e., if $p \geq .05$), no claim of a group difference can be made.

The catch is that test statistics (e.g., t-tests) and p-values don't indicate the magnitude of the difference between two groups. Both test statistics and p-values will vary depending on the number of participants in a study. The greater the number of subjects in a study, the more likely it is that even small differences will not be due to chance (meaning the p-value will shrink). This creates situations in which very large studies can lead to very small differences between groups being considered statistically significant, even if the difference between the groups is essentially meaningless. This is why most academic journals in psychology require indications of the size (i.e., magnitude) of the effects being studied. To measure the magnitude of group differences (and other types of research questions), scientists use a measure of *effect size*. There are many different types of effect sizes, but the most common type for measuring the differences between groups is called a d-statistic, effect-size d, or simply d (J. Cohen, 1988). One of the advantages of reporting effect-size statistics, like d, is that they are standardized. This allows comparisons of effects across studies. Just as Fahrenheit is a scale that indicates temperature across settings, d is an indication of the magnitude of group differences across studies and variables.

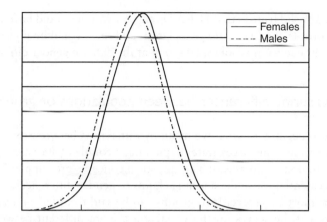

Figure 11 Do these two groups look very different? These are the normal distributions of males and females that approximate an effect size *d* of 0.21, which is considered a small effect. In Hyde's (2005) meta-analysis, 48% of the reported gender differences were considered small (*d* between 0.11 and 0.35) and another 30% considered trivial (*d* between 0 and 0.10), so the two distributions in this figure are typical of 78% of studies of gender differences. The above figure was originally from "Gender differences in self-esteem: A meta-analysis" by K. C. Kling, J. S. Hyde, C. J. Showers, & B. N. Buswell (1999, *Psychological Bulletin, 125*, p. 484) and reproduced in J. S. Hyde's (2005) article titled "The Gender similarities hypothesis" (*American Psychologist, 60*, p. 587). Copyright 1999 by the American Psychological Association.

The advantage of using *d* over other measures of effect size is that it's simple and specifically designed for measuring the magnitude of group differences, like the difference between men and women. The formula for *d* when measuring gender differences is as follows:

$$d = \frac{\text{Mean score of men} - \text{mean score of women}}{\text{Mean of the two within-sex standard deviations}}$$

Using this formula, you can see that positive *d*-values will mean men scored higher and negative *d*-values will mean women scored higher, which is the convention among those who study gender differences. What may be less obvious, but is one of the best features of *d*, is that it allows differences to be measured in terms of standard deviations (*SD*s, which are a measure of how much the scores on a variable differ from the mean). So, a *d* of 0.21 would mean that the two means are 0.21 standard deviations apart. To visualize this, look at Figure 11. Notice that the amount of overlap of the distributions of males and females is a measure of their

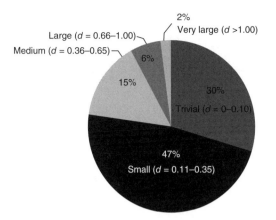

Figure 12 Of 124 studies of gender differences, these are the percentages of those with effect sizes (d) that fell into the trivial, small, medium, large, and very large categories (adapted from Hyde, 2005, p. 586).

similarity and the degree to which the distributions don't overlap is an indication of their differences (in the case of Figure 11, this is a measure of self-esteem). So, in looking at Figure 11, would you describe this as a small, medium, or large effect? If you thought "small," you think like Jacob Cohen (1988) who developed qualitative descriptors for effect-size d. He described effects sizes as follows: $d = 0.20$ as "small," $d = 0.50$ as "medium," and $d = 0.80$ as "large." Janet Shibley Hyde (2005) converted Cohen's descriptions into ranges and categorized 124 studies of gender differences and found that 78% of them were either trivial or small (see Figure 12).

Gender differences and similarities

So, are men and women really so different that they may as well be from different planets? Or, are the genders really more similar than different? To answer these questions, I'll begin with the two gender differences in the "very large" category of Figure 12, which are differences in throwing velocity ($d = 2.18$) and throwing distance ($d = 1.98$; Thomas & French, 1985). That men and women are about two standard deviations apart on throwing abilities is not especially surprising based on well-known differences in the average physicality of men and women. Nevertheless, when we start to think about other well-known differences between men and women – differences that are commonly accepted stereotypes – we begin to see a different picture. Figure 13 describes the magnitude of gender

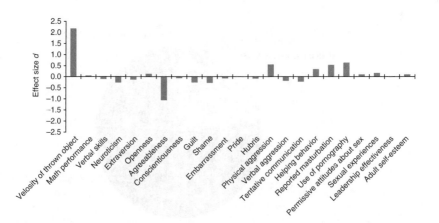

Figure 13 Meta-analytic findings regarding the differences between males and females on a variety of attitudes, behaviors, and skills. The effects are measured using effect size d, with positive scores reflecting higher scores for male than females and negative scores indicating higher scores for females compared to males. When interpreting the figure, note that $ds \approx 0.20$ are considered weak or small, $ds \approx 0.50$ are considered moderate or medium, $ds \approx 0.80$ are considered strong or large (J. Cohen, 1988); as such the majority of the psychological constructs in the figure have either null or weak gender differences (adapted from the following meta-analyses: Archer, 2004; Eagly, 2009; Eagly & Crowley, 1986; Eagly, Karau, & Makhijani, 1995; Else-Quest, Higgins, Allison, & Morton, 2012; Feingold, 1994; Hedges & Nowell, 1995; Hyde, 2014; Hyde, Lindberg, Linn, Ellis, & Williams, 2008; Hyde & Linn, 1988; Leaper & Robnett, 2011; Lindberg, Hyde, Petersen, & Linn, 2010; Petersen & Hyde, 2010; Thomas & French, 1985).

differences across a broad range of variables on which men and women are assumed to be different. Note that I have included the effect size of throwing velocity to give perspective on the size of the gender difference on the other variables. Each of these variables could be examined further to consider other factors, such as whether they vary by race (e.g., the self-esteem difference of $d = 0.21$ is based on mostly White samples and switches to $d = -0.03$ for Black samples; Kling, Hyde, Showers, & Buswell, 1999) or how the data were collected (e.g., gender differences in the reporting of sexual experiences disappear when participants think they're connected to a lie detector; Alexander & Fisher, 2003; Fisher, 2013; see also Myth 1). Overall, the effects described in Figure 13 contradict many stubborn stereotypes. For example, there are trivial or small gender differences for math performance, verbal skills, gregariousness, conscientiousness, neuroticism, relational aggression, tentative speech, attitudes about extramarital sex, attitudes about masturbation, leadership ability, and self-esteem (Hyde, 2014). Even in domains surrounding communication within couples, the differences are small. So it seems that men and women aren't so different.

There are other ways of thinking about gender in relationships beyond simply looking at the differences and similarities in the mean scores of variables of interest. Another way to determine whether men and women are so different that each should consider the other gender extraterrestrial beings capitalizes on advanced statistical methods (e.g., taxometric analysis). Bobbi Carothers and Harry Reis (2013) looked at 122 variables from 13 studies using a total of 13,301 participants. They started by seeing if they could actually put men and women on different metaphorical planets using the most obvious of variables, such as physical strength, certain leisure activities (e.g., hunting vs. knitting), and body measurements. On variables like these, they found that, sure enough, men are from Mars and women are from Venus. Knowing they could find inter-planetary differences, they examined personality variables, such as neuroticism, agreeableness, inclinations toward science, and fear of success. They also examined variables more associated with intimate relationships, such as masculinity, femininity, sexuality variables, mate preferences, empathy, and relationship dependence. No matter how they combined these variables, they kept finding that men and women are more similar than different. In other words, it appears that men and women are both *intra*-terrestrial.

The role of masculinity and femininity

If men and women are more similar than different, why do we have a sense that they are different? Partly, as discussed in Myth 6 (Opposites attract), we tend to focus on differences not on similarities. However, another way of thinking about gender is in terms of *sex role identity*, which is the degree to which individuals exhibit masculine and feminine traits regardless of the person's sex. So (according to Sandra Bem's Sex Role Inventory, 1974, 1981) masculine traits would include self-reliant, competitive, and analytical, whereas feminine traits would include empathic, gentle, and loyal (for comparison, examples of gender-neutral traits include happy, helpful, and likable). It's then possible to categorize people as high or low on masculinity and femininity. People high on masculinity and low on femininity are considered "masculine;" people high on femininity and low on masculinity are considered "feminine;" people low on both are considered "undifferentiated;" and people high on both are considered "androgynous." So, which is best for relationships?

Men and women characterized as androgynous (displaying high levels of both masculine and feminine traits) are the clear winners. They have higher self-esteem (Flaherty & Dusek, 1980), lower anxiety (Williams & D'Alessandro, 1994), better social skills (Guastello & Guastello, 2003), and better psychological adjustment (Cheng, 2005; Kring & Gordon, 1998). The benefits of androgyny are apparent in intimate relationships as well. Androgynous individuals are the most secure in their attachment to their partners (Shaver, Papalia, Clark, & Koski, 1996) and are the least likely to need relationship counseling (Peterson, Baucom, Elliott, & Farr, 1989). For all of these reasons, it's not surprising to learn that androgynous individuals are the most sought-after mates (Green & Kenrick, 1994). For a review of this literature, see Bradbury and Karney (2014). So, there's little risk and the potential for a lot of reward in being androgynous. Therefore, if you're searching for a partner, be sure to check out people like male nurses or female mechanics.

Conclusion

In summary, there's far more evidence supporting the "gender similarity hypothesis" than the "gender difference hypothesis" (Hyde, 2005, 2014). Additionally, individuals who possess both masculine and feminine traits make excellent relationship partners. So, let's all agree that men are from Earth and women are from Earth.

Myth #22   Only men perpetrate violence in intimate relationships

"Can you get someone over here now? ... He's back. Please. He's O.J. Simpson. I think you know his record. ... He showed up again. Could you just send somebody over here? He's in a white Bronco. But first of all, he broke the back door down to get in. ... He's fucking going nuts. ... He's going to beat the shit out of me!" This quote was from a 911 call made by Nicole Brown Simpson on October 25, 1993, eight months before she was murdered. The reporters for *The Los Angeles Times* who first reported on this phone call go on to note that

> authorities took no action after the October, 1993, emergency call because Nicole [Brown] Simpson declined to press charges. However, during the same month, she contacted the unit of the city attorney's office

that prosecuted her 1989 battery case against Simpson, saying she was terrified and in fear for her life. According to authorities familiar with that contact, Nicole [Brown] Simpson said there were "many, many incidents" in which Simpson had threatened her. (Meyer & Ford, 1994, p. 1)

The murders of Nicole Brown Simpson and Ronald Lyle Goldman have much to teach us about how a pattern of abuse within an intimate relationship can escalate to the point of homicide. The lessons of the case include the fact that interpersonal violence can occur even among the wealthy and respected. In the 911, call she goes on to describe the fact that she's trying to get Simpson to leave because she was with her two young children, so we learn that the presence of children doesn't prevent violence. Finally, we learn that we need to take the pleas of help from victims of domestic violence seriously when they request assistance. But, how universal is this case? In other words, do the lessons learned in this case apply to less severe cases of assault?

For a long time, it was assumed that aggression within intimate relationships fell along a continuum from minor to major acts of aggression. In fact, one of the most widely used measures of assessing violence in relationships, the Conflict Tactics Scale (Straus, 1979), begins with questions about negotiating with a partner and ends with questions about using a firearm against a partner. Nevertheless, as studies of interpersonal violence accumulated, a rift in the field became obvious. The studies were producing two distinct sets of results that appeared to contradict each other. Some studies were finding that men were almost always the ones perpetrating violence in other-sex intimate relationships. Other studies were finding that the perpetrators of violence were about equally split between men and women or, more perplexing still, were more often women! As you might imagine, the debate between these two camps was intense because of the – literally – life-and-death nature of the debate.

The debate was resolved when the differences in sampling strategies were found to be the reason for the different findings. Social scientists who were using large national samples (e.g., Slep & O'Leary, 2005; Straus & Gelles, 1986) were painting a very different picture of domestic violence than those who were reporting data from distressed couples. The differences were stark. For example, the prevalence rates differed when comparing nationally representative samples (10–12% reporting being a victim of intimate partner assault in the last year) to samples derived from marital therapy clinics (36–58% reporting being a victim of intimate partner assault in the last year; Jose & O'Leary, 2009). In addition to studies with nationally representative samples and samples derived from marital therapy clinics, advocates of battered women presented data from domestic violence shelters, emergency rooms, police reports, and national crime surveys that suggested that there was almost no female-to-male aggression resulting in serious harm. These studies were considered important from an advocacy perspective, but caused further confusion about the rates of domestic violence. Beyond methodologies, researchers began asking whether there are other differences in the types of violence couples experience (e.g., Dobash & Dobash, 1992; M. P. Johnson, 1995).

Two types of intimate partner violence

There's now a consensus among relationship scientists that there are two distinct types of intimate partner violence. The existence of these two types partially explains why there were such differences between the data collected in national samples and clinic samples compared to the daily experiences of people working in emergency rooms and domestic violence shelters. These two types of violence have been termed situational couple violence and intimate terrorism (Bell & Naugle, 2008; M. P. Johnson, 2008).

Situational couple violence
By far, the most common type of intimate partner violence is situational couple violence. This type of violence occurs when arguments escalate, becoming more and more intense. Then, at some point the anger boils over resulting in an assault. Don't be fooled by the name or the fact that it's the most common type of violence. The assaults can be severe and deadly. Punching, kicking, and threatening with (or using) a knife or firearm have all occurred during situational couple violence. Often arguments are spurred on by alcohol or other drugs, which also have a disinhibitory effect, rendering the partners more impulsive than they would be normally (for a review of the effects of alcohol on violence within couples, see Foran & O'Leary, 2008). More often than not, however, situational couple violence results in less severe violence, such as throwing objects, slapping, pushing, and grabbing. In this type of interpersonal violence, women are as likely or more likely than men to perpetrate an assault on an intimate partner (Jose & O'Leary, 2009).

Intimate terrorism
Whereas situational couple violence is characterized as reactive and angry, intimate terrorism is calculated and cold. This latter type of violence is about controlling a partner. Instead of being reactive, it's proactive in the

sense that the perpetrator uses violence as a means of controlling the behavior of a current or former partner. Therefore, from the perspective of the victim or other observers, it often seems that the violence is spontaneous and hard to predict. In the transcript from the 911 call made by Nicole Brown Simpson quoted at the beginning of this myth, she describes O.J. Simpson as breaking into her house while her children are asleep. Who can say what was going through his mind, but clearly this didn't escalate from an argument. This was out-of-the-blue terrorism. Consistent with intimate terrorism, Ms. Brown Simpson was apparently fearful and felt she was in danger (Meyer & Ford, 1994). In this type of violence, the assailants are almost always men. In fact, this type of intimate partner violence was originally called *patriarchal terrorism* (M. P. Johnson, 1995). In the comparatively few cases in which women have killed their husbands, nearly all of them have been the result of violent resistance. Some have argued that this is a third type of intimate partner violence, which is characterized by women using violence to protect themselves and their family members (M. P. Johnson, 2008). These cases are infrequent, but are one of the more common reasons women are incarcerated (Swan & Snow, 2002).

Interventions for domestic violence

The shockingly high prevalence rates of intimate partner violence suggest the need for stringent screening in multiple settings, including in primary care offices (Nelson, Bougatsos, & Blazina, 2012). But, do we know what works once violence has been reported?

The criminalization of intimate partner violence didn't begin in the United States until 1871 when Alabama led the way by rescinding husbands' right to physically punish their wives (Barner & Carney, 2011). In 1914 the Psychiatric Institute of the Municipal Court of Chicago added psychological treatment for offenders to their jail time and included social services for victims (Dobash & Dobash, 1992). This change led to the two-prong approach to the treatment of intimate partner violence using law enforcement and psychosocial interventions. Let's review the data on both types of interventions.

Following some highly publicized cases of intimate partner violence, there was a strong push for the police to make more arrests. There's a substantial literature on the factors that lead police to make arrests and the outcomes of those arrests. For example, arrests are more likely to be made if the victim is cooperative, injured, White, and suburban (it also helps if it's not within an hour of the end of a police shift; e.g., Robinson & Chandek, 2000).

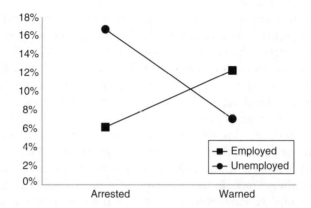

Figure 14 Percent of men who subsequently assaulted their female partners after an initial assault, separated by employment status and whether they were arrested for the primary assault (adapted from Pate & Hamilton, 1992, p. 695).

However, the question is, does arresting the offender prevent further violence? Unfortunately, the answer is: sometimes. Arresting a man for assaulting his partner reduces the likelihood of further assaults if he is employed, but appears to increase it if he is unemployed (see Figure 14; Pate & Hamilton, 1992). Evidence from a randomized outcome trial indicates that arresting the assailant increased the victim's chance of having died from homicide 23 years after the incident (Sherman & Harris, 2013). Thus, it seems unclear whether arresting an assailant – even when the victim wants him arrested – is helpful. Many have argued that averting the immediate danger is still worth it, noting that arresting the assailant has positive implications for prevention at a societal level and can provide a window for the abused partner to seek safety (for review of the impact of arresting versus warning, see Holtzworth-Munroe, Beatty, & Anglin, 1995). In any case, the nuances of the decision of whether to arrest or warn highlights the difficulty faced by police officers asked to make these decisions on a nightly basis.

In addition to arresting the perpetrators of violence, another common legal intervention is for victims to seek orders of protection. While these do an excellent job of creating a legal trail that empowers the legal system to act more firmly in protecting women and children from assailants, there's controversy about whether they actually help prevent violence. As Gavin de Becker (1997) has written, restraining orders are often used by police and prosecutors as a way to gauge how serious a woman is in resolving the matter. They also can demonstrate to the abuser or stalker that the woman (the odds are it's a woman) is serious about ending the relationship. For many stalkers, this is convincing evidence that the relationship is over and that it's time to move on. However, de Becker and domestic violence advocates want to make it clear that a restraining order doesn't actually restrain anyone. So, what should women in this situation do? They should make themselves unavailable to the person who is pursuing them, and "battered women's shelters provide the best way to be safe" (p. 200).

If the record of legal interventions is mixed, do psychosocial interventions have a better record of preventing further abuse? For couples experiencing violence and who wish to remain together, there's no empirically supported intervention (Dixon & Graham-Kevan, 2011). Indeed, the very idea of treating a couple for their violence is controversial. However, around 50% of couples who seek therapy report some episodes of violence, yet they rarely state that as their reason for coming to treatment. Therefore, in some cases therapists may decide that the violence is minimal enough to still treat the couple. In these cases, Amy Holtzworth-Munroe and her colleagues have developed a system that focuses on anger management and communication skills to reduce violence in the relationship (Holtzworth-Munroe, Beatty, et al., 1995; Holtzworth-Munroe, Clements, & Farris, 2005). However, she and her colleagues are quick to caution that couple therapy should be discouraged for some couples. In terms of treatment outside of the relationship, there's surprisingly little research on the effectiveness of programs for women. There's some evidence that the abuse of pregnant women (a common occurrence) can be reduced via multifaceted counseling programs (Van Parys, Verhamme, Temmerman, & Verstraelen, 2014). There's also some evidence that combining sheltering, advocacy, and counseling decreases the likelihood of a woman being abused again; however, there's little support for programs targeting men (Del Vecchio & O'Leary, 2004; Wathen & MacMillan, 2003). In the end, it seems that violence within a relationship is difficult to prevent and treat; however, it's clear that domestic violence shelters and agencies save lives. Therefore I urge you to support your local domestic violence shelter. To find one near you, go to http://ovc.ncjrs.gov/findvictimservices/ or contact the National Coalition Against Domestic Violence.

The best interventions are those that prevent intimate partner violence before it occurs. There have been efforts to integrate violence prevention into some relationship education programs (e.g., Holtzworth-Munroe, Markman, et al., 1995), but the results of these interventions are mixed (see Myth 15). On the other hand, large media campaigns have had a positive impact on preventing intimate partner violence (Biglan, 1995; Dixon & Graham-Kevan, 2011). The catch is that most of these are targeted toward men, which is not surprising given the prevalence of people believing the myth that only men initiate interpersonal violence. To truly break the cycle of violence in families, some have argued for media campaigns that target men and women. These might include messages that violence within families is not OK, no matter who is being violent. The added benefit of such messages is that it could break the cycle of abuse within couples and across generations while simultaneously addressing the overlap of violence between partners and child maltreatment (Dixon, Browne, & Hamilton-Giachritsis, 2005; O'Leary & Slep, 2012).

Conclusion

To summarize, men and women engage in intimate partner violence at about equal rates. The problem is that men are more likely to cause serious injury or death and men are more likely to engage in intimate terrorism, which is just as bad as it sounds. Women who are in dangerous situations should get away from their pursuer and we should all support our local domestic violence shelters so women and children have a safe place to go (for an excellent review of the issues of violence within intimate relationships, see Dixon & Graham-Kevan, 2011; O'Leary & Woodin, 2009).

Myth #23   Marital therapy doesn't work

"Dr. Johnson, I'm interested in marriage counseling, and you were recommended to me by my attorney David Thrower." This is a fairly typical beginning of a telephone call I might get from someone who is interested in couple therapy.[1] A little further into the conversation, the caller will often say something like "I'm not sure my husband will go for this. He doesn't think marriage counseling will do any good" (such skepticism about the outcome of couple therapy is seen in a significant number of people seeking treatment; Tambling, 2012; Tambling & Johnson, 2010). At this point, I suggest that they talk it over and make a joint decision about whether to begin treatment. I do this, in part, because I want them to at least buy in to the process enough that they both show up for the first session and because they might make some progress without me. In addition, I usually offer to speak with the reluctant partner if he or she would like to call me. They seldom do, but, if the skeptical partner does call me, I indicate that I too am a skeptic. I'm a skeptic because I know the outcome data on marital therapy, and there's good news and bad news in those data.

A brief history of marital therapy and why it's supposed to work

In the United States, the roots of marital counseling go back to the 1920s when Abraham and Hannah Stone, who were both physicians, were interested in assisting couples through marriage counseling and family planning services. Working in New York City, they authored a popular book called *A Marriage Manual: A Practical Guide-Book to Sex and Marriage* and were staunch advocates for assisting women who either did or didn't want to have children. They worked closely with Margaret Sanger, who went on to establish the International Planned Parenthood Federation in 1952. However, it was Paul Popenoe who, in 1939 with no formal training, opened the American Institute of Family Relations, based in Los Angeles, which became the country's leading marriage clinic. Paul Popenoe (not to be confused with his son, David Popenoe, who helped found the National Marriage Project) is considered by many to be the "father of marriage counseling" and went on to write the "Can This Marriage Be Saved?" feature for the *Ladies' Home Journal*. In addition, he wrote numerous marriage manuals, wrote a syndicated newspaper column, hosted a radio program, and was a judge on a television show (he also dabbled in eugenics and wrote positively about Hitler; Lepore, 2010). The greatest expansion of efforts to improve marriages came in the late 1940s and early 1950s when there was an uptick in divorces among young married couples following World War II (Prochaska & Prochaska, 1978). However, the early treatments were little more than psychoanalysis in which both members of the couple were treated individually. This form of concurrent marital therapy dominated until the early 1970s when conjoint approaches (i.e., seeing both members of the couple together) became the norm, but the field was still new and grasping for treatments that worked (for an interesting history of marital interventions, see Davis, 2010).

Everything changed in marital therapy (and in psychology more generally) with the increasing influence of behaviorism (Skinner, 1974; J. B. Watson, 1913) on psychological interventions. Social learning theory (Bandura, 1969, 1977), which suggested that people train each other through basic learning principles (rewarding and punishing behaviors), came to influence how psychologists conducted psychotherapy. As applied to couples, social learning theory posited that partners reward and punish the other person's behaviors. This idea became the basis for the behavioral model of marriage, which suggested that dysfunction develops when maladaptive behaviors are inadvertently rewarded and adaptive behaviors are punished (Stuart, 1969; Weiss et al., 1973). The goal of behavioral marital therapy was to alter the dysfunctional learning that had taken place and implement a new set of rewards to enhance more functional behaviors (Jacobson & Margolin, 1979; Stuart, 1980). In the years since behavioral marital therapy was first introduced, the theory behind it has become mainstream. People who call me for couple therapy often describe relationship problems as communication issues (see Myth 16). For example, a husband might say "mostly, we are having a communication problem," which I might later discover means that she's no longer speaking to him since she discovered his affair. However, couples and clinicians can be forgiven for couching relationship problems in behavioral terms; after all, the simple logic of the model is appealing and the exchange of behaviors is how humans connect to each other (Kelley et al., 1983). For more about how interpersonal behaviors predict success or failure in relationships, see Myths 16, 17, and 20.

Measuring treatment outcomes

Psychologists often refer to two types of therapy outcomes: *efficacy* – which answers the question of whether the patients who received the intervention demonstrated a statistically significant improvement compared with those in the control condition; and *effectiveness* – which answers the question of whether the patients who received the intervention demonstrated a clinically significant improvement compared to those in the control condition.

Statistical significance is determined by examining whether the p-value is less than .05 meaning there's less than a .05 probability that the treatment effect is due to chance (i.e., $p < .05$). As you may remember from your statistics class (or from Myth 21), there are two things that determine the p-value: the size of the treatment effect (in the case of outcome research, this is the size of the difference between the control group mean and the intervention group mean on whichever variable is considered the outcome variable) and the size of the sample (i.e., the N).

Demonstrating effectiveness, sometimes called "clinical efficacy," is usually more difficult than demonstrating efficacy because the presence of a statistical difference in a variable doesn't mean that there's a clinical difference. To better understand this, imagine that, instead of relationship satisfaction, the outcome is salary. If we compared two groups with a large enough sample size, we might find that one group had an average salary that was statistically higher than the other group. However, the difference might end up being $120 (average of control group = $57,892; average of intervention group = $58,012). You would then need to make a judgment call on whether that is clinically significant. To do so, you might break that down into smaller units (e.g., $10 a month) or put it in terms other than money (e.g., three tanks of gas). Either way, you might decide that while your intervention (whatever it was) was statistically significant – and therefore *efficacious* – it was not clinically significant – and therefore it wasn't *effective*.[2] For a more detailed discussion of efficacy and effectiveness, see a report written by a select committee of the Society for Prevention Research (Flay et al., 2005).

Does marital therapy work and, if so, which approach works best?

Since it first starting being used, there's been considerable research on the efficacy and effectiveness (see the inset) of behavioral marital therapy. In terms of efficacy, the intervention appears to have helped some couples by improving relationship satisfaction. A meta-analysis of behavioral marital therapy outcome studies described it as moderately more efficacious ($d = .59$) than no treatment control groups (Shadish & Baldwin, 2005). Nevertheless, if we switch to considering effectiveness, the data are less encouraging. In one study, clinical significance was defined as the couples improving to the point that they were no longer different from couples who were not seeking or receiving couple therapy (a tough criterion to meet). Using this effectiveness criterion, behavioral marital therapy was effective for slightly fewer than half of couples (Jacobson et al., 1984).

Another aspect of outcome research to consider is whether the benefits continue following the end of the treatment. Of the slightly fewer than half of couples for whom behavioral marital therapy was effective, about 70% of them maintained their relationship satisfaction at that level or better for two years (Jacobson, Schmaling, & Holtzworth-Munroe, 1987). In another study, of those couples who were rated as being satisfied with their relationship at the end of behavioral marital therapy, 15% dissolved their relationship within two years (Christensen, Atkins, Yi, George, & Baucom, 2006) and 30% dissolved their relationship within five years (Christensen, Atkins, Baucom, & Yi, 2010). Therefore, it appears that behavioral marital therapy is likely to lead to clinically significant improvements in relationship satisfaction in about half the couples at the end of treatment and, of those couples who were satisfied, about 70% will continue to be satisfied for two to five years.

When comparing different types of couple therapy, the outcomes are similar. For example, there are similar benefits when couples are treated with behavioral therapy versus insight-oriented therapy, which is a theoretical sibling to psychodynamic psychotherapy (Jacobson, 1991; Snyder & Wills, 1989; Snyder, Wills, & Grady-Fletcher, 1991a, 1991b). A comparison of behavioral therapy with a revised version of behavioral therapy, which included acceptance, revealed that the percent of couples who recovered or who reported substantial gains in marital satisfaction was similar for both groups, as was the percent who deteriorated and divorced (Christensen et al., 2010). Other analyses have found similar rates of effectiveness across other approaches to couple therapy (e.g., S. M. Johnson & Wittenborn, 2012; see also Lebow, Chambers, Christensen, & Johnson, 2012). Therefore, it seems that there's little difference between the models of couple therapy, so the key is to find a competent counselor who knows how to work with couples (Christensen et al., 2004).

Conclusion

In the end, the similarity of the outcome findings when comparing various psychological treatments for relationship distress doesn't change the fact that marital therapy, when it's conducted competently, has about a 50% chance of immediately improving intimate relationships to the point that the relationship satisfaction of couples seeking treatment is indistinguishable from couples who aren't seeking treatment. While relationship scientists and couple counselors would like to improve that number, knowing it allows me to have an informed conversation with those considering marital therapy. Therefore, when I speak with a person who is (or has a partner who is) reluctant to come to couple therapy because of doubts about its effectiveness (as in the example at the start of this myth),

I can say: "On average, 50% of couples who participate in marital therapy experience clinically significant improvement and most maintain that improvement over the long term even if they had severe relationship problems."

Myth #24   The first cut is the deepest

When using a metaphor, it's best to make sure that we're in agreement as to what is meant by the metaphor. So, perhaps the best place to start is with the lyrics of the song that Cat Stevens (now known as Yusuf Islam) wrote. Here are the opening lines of the song:

> I would have given you all of my heart
> but there's someone who's torn it apart
> and she's taking almost all that I've got
> but if you want, I'll try to love again
> baby I'll try to love again but I know

> The first cut is the deepest, baby I know
> The first cut is the deepest
> 'cause when it comes to being lucky she's cursed
> when it comes to lovin' me she's worst
> but when it comes to being loved she's first
> that's how I know

> The first cut is the deepest, baby I know
> The first cut is the deepest

Clearly, this song has resonance with a lot of people because it has been a hit song four times, by P. P. Arnold (in 1967), Keith Hampshire (1973), Rod Stewart (1977) and Sheryl Crow (2003), and it won an award from the American Society of Composers, Authors and Publishers. The song goes on to request that his new lover help him dry his eyes from his feelings for his first lover (a request that seems unwise). Nevertheless, the main message of the song was powerful enough that "the first cut is the deepest" has become a widely used expression.

Researching the validity of an expression or a metaphor from a song is probably a fool's errand because it could be interpreted in multiple ways. So, let's start with some assumptions. The idea seems to be that the singer's capacity for future relationships has been severely damaged by the singer's first love. With some coaxing, the singer may be willing to fall in love again, but the new partner will need to understand that the former partner will be considered "first" and, oddly, "worst." I assume that "worst" in this case means "best," just as when Michael Jackson taught us that "bad" means, in essence, "good" (these are the kinds of issues that crop up when science examines art).

Therefore, Mr. Stevens appears to have been suggesting the following with this song: (1) the psychological damage from being in love and breaking up for the first time is severe; (2) future intimate relationships are likely to suffer because of a first love; and (3) if we take "worst" and "deepest" at face value, the effects of a first breakup are the most damaging in one's life. Therefore, we get three myths for the price of one. However, we still need to define (scientists would say *operationalize*) a few things. First, what do we mean by first love? As a relationship scientist, I try to avoid the word "love" because defining it seems either too generic (e.g., intense liking) or too technical (e.g., flooding the central nervous system with affiliative neurochemicals such as oxytocin); however, we seem to have no choice. So, let's go with a definition that is fairly vague by defining "love" as having a relationship that has, minimally, the potential for sex (notice this is the same way I defined an "intimate relationship"). Now for the easier definition: "first." Using the definition of love as a close relationship with at least the potential of sex, I am excluding relationships that occurred before puberty. We also know that most people begin having their first sexual experiences in adolescence; therefore, I will limit the discussion of the empirical literature to adolescent intimate relationships. Now let's examine the research on whether the first cut is the deepest.

Sub-myth 1   The psychological damage from adolescent relationships and break-ups is severe

Many parents worry about the consequences of teenagers dating and even assume that dating will lead to sex and pregnancy (Guzman, Caal, Hickman, Golub, & Ramos, 2013). The belief that adolescent break-ups have long-term negative consequences has some truth to it. The top predictor of first-time depression in adolescents is the break-up of a romantic relationship, which can lead to future depressive episodes (Monroe, Rohde, Seeley, & Lewinsohn, 1999). However, as many articles and parenting books point out, the pain of a first break-up is also an important milestone in a person's life (e.g., Caron, 2010). While there are many individual cases where adolescent relationships may lead to severe psychological damage, this is not the norm. Indeed, more than half of U.S.

adolescents report having had an intimate relationship within the last 18 months (Carver, Joyner, & Udry, 2003). These numbers vary culturally and developmentally (Giordano, Manning, & Longmore, 2005; Meier & Allen, 2008; Upchurch, Levy-Storms, Sucoff, & Aneshensel, 1998) and the numbers are higher if looser definitions of intimate relationships are used (Furman & Hand, 2006). Therefore, given the facts that adolescent relationships are more common and last longer than most people estimate (W. A. Collins, Welsh, & Furman, 2009), it seems that they are developmentally appropriate. But, are they damaging?

There's clear evidence that the psychological factors associated with adolescent relationships vary a great deal depending on the qualities of the relationship, the circumstances, and the characteristics of the adolescent (Furman & Collins, 2009; Furman & Shaffer, 2003). However, in their review of adolescent relationships, W. Andrew Collins, Deborah Welsh, and Wyndol Furman (2009) describe how these relationships are associated with developmentally important psychological factors, including "forming a personal identity, adjusting to changes in familial relationships, furthering harmonious relations with peers, succeeding (or not) in school, looking ahead to future careers, and developing sexuality (regardless of the extent of sexual activity)" (p. 644).

So, being in adolescent relationships is associated with typical and well-functioning adolescent development. What about adolescent relationships that are especially strong? By defining "strength" of a relationship as relationship quality, we can examine the correlates of relationship quality during adolescence. It turns out that relationship quality is associated with greater social competence as well as self-esteem and confidence (M. J. Pearce, Boergers, & Prinstein, 2002; Zimmer-Gembeck, Siebenbruner, & Collins, 2001).

On the other hand, bad relationships can be quite problematic. Collins and colleagues (2009) note that dysfunctional adolescent relationships are associated with higher rates of alcohol and other drug use, poor academic and job performance, and mental health problems (Zimmer-Gembeck et al., 2001; Zimmer-Gembeck, Siebenbruner, & Collins, 2004). One way in which adolescent relationships can be dysfunctional is when one member of the couple is afraid to express herself or himself out fear of being dumped. Indeed, many adolescents report stifling themselves in an effort to sustain a relationship, even in comparably strong relationships. This type of self-silencing is associated with increased rates of depression and sensitivity to rejection. As you might imagine, it's also associated with communication problems within the relationship (Harper, Dickson, & Welsh, 2006; Harper & Welsh, 2007).

In summary, to the extent that someone describing his or her "first cut" or "first love" means they are talking about a reasonably functional relationship, there's evidence that these can have a positive impact on adolescent development. In fact, there's some evidence that first sexual experiences, whether kissing or intercourse, relieve some anxiety and often result in improved emotional states (L. M. Langer, Zimmerman, & Katz, 1995; Regan, Shen, De La Peña, & Gosset, 2007).

Sub-myth 2   Future intimate relationships are likely to suffer because of adolescent relationships

There's evidence that early negative experiences with intimate relationships increase later pessimism about relationships (Carnelley & Janoff-Bulman, 1992). In addition, involvement in intimate relationships in early adolescence is associated with academic, psychological, and behavioral problems (for a review, see B. B. Brown, Feiring, & Furman, 1999).

However, rather than having a negative association on later relationship functioning as many believe, mid- and late-adolescent relationships actually appear to have a positive effect (W. A. Collins et al., 2009). For example, Ann Meier and Gina Allen (2009) found that having intimate relationships in adolescence increased the likelihood of marriage in young adults and increased the age at which they were married. However, this association varied by race. Specifically, African American adolescents in a steady relationship were less likely to marry and more likely to cohabit with a partner as adults (the opposite was found for the rest of their sample). A similar study in Germany demonstrated that the quality of adolescent relationships (specifically, partner support) is associated with early adulthood relationship quality (Seiffge-Krenke, 2003). In summary, the findings on the impact of adolescent relationships on adult relationships is strong enough to lead Meier and Allen to write that "rather than being trivial or fleeting, adolescent romantic relationships are an integral part of the social scaffolding on which young-adult romantic relationships rest" (2009, p. 308).

It should be noted that all of the aforementioned associations are for consensual intimate relationships in mid- to late-adolescent development, without violence (Haugaard & Seri, 2003). Indeed, the romantic experiences taking place in late childhood or early adolescence are associated with future relationship problems (as well as misconduct and academic problems; Furman, Ho, & Low, 2007; Zimmer-Gembeck, Siebenbruner, & Collins, 2001). In addition, adolescents in relationships who are also engaging in casual sex and have disengaged families are more likely to have later relationship problems (Ayduk, Downey, & Kim, 2001; Davila, Steinberg, Kachadourian, Cobb, & Fincham, 2004; Grello, Welsh, Harper, & Dickson, 2003). Therefore, as with most correlational findings, there are many qualifiers and ways in which adolescent relationships could potentially have negative consequences for later relationships.

Sub-myth 3   The effects of one's first break-up are the most damaging in one's life

The first sexual experience is one that people don't forget. It has such an impact that there's a play called *My First Time* (Davenport, 2007). In the play, actors describe various "first-time" sexual experiences. Sexual firsts are such a cultural touchstone that just the phrase "my first time" usually needs no explanation. Clearly, there's a mythology about our first sexual experiences and the dissolution of the relationships behind those first sexual experiences. The question is whether the dissolution of that first romance is the most difficult that people experience.

Adolescence is a difficult time on many levels and one of those has to be the development of emotion regulation, including how adolescents learn to cope with disappointment. This partially explains why adolescence is a time of increased suicidal thoughts, with 4.1% of adolescents attempting suicide (Nock et al., 2013). Although romantic disappointments are usually only a small part of why youth attempt suicide, it is worth reaching out to adolescents who are in serious distress about a break-up. By asking someone about their suffering and whether they are considering suicide, you may prevent a tragedy (for reviews, see Andover, Morris, Wren, & Bruzzese, 2012; Gould, Fisher, Parides, Flory, & Shaffer, 1996).

For further information about suicide prevention, contact your local mental health agency or call a suicide prevention lifeline:
- In the United States and Canada: 1-800-273-TALK (8255; http://www.suicidepreventionlifeline.org/ or http://suicide prevention.ca/)
- In Australia: 13 11 14 (https://www.lifeline.org.au/)
- In the UK: 116 123 (http://www.nhs.uk/Conditions/Suicide/Pages/Getting-help.aspx)

Returning to the question of whether the effects of adolescent relationship dissolution are worse than the dissolution of later intimate relationships (e.g., divorce), it's not even close. The effects of divorce are far more profound. On nearly any measure, being divorced is worse than being married or single (the effects of being widowed come close to the effects of divorce on a few variables). To keep it simple, let's limit our discussion to one variable: life satisfaction. Divorce is one of very few common variables that can permanently alter your life satisfaction (see Myth 25). Most of the events that people experience may raise or lower their life satisfaction, but sooner or later they come back to their average level of satisfaction. Not so with divorce. It knocks you down and tends to keep you down (for a review, see Diener et al., 1999). In addition, it's universal. Ed Diener, Carol Gohm, Eunkook Suh, and Shigehiro Oishi (2000) collected a sample of 59,169 people in 42 nations and evaluated the association between marital status and life satisfaction (also called *subjective well-being*). In every culture and nation that they assessed, people who were divorced reported lower life satisfaction than people who were married. Although there were small changes in the size of the effect depending on each country's cultural tolerance of divorce, the findings were consistent across the world. So, clearly divorce is a very deep cut (for a more detailed discussion of the effects of divorce see Myth 25; see also Smock, Manning, & Gupta, 1999).

The cut of an adolescent relationship dissolving is simply not as deep as that of a marriage dissolving. In fact, adolescent relationships that don't dissolve but continue into adulthood and lead to marriage are more likely to experience marital distress and divorce (Karney & Bradbury, 1995). Given the developmental benefits of appropriate adolescent intimate relationships, it's reasonable to assume that dissolving intimate relationships is an important developmental milestone for adolescents. Whether one is the dumper or the dumpee, there's much to be learned from this type of experience and lessons for later life. Although there's little research on the termination of adolescent relationships, it's clear that families and peers play important roles in assisting with the onset, continuation, and dissolution of adolescent relationships (W. A. Collins et al., 2009). But, in the end divorce is a much deeper cut (see the next Myth).

Conclusion

In almost no way is the first cut the deepest. It probably just feels that way because – to borrow from yet another song – breaking up is hard to do, no matter what your age. If we define the "first cut" as being an adolescent intimate relationship, we know that adolescent relationships are more common and longer lasting than most people think. They're associated with both positive and negative events, depending on a number of other factors; however, appropriate and functional relationships tend to be associated with better long-term relationship functioning (for a positive reframing of adolescent sexuality, see Harden, 2014). Finally, as bad as adolescent break-ups are, they tend to be experienced as worse because the pain is a new experience and because adolescents are still developing their ability to understand their emotions, but from a perspective of overall life satisfaction the experience of divorce is far worse than that of an adolescent breakup. In the end, the first cut may feel deep, but it is more like a blister that precedes thicker skin. Perhaps there's another song in there somewhere.

Myth #25 Things will improve once you're divorced

"Life's short. Get a divorce." This trademarked message was on a billboard that went up in Chicago on May 1, 2007 (Pallasch, 2007). The billboard implied that divorce can lead to increases in your subjective well-being or life satisfaction (see the introduction and Myth 24 for more on this concept). Based on surveys of attitudes and expectations about divorce, it seems that many people agree with the sentiment expressed in the billboard (e.g., Diaz, Molina, MacMillan, Duran, & Swart, 2013; S. P. Martin & Parashar, 2006; Trail & Karney, 2012). So, does it work? Does getting out of an unhappy marriage improve life satisfaction? Let's look at the data.

Bonus myth: The divorce rate is climbing

Contrary to what many think, the divorce rate is not climbing. In fact, it's dropping in the United States. For every 1,000 people in the United States, 4.7 of them got a divorce in 1990, 4.1 did in 2000, and 3.4 did in 2009 (Kreider & Ellis, 2011). These data aren't unusual in comparison with historical trends. The divorce rate has fluctuated quite a bit over time, going down in the 1950s and 1960s and back up in the 1970s and 1980s. In addition, these rates vary across nations and states. Regardless of the rate, divorce is associated with lower well-being. Read on as I explore these associations in both adults and children as well as what might be the explanatory mechanisms of the associations.

We know that marital status is associated with life satisfaction in cross-sectional studies (in other words, studies that compare life satisfaction across married, single, and divorced couples), with married people reporting greater life satisfaction than divorced people (Haring-Hidore, Stock, Okun, & Witter, 1985; Myers, 1999) and these correlations appear to be similar around the world (Diener et al., 2000). However, cross-sectional studies are unable to differentiate whether people who are more satisfied with their lives are less likely to divorce or whether divorce leads to lower life satisfaction. To address this question, we turn to longitudinal studies in which researchers assess people before and after their divorces (for more on longitudinal studies, see the introduction to Chapter 5 "Predicting Success in Relationships"). This is exactly what Richard Lucas (2005) did. Using the German Socio-Economic Panel Study collected by the German Institute for Economic Research in Berlin, he was able to track the life satisfaction of more than 30,000 Germans over 18 years.

Before I describe the results of this study, let me give a little background on the research on life satisfaction. People are often surprised to learn that most events don't permanently impact life satisfaction. Even though people play the lottery, work hard for a promotion, or set goals they think will make them happy, attaining these goals tends to result in only a transient increase in life satisfaction. Similarly, people fear losing their jobs, becoming disabled, or losing a friend. Yet these events, as well, tend to result in reductions in life satisfaction that are temporary. The resilience to set-backs and the existential ennui that can follow successes has been replicated so many times (e.g., Brickman, Coates, & Janoff-Bulman, 1978; Suh, Diener, & Fujita, 1996) that scientists have come to believe that people tend to have a fairly stable level of life satisfaction to which they return following most of the events in their lives. In other words, humans work hard at increasing – or at least preventing the decrease of – our life satisfaction without ever really having an impact on it. This has led to the concept of a *hedonic treadmill* on which we're running to achieve happiness without ever quite getting to the blissful destination of our dreams (Brickman & Campbell, 1971; Headey & Wearing, 1989). Having noted how few events can permanently alter one's life satisfaction, let's return to Lucas' (2005) 18-year study of life satisfaction.

Lucas (2005) found that divorce appears to have a permanent – or at least a long-term – effect on life satisfaction. Just to reiterate: of the many major life events humans may experience, divorce appears to be one of

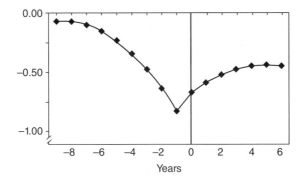

Figure 15 The graph above shows the average trajectories of life satisfaction in the years before and after divorce. Thus, in this graph, the overall mean of life satisfaction for the whole sample (regardless of whether the participants were single, married, divorced, etc.) was recalculated to equal zero (thus negative numbers represent values below the mean) and the year of the divorce is year zero. As you can see, the life satisfaction of people who experienced a divorce does not make it back up to their baseline level as it does with most other major life events. (Figure is from Lucas, 2005, p. 947).

the very few events that can permanently alter overall life satisfaction (for a review of other events that can permanantly lower life satisfaction, see Diener, Lucas, & Scollon, 2006). Figure 15 describes how individuals who divorce don't make it back to their original levels of life satisfaction. However, Figure 15 doesn't address the possibility that there may be a pre-existing difference between those who go on to divorce and those who don't divorce that is present even before they get married and that the early years of their marriage might have been unusually satisfying for people who eventually divorced. Lucas looked at that as well. Indeed, there was a difference in the levels of life satisfaction before marriage, with those who would later go on to get married and divorced having lower levels of life satisfaction than those who would go on to get married and stay married. Nevertheless, this difference couldn't account for the stable drop in life satisfaction that followed a divorce. Thus, there's compelling evidence that on average divorce lowers your life satisfaction.

Despite these findings, it should be noted that there are clear individual differences in how people respond to divorce (Mancini, Bonanno, & Clark, 2011) that serve to remind us that findings like these are general and may not apply to everyone who gets divorced. For example, if your partner is violent or abusive, dissolving the relationship and making yourself unavailable to your partner will likely improve your life satisfaction and possibly prolong your life (as discussed in Myth 22; de Becker, 1997). In fact, it's clear that one of the ways to drive a romantic partner away from a relationship is by being aggressive or violent (e.g., Rogge & Bradbury, 1999).

Children and divorce

If divorce is hard on spouses, what are the effects on children? Again, let's start with the cross-sectional data. Adults whose parents divorced when they were children tend to have more mental illness, lower marital quality, higher rates of divorce, lower educational attainment, lower income, and worse physical health (for review, see M. D. Johnson & Bradbury, 1998). The question – as with spouses – is whether we can identify the mechanism for the impact of divorce on children. Paul Amato and Bruce Keith (1991b) conducted a meta-analysis that considered 34 childhood outcomes and found that children from divorced parents did worse on 27 of them. They then considered three possible mechanisms for the apparent negative impact of divorce on children.

First, Amato and Keith (1991b) considered the fact that divorce usually means the same income has to support two households, which effectively reduces the financial resources of the family. This reduction in turn can mean a loss of opportunities for children experiencing the divorce of their parents. They tested whether the financial impact and subsequent loss of opportunities accounted for the impact of divorce on children by comparing children with divorced parents to children with married parents, while statistically controlling for income. They found partial support for this hypothesis. If the effects of income inequality are removed from the analyses, the number of child well-being outcomes showing a difference between married and divorced families dropped from 27 to 13. They also found evidence that the effects are even more substantial when the divorce causes a substantial drop in the families' socio-economic standing. Thus, there's modest support for the finding that the economic repercussions of divorce adversely impacts children.

Second, they considered whether the change in family structure was accounting for the worse child outcomes in families who had experienced a divorce. This was a tougher hypothesis to test. First, they noted that the big change in family structure that comes with divorce usually involves the father's absence from the home. So, they looked at studies that compared children in single-mother families with families that included an active step-father. In the six studies that examined this difference, they found that the presence of a step-father in the home improved the outcomes for sons and worsened the outcome for daughters. When they examined this hypothesis by simply using time spent with the non-custodial parent, they again found that greater father–son time was associated with improved outcomes, but the effect was not there for father–daughter time. This is consistent with the fact that fathers tend to be less active in parenting daughters compared to sons (Amato & Keith, 1991b). Therefore, it seems that family disruption may account for some of the deleterious effects of divorce on boys but not girls.

Third, Amato and Keith examined studies that considered whether the increase in conflict expressed in the home prior to and during divorce might account for the effects of divorce on children. This was the strongest of the three effects. There's a large empirical literature detailing the impact of family conflict on children (Amato & Keith, 1991b). In fact, this hypothesis was studied in two large studies that examined the effects of divorce on children (one in the United States and one in Great Britain). These studies found that the effects of divorce were ameliorated when the inter-parental conflict was statistically removed from the analyses (Cherlin et al., 1991). Therefore, it seems that parental conflict is a powerful predictor of problematic childhood outcomes.

Given that there appear to be negative effects of parental conflict and divorce on children, the next question is whether these effects are long-lasting. Amato and Keith conducted another meta-analysis (1991a) that confirmed that the effects are long-lasting. However, even more compelling evidence came from a 12-year study that Amato conducted with Laura Spencer Loomis and Alan Booth (1995) looking at the effects of parental divorce on the children's well-being as young adults. Specifically, they assessed the adult offspring's life satisfaction, psychological well-being, marital satisfaction, and social support. Most importantly, they used both parental conflict and divorce as predictors of these outcomes. They found that the negative impact of the divorce actually decreased to the extent that the there was more conflict between the parents in the marriage. In other words, it seems that divorces that curtail the conflict between the parents can benefit children in the long run; whereas, divorces in low-conflict couples appear to have a negative impact on children (see Figure 16). Thus, it appears that the long-term benefits or detriments of divorce on children depend on the amount of conflict within the parents' marriage.

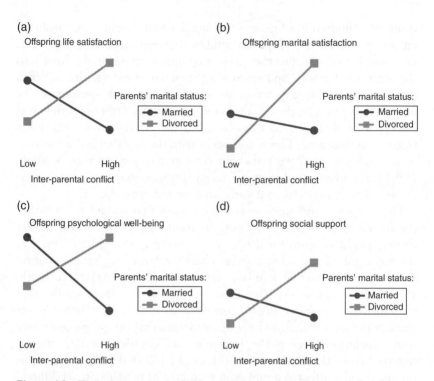

Figure 16 These four graphs represent the impact of parental conflict and divorce on the adult well-being of children (adapted from Amato et al., 1995, p. 910).

Conclusion

Those considering divorce have many factors to weigh, and the very fact that they are considering divorce demonstrates that there's a level of dissatisfaction with their marriage that they may not be able to overcome. Although people vary in what they consider the threshold at which a marriage can't be saved, the data on the impact of divorce – both on spouses and on children – make it clear that it's not a decision to be taken lightly. In the end, the lesson of the negative impact of marital discord and divorce is that one should choose a spouse very carefully. In terms of life satisfaction, it's the most important decision of your life. This lesson seems to have been learned well as evidenced by the dropping rate of both marriage and divorce in the United States, such that now only around 40% of first marriages end in divorce (Kreider & Ellis, 2011).

Notes

1 I consider the following terms synonyms: "couple therapy," "marital therapy," "couple counseling," and "marital counseling." I treat them as synonyms because the differences in treating married vs. unmarried couples are no different than other contextual factors that a therapist would consider. In addition, while the field of psychology considers there to be a difference between counseling and psychotherapy, the general public tends to treat them as synonyms.

2 This is not to be confused with *effectiveness research*, which refers to treatment outcome research that is done in community settings as opposed to the more controlled confines of a psychological lab. In this way, the impact of a treatment is evaluated in a manner that more realistically simulates how the treatment would typically be provided if deployed widely.

CODA

I didn't start out with the intention of citing more than 800 sources, and I fear that my effort to carefully support my claims may have conveyed an overwhelming level of complexity. So, let me sum up the thesis of my book with a simple idea.

In nearly every religious tradition and in many spiritual practices, an overriding theme is a commandment to love one another. So it is here.

When I speak with couples or friends about their relationship problems, I always try to come back to love. You're angry because your partner did or didn't do something. Beneath the anger is hurt or maybe fear. Fear that your partner's action or inaction may mean that your needs or desires aren't being respected. And, if your partner doesn't meet the low bar of respecting you, how can you know that you're loved? From the other perspective, you may see that your partner is angry or withdrawn. You may think that it was such a little thing that you did or didn't do. What could it matter? How could your partner be so upset over something so small? Your partner should just get over it. By examining relationship conflicts closely, I try to help people understand that their action or inaction conveys a message about their love. Understanding this simple idea may help.

In other words, I hope that in writing this book, I have helped you understand – to quote a poem by Robert Hayden (1975, p. 113) – "love's austere and lonely offices."

Great Myths of Intimate Relationships: Dating, Sex, and Marriage,
First Edition. Matthew D. Johnson.
© 2016 John Wiley & Sons, Inc. Published 2016 by John Wiley & Sons, Inc.

REFERENCES

Abbey, A., & Melby, C. (1986). The effects of nonverbal cues on gender differences in perceptions of sexual intent. *Sex Roles*, *15*, 283–298. doi: 10.1007/BF00288318

Ablow, K. (2012). Study finds host of challenges for kids of gay parents. *Fox News*. Retrieved March 27, 2014, from http://www.foxnews.com/opinion/2012/06/12/study-finds-host-challenges-for-kids-gay-parents/

Adultery and Fornication; Unlawful Cohabitation, Unannotated Mississippi Code (2013) § 97-29-1 (1848).

Alexander, M. G., & Fisher, T. D. (2003). Truth and consequences: Using the bogus pipeline to examine sex differences in self-reported sexuality. *Journal of Sex Research*, *40*, 27–35. doi: 10.1080/00224490309552164

Allen, E. S., Rhoades, G. K., Stanley, S. M., Loew, B., & Markman, H. J. (2012). The effects of marriage education for army couples with a history of infidelity. *Journal of Family Psychology*, *26*, 26–35. doi: 10.1037/a0026742

Al Sughayir, M. A. (2004). Unconsummated marriage: A Saudi version. *Arab Journal of Psychiatry*, *15*, 122–130.

Amato, P. R., & Keith, B. (1991a). Parental divorce and adult well-being: A meta-analysis. *Journal of Marriage and the Family*, *53*, 43–58. doi: 10.2307/353132

Amato, P. R., & Keith, B. (1991b). Parental divorce and the well-being of children: A meta-analysis. *Psychological Bulletin*, *110*, 26–46. doi: 10.1037/0033-2909.110.1.26

Amato, P. R., Loomis, L. S., & Booth, A. (1995). Parental divorce, marital conflict, and offspring well-being during early adulthood. *Social Forces*, *73*, 895–915. doi: 10.2307/2580551

Ambrosino, B. (2014). I wasn't born this way. I choose to be gay. *The New Republic*. Retrieved October 19, 2014, from http://www.newrepublic.com/article/116378/macklemores-same-love-sends-wrong-message-about-being-gay

American Psychiatric Association. (2013). *Diagnostic and statistical manual of mental disorders* (5th ed.). Washington, DC: American Psychiatric Publishing.

American Sociological Association. (2012). Brief of *amicus curiae* American Sociological Association in support of respondent Kristin M. Perry and respondent Edith Schlain Windsor. Washington, DC: Supreme Court of the United States.

Anderson, N. H. (1968). Likableness ratings of 555 personality-trait words. *Journal of Personality and Social Psychology, 9*, 272–279. doi: 10.1037/h0025907

Andersson, G., Noack, T., Seierstad, A., & Weedon-Fekjær, H. (2006). The demographics of same-sex marriages in Norway and Sweden. *Demography, 43*, 79–98. doi: 10.1353/dem.2006.0001

Andover, M. S., Morris, B. W., Wren, A., & Bruzzese, M. E. (2012). The co-occurrence of non-suicidal self-injury and attempted suicide among adolescents: Distinguishing risk factors and psychosocial correlates. *Child and Adolescent Psychiatry and Mental Health, 6*, ArtID: 11. doi: 10.1186/1753-2000-6-11

Antheunis, M. L., Schouten, A. P., Valkenburg, P. M., & Peter, J. (2012). Interactive uncertainty reduction strategies and verbal affection in computer-mediated communication. *Communication Research, 39*, 757–780. doi: 10.1177/0093650211410420

Antheunis, M. L., Valkenburg, P. M., & Peter, J. (2007). Computer-mediated communication and interpersonal attraction: An experimental test of two explanatory hypotheses. *CyberPsychology & Behavior, 10*, 831–835. doi: 10.1089/cpb.2007.9945

Antheunis, M. L., Valkenburg, P. M., & Peter, J. (2010). Getting acquainted through social network sites: Testing a model of online uncertainty reduction and social attraction. *Computers in Human Behavior, 26*, 100–109. doi: 10.1016/j.chb.2009.07.005

Antill, J. K. (1983). Sex role complementarity versus similarity in married couples. *Journal of Personality and Social Psychology, 45*, 145–155. doi: 10.1037/0022-3514.45.1.145

Archer, J. (2004). Sex differences in aggression in real-world settings: A meta-analytic review. *Review of General Psychology, 8*, 291–322. doi: 10.1037/1089-2680.8.4.291 & 10.1037/1089-2680.8.4.291.supp (Supplemental)

Ariely, D. (2010). *The upside of irrationality: The unexpected benefits of defying logic at work and at home*. New York: Harper.

Armstrong, E. A., England, P., & Fogarty, A. C. K. (2012). Accounting for women's orgasm and sexual enjoyment in college hookups and relationships. *American Sociological Review, 77*, 435–462. doi: 10.1177/0003122412445802

Armstrong, E. A., Hamilton, L., & England, P. (2010). Is hooking up bad for young women? *Contexts, 9*, 22–27.

Aronson, E., Willerman, B., & Floyd, J. (1966). The effect of a pratfall on increasing interpersonal attractiveness. *Psychonomic Science, 4,* 227–228.

Asch, S. E. (1946). Forming impressions of personality. *The Journal of Abnormal and Social Psychology, 41,* 258–290. doi: 10.1037/h0055756

Aube, J., & Koestner, R. (1995). Gender characteristics and relationship adjustment: Another look at similarity-complementarity hypotheses. *Journal of Personality, 63,* 879–904. doi: 10.1111/j.1467-6494.1995.tb00319.x

Avishai, O., Heath, M., & Randles, J. (2012). Marriage goes to school. *Contexts, 11,* 34–38. doi: 10.1177/1536504212456180

Axinn, W. G., & Barber, J. S. (1997). Living arrangements and family formation attitudes in early adulthood. *Journal of Marriage and The Family, 59,* 595–611. doi: 10.2307/353948

Axinn, W. G., & Thornton, A. (1992). The relationship between cohabitation and divorce: Selectivity or causal influence? *Demography, 29,* 357–374. doi: 10.2307/2061823

Ayduk, O., Downey, G., & Kim, M. (2001). Rejection sensitivity and depressive symptoms in women. *Personality and Social Psychology Bulletin, 27,* 868–877. doi: 10.1177/0146167201277009

Bailey, J. M., Gaulin, S., Agyei, Y., & Gladue, B. A. (1994). Effects of gender and sexual orientation on evolutionarily relevant aspects of human mating psychology. *Journal of Personality and Social Psychology, 66,* 1081–1093. doi: 10.1037/0022-3514.66.6.1081

Balsam, K. F., Beauchaine, T. P., Mickey, R. M., & Rothblum, E. D. (2005). Mental health of lesbian, gay, bisexual, and heterosexual siblings: Effects of gender, sexual orientation, and family. *Journal of Abnormal Psychology, 114,* 471–476. doi: 10.1037/0021-843x.114.3.471

Bandura, A. (1969). *Principles of behavior modification.* New York: Holt, Rinehart and Winston.

Bandura, A. (1977). *Social learning theory.* Englewood Cliffs, NJ: Prentice-Hall.

Bargh, J. A., McKenna, K. Y. A., & Fitzsimons, G. M. (2002). Can you see the real me? Activation and expression of the "true self" on the Internet. *Journal of Social Issues, 58,* 33–48. doi: 10.1111/1540-4560.00247

Bar-Kalifa, E., & Rafaeli, E. (2013). Disappointment's sting is greater than help's balm: Quasi-signal detection of daily support matching. *Journal of Family Psychology, 27,* 956–967. doi: 10.1037/a0034905

Barner, J. R., & Carney, M. M. (2011). Interventions for intimate partner violence: A historical review. *Journal of Family Violence, 26,* 235–244. doi: 10.1007/s10896-011-9359-3

Baron, R. (2011). *Opposites attract: How to use the secrets of personality type to create a love that lasts.* New York: HarperCollins.

Bartlett, T. (2012). Controversial gay-parenting study is severely flawed, journal's audit fFinds. *The Chronicle of Higher Education.* Retrieved Marth 27, 2014, from http://chronicle.com/blogs/percolator/controversial-gay-parenting-study-is-severely-flawed-journals-audit-finds/30255

Baucom, D. H., & Epstein, N. (1990). *Cognitive-behavioral marital therapy.* Philadelphia, PA: Brunner/Mazel.

Baumeister, R. F. (2000). Gender differences in erotic plasticity: The female sex drive as socially flexible and responsive. *Psychological Bulletin, 126,* 347–374. doi: 10.1037/0033-2909.126.3.347

Baumeister, R. F., Catanese, K. R., & Vohs, K. D. (2001). Is there a gender difference in strength of sex drive? Theoretical views, conceptual distinctions, and a review of relevent evidence. *Personality and Social Psychology Review, 5,* 242–273. doi: 10.1207/S15327957PSPR0503_5

Baumeister, R. F., & Twenge, J. M. (2002). Cultural suppression of female sexuality. *Review of General Psychology, 6,* 166–203. doi: 10.1037/1089-2680.6.2.166

Bayer, R. S., & Shunaigat, W. M. (2001). Psychological, social and cultural aspects of unconsummated marriage. *Arab Journal of Psychiatry, 12,* 43–52.

Baym, N. K. (2006). Interpersonal life online. In L. A. Lievrouw & S. Livingstone (Eds.), *The handbook of new media: Updated, student edition* (pp. 35–54). London: Sage.

Beach, S. R. H., & Fincham, F. D. (1994). Toward an integrated model of negative affectivity in marriage. In S. M. Johnson & L. S. Greenberg (Eds.), *The heart of the matter: Perspectives on emotion in marital therapy* (pp. 227–255). Philadelphia, PA: Brunner/Mazel.

Beach, S. R. H., Whitaker, D. J., Jones, D. J., & Tesser, A. (2001). When does performance feedback prompt complementarity in romantic relationships? *Personal Relationships, 8,* 231–248. doi: 10.1111/j.1475-6811.2001.tb00038.x

Beauvoir, S. de. (1953). *The second sex* (H. M. Parshley, Trans.). New York: Knopf.

Becker, G. S., Landes, E. M., & Michael, R. T. (1977). An economic analysis of marital instability. *Journal of Political Economy, 85,* 1141–1187. doi: 10.2307/1837421

Bell, K. M., & Naugle, A. E. (2008). Intimate partner violence theoretical considerations: Moving towards a contextual framework. *Clinical Psychology Review, 28,* 1096–1107. doi: 10.1016/j.cpr.2008.03.003

Belsky, J. (1985). Exploring individual differences in marital change across the transition to parenthood: The role of violated expectations. *Journal of Marriage and the Family, 47,* 1037–1044.

Belsky, J., & Hsieh, K.-H. (1998). Patterns of marital change during the early childhood years: Parent personality, coparenting, and division-of-labor correlates. *Journal of Family Psychology, 12,* 511–528. doi: 10.1037/0893-3200.12.4.511

Belsky, J., & Kelly, J. (1994). *The transition to parenthood: How a first child changes a marriage: Why some couples grow closer and others apart.* New York: Delacorte Press.

Belsky, J., & Pensky, E. (1988). Marital change across the transition to parenthood. *Marriage and Family Review, 12,* 133–156. doi: 10.1300/J002v12n03_08

Belsky, J., & Rovine, M. (1990). Patterns of marital change across the transition to parenthood: Pregnancy to three years postpartum. *Journal of Marriage and the Family, 52,* 5–19. doi: 10.2307/352833

Bem, S. L. (1974). The measurement of psychological androgyny. *Journal of Consulting and Clinical Psychology, 42*, 155–162. doi: 10.1037/h0036215

Bem, S. L. (1981). Gender schema theory: A cognitive account of sex typing. *Psychological Review, 88*, 354–364. doi: 10.1037/0033-295x.88.4.354

Bennett, N. G., Blanc, A. K., & Bloom, D. E. (1988). Commitment and the modern union: Assessing the link between premarital cohabitation and subsequent marital stability. *American Sociological Review, 53*, 127–138. doi: 10.2307/2095738

Berger, L. M., Carlson, M. J., Bzostek, S. H., & Osborne, C. (2008). Parenting practices of resident fathers: The role of marital and biological ties. *Journal of Marriage and Family, 70*, 625–639. doi: 10.1111/j.1741-3737.2008.00510.x

Bergner, D. (2013). *What do women want? Adventures in the science of female desire.* New York: HarperCollins.

Bergsma, A., Poot, G., & Liefbroer, A. (2008). Happiness in the garden of Epicurus. *Journal of Happiness Studies, 9*, 397–423. doi: 10.1007/s10902-006-9036-z

Berkman, L. F. (1985). The relationship of social networks and social support to morbidity and mortality. In S. Cohen & S. L. Syme (Eds.), *Social support and health.* (pp. 241–262). San Diego, CA: Academic Press.

Biglan, A. (1995). Translating what we know about the context of antisocial behavior into a lower prevalence of such behavior. *Journal of Applied Behavior Analysis, 28*, 479–492. doi: 10.1901/jaba.1995.28-479

Bir, A., Corwin, E., MacIlvain, B., Beard, A., Richburg, K., Smith, K., & Lerman, R. I. (2012). *The community healthy marriage initiative evaluation: Impacts of a community approach to strengthening families* (OPRE Report #2012-34A). Washington DC: Office of Planning, Research and Evaluation, Administration for Children and Families, U.S. Department of Health and Human Services.

Blankenhorn, D. (1995). *Fatherless America: Confronting our most urgent social problem.* New York: Harper Perennial.

Blazer, J. A. (1964). Married virgins: A study of unconsummated marriage. *Journal of Marriage and The Family, 26*, 213–214. doi: 10.2307/349732

Blumstein, P., & Schwartz, P. (1983). *American couples: Money, work, sex* (1st ed.). New York: Morrow.

Bluth, K., Roberson, P. N. E., Billen, R. M., & Sams, J. M. (2013). A stress model for couples parenting children with autism spectrum disorders and the introduction of a mindfulness intervention. *Journal of Family Theory & Review, 5*, 194–213. doi: 10.1111/jftr.12015

Bolger, N., & Eckenrode, J. (1991). Social relationships, personality, and anxiety during a major stressful event. *Journal of Personality and Social Psychology, 61*, 440–449. doi: 10.1037/0022-3514.61.3.440

Bolger, N., Foster, M., Vinokur, A. D., & Ng, R. (1996). Close relationships and adjustments to a life crisis: The case of breast cancer. *Journal of Personality and Social Psychology, 70*, 283–294. doi: 10.1037/0022-3514.70.2.283

Bolger, N., Zuckerman, A., & Kessler, R. C. (2000). Invisible support and adjustment to stress. *Journal of Personality and Social Psychology, 79*, 953–961. doi: 10.1037/0022-3514.79.6.953

Bornstein, R. F., & D'Agostino, P. R. (1994). The attribution and discounting of perceptual fluency: Preliminary tests of a perceptual fluency/attributional model of the mere exposure effect. *Social Cognition*, *12*, 103–128. doi: 10.1521/soco.1994.12.2.103

Bouchard, S., Sabourin, S., Lussier, Y., & Villeneuve, E. (2009). Relationship quality and stability in couples when one partner suffers from borderline personality disorder. *Journal of Marital and Family Therapy*, *35*, 446–455. doi: 10.1111/j.1752-0606.2009.00151.x

Bradbury, T. N., & Fincham, F. D. (1987). Affect and cognition in close relationships: Towards an integrative model. *Cognition and Emotion*, *1*, 59–87. doi: 10.1080/02699938708408364

Bradbury, T. N., & Fincham, F. D. (1988). Individual difference variables in close relationships: A contextual model of marriage as an integrative framework. *Journal of Personality and Social Psychology*, *54*, 713–721. doi: 10.1037/0022-3514.54.4.713

Bradbury, T. N., & Fincham, F. D. (1990). Attributions in marriage: Review and critique. *Psychological Bulletin*, *107*, 3–33. doi: 10.1037/0033-2909.107.1.3

Bradbury, T. N., & Karney, B. R. (2014). *Intimate Relationships* (2nd ed.). New York: W. W. Norton.

Bradley Foundation. (2006). *The Bradley Foundation's Mission*. Retrieved March 27, 2014, from http://www.bradleyfdn.org/foundations_mission.asp

Bramlett, M. D., & Mosher, W. D. (2002). *Cohabitation, marriage, divorce, and remarriage in the United States* (Vital and Health Statistics, Vol. *23*). Hyattsville, MD: National Center for Health Statistics.

Brickman, P., & Campbell, D. T. (1971). Hedonic relativism and planning the good society. In M. H. Appley (Ed.), *Adaptation-level theory* (pp. 287–305). New York: Academic Press.

Brickman, P., Coates, D., & Janoff-Bulman, R. (1978). Lottery winners and accident victims: Is happiness relative? *Journal of Personality and Social Psychology*, *36*, 917–927. doi: 10.1037/0022-3514.36.8.917

Bringle, R. G. (1995). Sexual jealousy in the relationships of homosexual and heterosexual men: 1980 and 1992. *Personal Relationships*, *2*, 313–325. doi: 10.1111/j.1475-6811.1995.tb00095.x

Brown, B. B., Feiring, C., & Furman, W. (1999). Missing the love boat: Why researchers have shied away from adolescent romance. In W. Furman, B. B. Brown, & C. Feiring (Eds.), *The development of romantic relationships in adolescence* (pp. 1–16). New York: Cambridge University Press.

Brown, S. L. (2004). Moving from cohabitation to marriage: Effects on relationship quality. *Social Science Research*, *33*, 1–19. doi: 10.1016/S0049-089X(03)00036-X

Bryant, A. S., & Demian. (1994). Relationship characteristics of American gay and lesbian couples: Findings from a national survey. *Journal of Gay & Lesbian Social Services*, *1*, 101–117. doi: 10.1300/J041v01n02_06

Buehlman, K. T., Gottman, J. M., & Katz, L. F. (1992). How a couple views their past predicts their future: Predicting divorce from an oral history review. *Journal of Family Psychology, 5,* 295–318. doi: 10.1037/0893-3200.5.3-4.295

Bumpass, L., & Sweet, J. (1989). National estimates of cohabitation. *Demography, 26,* 615–625. doi: 10.2307/2061261

Burke, L. K., & Follingstad, D. R. (1999). Violence in lesbian and gay relationships: Theory, prevalence, and correlational factors. *Clinical Psychology Review, 19,* 487–512. doi: 10.1016/S0272-7358(98)00054-3

Burnett, A. L. (2012). Evaluation and management of erectile dysfunction. In A. J. Wein, L. R. Kavoussi, A. W. Partin, C. A. Peters & A. C. Novick (Eds.), *Campbell-Walsh Urology* (10th ed., Vol. *1,* pp. 721–748). Philadelphia, PA: Saunders.

Buss, D. M. (1989). Sex differences in human mate preferences: Evolutionary hypotheses tested in 37 cultures. *Behavioral and Brain Sciences, 12,* 1–49. doi: 10.1017/s0140525x00023992

Buss, D. M., & Schmitt, D. P. (1993). Sexual strategies theory: An evolutionary perspective on human mating. *Psychological Review, 100,* 204–232. doi: 10.1037/0033-295X.100.2.204

Buss, D. M., Shackelford, T. K., Kirkpatrick, L. A., & Larsen, R. J. (2001). A half century of mate preferences: The cultural evolution of values. *Journal of Marriage and Family, 63,* 491–503. doi: 10.1111/j.1741-3737.2001.00491.x

Cacioppo, J. T., Cacioppo, S., Gonzaga, G. C., Ogburn, E. L., & VanderWeele, T. J. (2013). Marital satisfaction and break-ups differ across on-line and off-line meeting venues. *Proceedings of the National Academy of Sciences.* doi: 10.1073/pnas.1222447110

Caffrey, N., & O'Neill, D. (2007). Sexuality and health among older adults in the United States: Comment. *The New England Journal of Medicine, 357,* 2732.

Cameron, J. J., Stinson, D. A., & Wood, J. V. (2013). The bold and the bashful: Self-esteem, gender, and relationship initiation. *Social Psychological and Personality Science.* doi: 10.1177/1948550613476309

Campbell, D. T., & Fiske, D. W. (1959). Convergent and discriminant validation by the multitrait-multimethod matrix. *Psychological Bulletin, 56,* 81–105. doi: 10.1037/h0046016

Camperio-Ciani, A., Corna, F., & Capiluppi, C. (2004). Evidence for maternally inherited factors favouring male homosexuality and promoting female fecundity. *Proceedings of the Royal Society of Biological Sciences, 271,* 2217–2221. doi: 10.1098/rspb.2004.2872

Campos, B., Graesch, A. P., Repetti, R. L., Bradbury, T. N., & Ochs, E. (2009). Opportunity for interaction? A naturalistic observation study of dual-earner families after work and school. *Journal of Family Psychology, 23,* 798–807. doi: 10.1037/a0015824

Caplan, G. (1964). *Principles of preventive psychiatry.* New York: Basic Books.

Carden, M. L. (1969). *Oneida: Utopian community to modern corporation.* Baltimore: Johns Hopkins Press.

Carlson, M. J., & VanOrman, A. G. (2014). Trajectories of couple relationship quality after childbirth: Does marriage matter? *Working paper WP13-14-FF.* Princeton, NJ: The Bendheim-Thoman Center for Research on Child Wellbeing.

Carlson, M. J., McLanahan, S., & England, P. (2004). Union formation in fragile families. *Demography, 41*, 237–261. doi: 10.1353/dem.2004.0012

Carlson, M. J., Pilkauskas, N. V., McLanahan, S. S., & Brooks-Gunn, J. (2011). Couples as partners and parents over children's early years. *Journal of Marriage & Family, 73*, 317–334. doi: 10.1111/j.1741-3737.2010.00809.x

Carnelley, K. B., & Janoff-Bulman, R. (1992). Optimism about love relationships: General vs specific lessons from one's personal experiences. *Journal of Social and Personal Relationships, 9*, 5–20. doi: 10.1177/0265407592091001

Caron, S. W. (2010). Teen girls and breakups: Helping them move on: Lessons learned from first breakups. *SheKnows.com*. Retrieved November 3, 2014, from http://www.sheknows.com/parenting/articles/813548/teen-girls-and-breakups-helping-them-move-on-1

Carothers, B. J., & Reis, H. T. (2013). Men and women are from Earth: Examining the latent structure of gender. *Journal of Personality and Social Psychology, 104*, 385–407. doi: 10.1037/a0030437 & 10.1037/a0030437.supp (Supplemental)

Carver, K., Joyner, K., & Udry, J. R. (2003). National estimates of adolescent romantic relationships. In P. Florsheim (Ed.), *Adolescent romantic relations and sexual behavior: Theory, research, and practical implications* (pp. 23–56). Mahwah, NJ: Lawrence Erlbaum.

Cary, M. S. (1976). *Talk? Do you want to talk? Negotiation for the initiation of conversation between the unacquainted*. Pennsylvania University, Philadelphia. Available from Dissertation Abstracts International Section B: The Sciences and Engineering, Vol. 36(8-B) database.

Casper, L. M., & Bianchi, S. M. (2002). *Continuity and change in the American family*. Thousand Oaks, CA: Sage.

Caspi, A., & Gorsky, P. (2006). Online deception: Prevalence, motivation, and emotion. *CyberPsychology & Behavior, 9*, 54–59. doi: 10.1089/cpb.2006.9.54

Catalano, S. (2007). *Intimate partner violence in the United States*. Washington, DC: Bureau of Justice Statistics. Retrieved May 19, 2014, from http://www.bjs.gov/content/pub/pdf/ipvus.pdf

Caughlin, J. P. (2002). The demand/withdraw pattern of communication as a predictor of marital satisfaction over time. *Human Communication Research, 28*, 49–85. doi: 10.1093/hcr/28.1.49

Centers for Disease Control and Prevention. (2011). *Diagnoses of HIV infection and AIDS in the United States and dependent areas, 2009*. Atlanta, GA: HIV Surveillance Report. Retrieved May 19, 2014, from http://www.cdc.gov/hiv/pdf/statistics_2009_HIV_Surveillance_Report_vol_21.pdf

Centers for Disease Control and Prevention. (2012). *Youth risk behavior surveillance – United States, 2011*. Atlanta, GA: Morbidity and Mortality Weekly Report.

Chen, H., Luo, S., Yue, G., Xu, D., & Zhaoyang, R. (2009). Do birds of a feather flock together in China? *Personal Relationships, 16*, 167–186. doi: 10.1111/j.1475-6811.2009.01217.x

Cheng, C. (2005). Processes underlying gender-role flexibility: Do androgynous individuals know more or know how to cope? *Journal of Personality, 73*, 645-673. doi: 10.1111/j.1467-6494.2005.00324.x

Cherlin, A. J., Furstenberg, F. F., Chase-Lansdale, P. L., Kiernan, K. E., Robins, P. K., Morrison, D. R., & Teitler, J. O. (1991). Longitudinal studies of effects of divorce on children in Great Britain and the United States. *Science, 252,* 1386–1389. doi: 10.1126/science.2047851

Chernev, A., Böckenholt, U., & Goodman, J. (2010). Commentary on Scheibehenne, Greifeneder, and Todd choice overload: Is there anything to it? *Journal of Consumer Research, 37,* 426–428. doi: 10.1086/655200

Chivers, M. L. (2005). A brief review and discussion of sex differences in the specificity of sexual arousal. *Sexual and Relationship Therapy, 20,* 377–390. doi: 10.1080/14681990500238802

Chivers, M. L. (2006). Psychophysiological and subjective sexual arousal to visual sexual stimuli in new women. *Journal of Psychosomatic Obstetrics & Gynecology, 27,* 125–126. doi: 10.1080/01674820600888634

Chivers, M. L. (2010). A brief update on the specificity of sexual arousal. *Sexual and Relationship Therapy, 25,* 407–414. doi: 10.1080/14681994.2010. 495979

Chivers, M. L., & Bailey, J. M. (2005). A sex difference in features that elicit genital response. *Biological Psychology, 70,* 115–120. doi: 10.1016/j. biopsycho.2004.12.002

Chivers, M. L., Rieger, G., Latty, E., & Bailey, J. M. (2004). A sex difference in the specificity of sexual arousal. *Psychological Science, 15,* 736–744. doi: 10.1111/j.0956-7976.2004.00750.x

Chivers, M. L., Seto, M. C., & Blanchard, R. (2007). Gender and sexual orientation differences in sexual response to sexual activities versus gender of actors in sexual films. *Journal of Personality and Social Psychology, 93,* 1108–1121. doi: 10.1037/0022-3514.93.6.1108

Chivers, M. L., Seto, M. C., Lalumière, M. L., Laan, E., & Grimbos, T. (2010). Agreement of self-reported and genital measures of sexual arousal in men and women: A meta-analysis. *Archives of Sexual Behavior, 39,* 5–56. doi: 10.1007/ s10508-009-9556-9

Chivers, M. L., & Timmers, A. D. (2012). Effects of gender and relationship context in audio narratives on genital and subjective sexual response in heterosexual women and men. *Archives of Sexual Behavior, 41,* 185–197. doi: 10.1007/s10508-012-9937-3

Christensen, A., Atkins, D. C., Baucom, B., & Yi, J. (2010). Marital status and satisfaction five years following a randomized clinical trial comparing traditional versus integrative behavioral couple therapy. *Journal of Consulting and Clinical Psychology, 78,* 225–235. doi: 10.1037/a0018132

Christensen, A., Atkins, D. C., Berns, S., Wheeler, J., Baucom, D. H., & Simpson, L. E. (2004). Traditional versus integrative behavioral couple therapy for significantly and chronically distressed married couples. *Journal of Consulting and Clinical Psychology, 72,* 176–191. doi: 10.1037/0022-006x.72.2.176

Christensen, A., Atkins, D. C., Yi, J., George, W. H., & Baucom, D. H. (2006). Couple and individual adjustment for 2 years following a randomized clinical trial comparing traditional versus integrative behavioral couple therapy.

Journal of Consulting and Clinical Psychology, *74*, 1180–1191. doi: 10.1037/0022-006X.74.6.1180

Christensen, A., & Jacobson, N. S. (2000). *Reconcilable differences*. New York: Guilford.

Chung, G. H., Tucker, M. B., & Takeuchi, D. (2008). Wives' relative income production and household male dominance: Examining violence among Asian American enduring couples. *Family Relations*, *57*, 227–238. doi: 10.1111/j.1741-3729.2008.00496.x

Clarkin, J. F., Levy, K. N., Lenzenweger, M. F., & Kernberg, O. F. (2007). Evaluating three treatments for borderline personality disorder: A multiwave study. *The American Journal of Psychiatry*, *164*, 922–928. doi: 10.1176/appi. ajp.164.6.922

Claxton, A., & Perry-Jenkins, M. (2008). No fun anymore: Leisure and marital quality across the transition to parenthood. *Journal of Marriage and Family*, *70*, 28–43. doi: 10.1111/j.1741-3737.2007.00459.x

Claxton, S. E., & van Dulmen, M. H. (2013). Casual sexual relationships and experiences in emerging adulthood. *Emerging Adulthood*, *1*, 138–150. doi: 10.1177/2167696813487181

Clinton, H. R. (1996). *It takes a village: And other lessons children teach us*. New York: Simon & Schuster.

Cobb, R. J., Davila, J., & Bradbury, T. N. (2001). Attachment security and marital satisfaction: The role of positive perceptions and social support. *Personality and Social Psychology Bulletin,27,*1131–1143.doi:10.1177/0146167201279006

Cochran, S. D., & Mays, V. M. (2009). Burden of psychiatric morbidity among lesbian, gay, and bisexual individuals in the California Quality of Life Survey. *Journal of Abnormal Psychology*, *118*, 647–658. doi: 10.1037/a0016501Code of Canon Law, 1697–1706 (n.d.).

Cohan, C. L. (2013). The cohabitation conundrum. In M. A. Fine & F. D. Fincham (Eds.), *Handbook of family theories: A content-based approach* (pp. 105–122). New York: Routledge.

Cohan, C. L., & Bradbury, T. N. (1997). Negative life events, marital interaction, and the longitudinal course of newlywed marriage. *Journal of Personality and Social Psychology*, *73*, 114–128. doi: 10.1037/0022-3514.73.1.114

Cohan, C. L., Cole, S., & Davila, J. (2005). Marital transitions among Vietnam-era repatriated prisoners of war. *Journal of Social and Personal Relationships*, *22*, 777–795. doi: 10.1177/0265407505058680

Cohan, C. L., & Cole, S. W. (2002). Life course transitions and natural disaster: Marriage, birth, and divorce following Hurricane Hugo. *Journal of Family Psychology*, *16*, 14–25. doi: 10.1037/0893-3200.16.1.14

Cohan, C. L., & Kleinbaum, S. (2002). Toward a greater understanding of the cohabitation effect: Premarital cohabitation and marital communication. *Journal of Marriage and Family*, *64*, 180–192. doi: 10.1111/j.1741-3737.2002. 00180.x

Cohen, J. (1988). *Statistical power analysis for the behavioral sciences* (2nd ed.). Hillsdale, NJ: Lawrence Erlbaum.

Cohen, P. N. (2011). Homogamy unmodified. *Journal of Family Theory & Review*, 3, 47–51. doi: 10.1111/j.1756-2589.2010.00080.x

Cohen, P. N. (2012, June 18). Time travel: Regnerus study timeline suggests superhuman abilities. Retrieved March 27, 2014, from https://familyinequality.wordpress.com/2012/06/18/regnerus-study-timeline/

Cohen, P. N. (2013, March 11). "More managerial than intellectual": How right-wing Christian money brought us the Regnerus study. Retrieved March 27, 2014,fromhttp://familyinequality.wordpress.com/2013/03/11/more-managerial-than-intellectual/

Cohen, S., & Wills, T. A. (1985). Stress, social support, and the buffering hypothesis. *Psychological Bulletin*, 98, 310–357. doi: 10.1037/0033-2909.98.2.310

Collins, N. L., & Feeney, B. C. (2000). A safe haven: An attachment theory perspective on support seeking and caregiving in intimate relationships. *Journal of Personality and Social Psychology*, 78, 1053–1073. doi: 10.1037/0022-3514.78.6.1053

Collins, W. A., Welsh, D. P., & Furman, W. (2009). Adolescent romantic relationships. *Annual Review of Psychology*, 60, 631–652. doi: 10.1146/annurev.psych.60.110707.163459

Cooper, A., & Sportolari, L. (1997). Romance in cyberspace: Understanding online attraction. *Journal of Sex Education & Therapy*, 22, 7–14.

Cowan, C. P. (1996). Becoming parents: What has to change? In C. F. Clulow (Ed.), *Partners becoming parents* (pp. 119–139). Northvale, NJ: J. Aronson.

Cowan, C. P., & Cowan, P. A. (1992). *When partners become parents: The big life change for couples*. New York: Basic Books.

Cowan, C. P., Cowan, P. A., Heming, G., Garrett, E., Coysh, W. S., Curtis-Boles, H., & Boles, A. J. (1985). Transitions to parenthood: His, hers, and theirs. *Journal of Family Issues*, 6, 451–481. doi: 10.1177/019251385006004004

Cowan, C. P., Cowan, P. A., Heming, G., & Miller, N. B. (1991). Becoming a family: Marriage, parenting, and child development. In P. A. Cowan & E. M. Hetherington (Eds.), *Family transitions* (pp. 79–109). Hillside, NJ: Lawrence Erlbaum.

Cox, M. J., Owen, M. T., Lewis, J. M., & Henderson, V. K. (1989). Marriage, adult adjustment, and early parenting. *Child Development*, 60, 1015–1024. doi: 10.2307/1130775

Cox, M. J., Paley, B., Burchinal, M., & Payne, C. C. (1999). Marital perceptions and interactions across the transition to parenthood. *Journal of Marriage and the Family*, 61, 611–625. doi: 10.2307/353564

Coyne, J. C., & DeLongis, A. (1986). Going beyond social support: The role of social relationships in adaptation. *Journal of Consulting and Clinical Psychology*, 54, 454–460. doi: 10.1037/0022-006X.54.4.454

Coyne, J. C., Rohrbaugh, M. J., Shoham, V., Sonnega, J. S., Nicklas, J. M., & Cranford, J. A. (2001). Prognostic importance of marital quality for survival of congestive heart failure. *The American Journal of Cardiology*, 88, 526–529. doi: 10.1016/S0002-9149(01)01731-3

Critelli, J. W., & Bivona, J. M. (2008). Women's erotic rape fantasies: An evaluation of theory and research. *Journal of Sex Research*, 45, 57–70. doi: 10.1080/00224490701808191

Crown, C. L. (1991). Coordinated interpersonal timing of vision and voice as a function of interpersonal attraction. *Journal of Language and Social Psychology*, *10*, 29–46. doi: 10.1177/0261927x91101002

Cunningham, M., & Thornton, A. (2005). The influence of union transitions on white adults' attitudes toward cohabitation. *Journal of Marriage and Family*, *67*, 710–720. doi: 10.1111/j.1741-3737.2005.00164.x

Cunningham, M. R. (1989). Reactions to heterosexual opening gambits: Female selectivity and male responsiveness. *Personality and Social Psychology Bulletin*, *15*, 27–41. doi: 10.1177/0146167289151003

Cutrona, C. E. (1996). *Social support in couples: Marriage as a resource in times of stress*. Thousand Oaks, CA: Sage.

D'Onofrio, B. M., Eaves, L. J., Murrelle, L., Maes, H. H., & Spilka, B. (1999). Understanding biological and social influences on religious affiliation, attitudes and behaviors: A behavior genetic perspective. *Journal of Personality*, *67*, 953–984. doi: 10.1111/1467-6494.00079

Dabhoiwala, F. (2012). *The origins of sex: A history of the first sexual revolution*. New York: Oxford University Press.

Dauw, F., & Maroney, J. (Directors), & Metzler, D., Murphy, B. & Jarlstedt, K. (Producers). (2012). *Catfish: The TV show* [Cable television show]. USA: Music Television.

Davenport, K. (Director and Producer). (2007). *My first time* [play].

Davila, J., Bradbury, T. N., & Fincham, F. D. (1998). Negative affectivity as a mediator of the association between adult attachment and marital satisfaction. *Personal Relationships*, *5*, 467–484. doi: 10.1111/j.1475-6811.1998.tb00183.x

Davila, J., Karney, B. R., Hall, T. W., & Bradbury, T. N. (2003). Depressive symptoms and marital satisfaction: Within-subject associations and the moderating effects of gender and neuroticism. *Journal of Family Psychology*, *17*, 557–570. doi: 10.1037/0893-3200.17.4.557

Davila, J., & Kashy, D. A. (2009). Secure base processes in couples: Daily associations between support experiences and attachment security. *Journal of Family Psychology*, *23*, 76–88. doi: 10.1037/a0014353

Davila, J., Steinberg, S. J., Kachadourian, L., Cobb, R. J., & Fincham, F. D. (2004). Romantic involvement and depressive symptoms in early and late adolescence: The role of a preoccupied relational style. *Personal Relationships*, *11*, 161–178. doi: 10.1111/j.1475-6811.2004.00076.x

Davis, R. L. (2010). *More perfect unions: The American search for marital bliss*. Cambridge, MA: Harvard University Press.

de Becker, G. (1997). *The gift of fear: Survival signals that protect us from violence*. New York: Little, Brown and Company.

de Weerth, C., & Kalma, A. (1995). Gender differences in awareness of courtship initiation tactics. *Sex Roles*, *32*, 717–734. doi: 10.1007/bf01560186

Deboer v. Snyder, 12-CV-10285 (E.D. Mich. 2014).

Deficit Reduction Act of 2005, Pub. L. No. 109-171, 120 Stat. 4 (2006).

Del Vecchio, T., & O'Leary, K. D. (2004). Effectiveness of anger treatments for specific anger problems: A meta-analytic review. *Clinical Psychology Review*, *24*, 15–34. doi: 10.1016/j.cpr.2003.09.006

Derks, D., Bos, A. E. R., & von Grumbkow, J. (2007). Emoticons and social interaction on the Internet: The importance of social context. *Computers in Human Behavior, 23*, 842–849. doi: 10.1016/j.chb.2004.11.013

Diamond, L. M. (2006a). Careful what you ask for: Reconsidering feminist epistemology and autobiographical narrative in research on sexual identity development. *Signs, 31*, 471–491. doi: 10.1086/491684

Diamond, L. M. (2006b). The evolution of plasticity in female-female desire. *Journal of Psychology & Human Sexuality, 18*, 245–274. doi: 10.1300/J056v18n04_01

Diamond, L. M. (2006c). The intimate same-sex relationships of sexual minorities. In A. L. Vangelisti & D. Perlman (Eds.), *The Cambridge handbook of personal relationships* (pp. 293–312). New York: Cambridge.

Diamond, L. M. (2008a). Female bisexuality from adolescence to adulthood: Results from a 10-year longitudinal study. *Developmental Psychology, 44*, 5–14. doi: 10.1037/0012-1649.44.1.5

Diamond, L. M. (2008b). *Sexual fluidity: Understanding women's love and desire*. Cambridge, MA: Harvard University Press.

Diaz, N., Molina, O., MacMillan, T., Duran, L., & Swart, E. (2013). Attitudes toward divorce and their relationship with psychosocial factors among social work students. *Journal of Divorce & Remarriage, 54*, 505–518. doi: 10.1080/10502556.2013.810983

Diener, E., Gohm, C. L., Suh, E., & Oishi, S. (2000). Similarity of the relations between marital status and subjective well-being across cultures. *Journal of Cross-Cultural Psychology, 31*, 419–436. doi: 10.1177/0022022100031004001

Diener, E., Lucas, R. E., & Scollon, C. N. (2006). Beyond the hedonic treadmill: Revising the adaptation theory of well-being. *American Psychologist, 61*, 305–314. doi: 10.1037/0003-066x.61.4.305

Diener, E., Suh, E. M., Lucas, R. E., & Smith, H. L. (1999). Subjective well-being: Three decades of progress. *Psychological Bulletin, 125*, 276–302. doi: 10.1037/0033-2909.125.2.276

Dijkstra, P., & Barelds, D. P. H. (2008). Do people know what they want: A similar or complementary partner? *Evolutionary Psychology, 6*, 595–602.

Dixon, L., Browne, K., & Hamilton-Giachritsis, C. (2005). Risk factors of parents abused as children: A mediational analysis of the intergenerational continuity of child maltreatment (Part I). *Journal of Child Psychology and Psychiatry, 46*, 47–57. doi: 10.1111/j.1469-7610.2004.00339.x

Dixon, L., & Graham-Kevan, N. (2011). Understanding the nature and etiology of intimate partner violence and implications for practice and policy. *Clinical Psychology Review, 31*, 1145–1155. doi: 10.1016/j.cpr.2011.07.001

Dobash, R. E., & Dobash, R. P. (1992). *Women, violence, and social change*. London: Routledge.

Don, B. P., & Mickelson, K. D. (2014). Relationship satisfaction trajectories across the transition to parenthood among low-risk parents. *Journal of Marriage and Family, 76*, 677–692. doi: 10.1111/jomf.12111

Donen, S. (Director and Producer). (1967). *Two for the road* [Motion picture]. United Kingdom: 20th Century Fox.

Doss, B. D., Rhoades, G. K., Stanley, S. M., & Markman, H. J. (2009). The effect of the transition to parenthood on relationship quality: An 8-year prospective study. *Journal of Personality and Social Psychology, 96,* 601–619. doi: 10.1037/a0013969

Doss, B. D., Simpson, L. E., & Christensen, A. (2004). Why do couples seek marital therapy? *Professional Psychology: Research and Practice, 35,* 608–614. doi: 10.1037/0735-7028.35.6.608

Dryer, D. C., & Horowitz, L. M. (1997). When do opposites attract? Interpersonal complementarity versus similarity. *Journal of Personality and Social Psychology, 72,* 592–603. doi: 10.1080/00223891.1990.9674088

Dyer, E. D. (1963). Parenthood as crisis: A re-study. *Marriage and Family Living, 25,* 196–201. doi: 10.2307/349182

Dyrenforth, P. S., Kashy, D. A., Donnellan, M. B., & Lucas, R. E. (2010). Predicting relationship and life satisfaction from personality in nationally representative samples from three countries: The relative importance of actor, partner, and similarity effects. *Journal of Personality and Social Psychology, 99,* 690–702. doi: 10.1037/a0020385

Eagly, A. H. (2009). The his and hers of prosocial behavior: An examination of the social psychology of gender. *American Psychologist, 64,* 644–658. doi: 10.1037/0003-066x.64.8.644

Eagly, A. H., & Crowley, M. (1986). Gender and helping behavior: A meta-analytic review of the social psychological literature. *Psychological Bulletin, 100,* 283–308. doi: 10.1037/0033-2909.100.3.283

Eagly, A. H., Karau, S. J., & Makhijani, M. G. (1995). Gender and the effectiveness of leaders: A meta-analysis. *Psychological Bulletin, 117,* 125–145. doi: 10.1037/0033-2909.117.1.125

Eastwick, P. W., Eagly, A. H., Finkel, E. J., & Johnson, S. E. (2011). Implicit and explicit preferences for physical attractiveness in a romantic partner: A double dissociation in predictive validity. *Journal of Personality and Social Psychology, 101,* 993–1011. doi: 10.1037/a0024061

Eastwick, P. W., & Finkel, E. J. (2008a). Sex differences in mate preferences revisited: Do people know what they initially desire in a romantic partner? *Journal of Personality and Social Psychology, 94,* 245–264. doi: 10.1037/0022-3514.94.2.245

Eastwick, P. W., & Finkel, E. J. (2008b). Speed-dating: A powerful and flexible paradigm for studying romantic relationship initiation. In S. Sprecher, A. Wenzel, & J. Harvey (Eds.), *Handbook of relationship initiation* (pp. 217–234). New York: Psychology Press.

Eastwick, P. W., Finkel, E. J., & Eagly, A. H. (2011). When and why do ideal partner preferences affect the process of initiating and maintaining romantic relationships? *Journal of Personality and Social Psychology, 101,* 1012–1032. doi: 10.1037/a0024062

Ebbesen, E. B., Kjos, G. L., & Konecni, V. J. (1976). Spatial ecology: Its effects on the choice of friends and enemies. *Journal of Experimental Social Psychology, 12,* 505–518. doi: 10.1016/0022-1031(76)90030-5

Eckholm, E. (2014b, February 23). Opponents of same-sex marriage take bad-for-children argument to court. *The New York Times*, p. A16.

Eckholm, E. (2014a, March 8). In gay marriage suit, a battle over research. *The New York Times*, p. A10.

Edin, K., & Kefalas, M. (2005). *Promises I can keep: Why poor women put motherhood before marriage*. Berkley: University of California Press.

Edin, K., & Reed, J. M. (2005). Why don't they just get married? Barriers to marriage among the disadvantaged. *The Future of Children*, *15*, 117–137. doi: 10.1353/foc.2005.0017

eHarmony. (2012). Scientific match making. Retrieved October 9, 2012, from http://www.eharmony.com/why/science-of-compatibility/

Eibl-Eibesfeldt, I. (1979). Human ethology: Concepts and implications for the sciences of man. *Behavioral and Brain Sciences*, *2*, 1–57. doi: 10.1017/s0140525x00060416

Eliot, G. (1872). *Middlemarch*. New York: Harper & Bros.

Ellison, C. (1968). Psychosomatic factors in the unconsummated marriage. *Journal of Psychosomatic Research*, *12*, 61–65. doi: 10.1016/0022-3999(68)90009-3

Ellison, N., Heino, R., & Gibbs, J. (2006). Managing impressions online: Self-presentation processes in the online dating environment. *Journal of Computer-Mediated Communication*, *11*, 415–441. doi: 10.1111/j.1083-6101.2006.00020.x

Ellwood, D. T., & Crane, J. (1990). Family change among Black Americans: What do we know? *The Journal of Economic Perspectives*, *4*, 65–84. doi: 10.2307/1942722

Else-Quest, N. M., Higgins, A., Allison, C., & Morton, L. C. (2012). Gender differences in self-conscious emotional experience: A meta-analysis. *Psychological Bulletin*, *138*, 947–981. doi: 10.1037/a0027930

Elze, D. E. (2002). Against all odds: The dating experiences of adolescent lesbian and bisexual women. *Journal of Lesbian Studies*, *6*, 17–29. doi: 10.1300/J155v06n01_03

Engell, A. D., Haxby, J. V., & Todorov, A. (2007). Implicit trustworthiness decisions: Automatic coding of face properties in the human amygdala. *Journal of Cognitive Neuroscience*, *19*, 1508–1519. doi: 10.1162/jocn.2007.19.9.1508

England, P., Shafer, E. F., & Fogarty, A. C. (2008). Hooking up and forming romantic relationships on today's college campuses. In M. S. Kimmel & A. Aronson (Eds.), *The gendered society reader* (3rd ed., pp. 531–547). New York: Oxford University Press.

Epstein, N. B., & Baucom, D. H. (2002). *Enhanced cognitive-behavioral therapy for couples: A contextual approach*. Washington, DC: American Psychological Association.

Ericson, J. T., & Robertson, C. N. (1973). *Oneida Community books, pamphlets, and serials, 1834–1972*. Glen Rock, NJ: Microfilming Corp. of America.

Erskine, M. S. (1989). Solicitation behavior in the estrous female rat: A review. *Hormones and Behavior*, *23*, 473–502. doi: 10.1016/0018-506X(89)90037-8

Fagan, J. (2013). Effects of divorce and cohabitation dissolution on preschoolers' literacy. *Journal of Family Issues, 34,* 460–483. doi: 10.1177/0192513x 12445164

Fausto-Sterling, A. (2007). Frameworks of desire. *Daedalus, 136,* 47–57.

Feeney, B. C., & Collins, N. L. (2003). Motivations for caregiving in adult intimate relationships: Influences on caregiving behavior and relationship functioning. *Personality and Social Psychology Bulletin, 29,* 950–968. doi: 10.1177/ 0146167203252807

Feeney, J. A. (2004). Hurt feelings in couple relationships: Towards integrative models of the negative effects of hurtful events. *Journal of Social and Personal Relationships, 21,* 487–508. doi: 10.1177/0265407504044844

Feeney, M. (2005, January 5). Beauty and the beast: Why are fat sitcom husbands paired with great-looking wives? *Slate.*

Fein, E., & Schneider, S. (1995). *The rules: Time-tested secrets for capturing the heart of Mr. Right.* New York: Warner Books.

Feingold, A. (1990). Gender differences in effects of physical attractiveness on romantic attraction: A comparison across five research paradigms. *Journal of Personality and Social Psychology, 59,* 981–993. doi: 10.1037/0022-3514. 59.5.981

Feingold, A. (1994). Gender differences in personality: A meta-analysis. *Psychological Bulletin, 116,* 429–456. doi: 10.1037/0033-2909.116.3.429

Feinstein, B. A., Goldfried, M. R., & Davila, J. (2012). The relationship between experiences of discrimination and mental health among lesbians and gay men: An examination of internalized homonegativity and rejection sensitivity as potential mechanisms. *Journal of Consulting and Clinical Psychology, 80,* 917–927. doi: 10.1037/a0029425

Festinger, L., Schachter, S., & Back, K. (1950). *Social pressures in informal groups: A study of human factors in housing.* New York: Harper.

Fichten, C. S., Tagalakis, V., Judd, D., Wright, J., & Amsel, R. (1992). Verbal and nonverbal communication cues in daily conversations and dating. *The Journal of Social Psychology, 132,* 751–769. doi: 10.1080/00224545.1992. 9712105

Fincham, F. D., & Bradbury, T. N. (1987a). Cognitive processes and conflict in close relationships: An attribution-efficacy model. *Journal of Personality and Social Psychology, 53,* 1106–1118. doi: 10.1037/0022-3514.53.6.1106

Fincham, F. D., & Bradbury, T. N. (1987b). The impact of attributions in marriage: A longitudinal analysis. *Journal of Personality and Social Psychology, 53,* 510–517. doi: 10.1037/0022-3514.53.3.510

Fincham, F. D., & Bradbury, T. N. (1988). The impact of attributions in marriage: An experimental analysis. *Journal of Social and Clinical Psychology, 7,* 147–162. doi: 10.1521/jscp.1988.7.2-3.147

Fincham, F. D., & Bradbury, T. N. (1989). The impact of attributions in marriage: An individual difference analysis. *Journal of Social and Personal Relationships, 6,* 69–85. doi: 10.1177/026540758900600105

Fincham, F. D., & Bradbury, T. N. (1993). Marital satisfaction, depression, and attributions: A longitudinal analysis. *Journal of Personality and Social Psychology, 64*, 442–452. doi: 10.1037/0022-3514.64.3.442

Fincham, F. D., Harold, G. T., & Gano Phillips, S. (2000). The longitudinal association between attributions and marital satisfaction: Direction of effects and role of efficacy expectations. *Journal of Family Psychology, 14*, 267–285. doi: 10.1037/0893-3200.14.2.267

Finkel, E. J., & Eastwick, P. W. (2008). Speed-dating. *Current Directions in Psychological Science, 17*, 193–197. doi: 10.1111/j.1467-8721.2008.00573.x

Finkel, E. J., Eastwick, P. W., Karney, B. R., Reis, H. T., & Sprecher, S. (2012). Online dating: A critical analysis from the perspective of psychological science. *Psychological Science in the Public Interest, 13*, 3–66. doi: 10.1177/1529100612436522

Finkel, E. J., Eastwick, P. W., & Matthews, J. (2007). Speed-dating as an invaluable tool for studying romantic attraction: A methodological primer. *Personal Relationships, 14*, 149–166. doi: 10.1111/j.1475-6811.2006.00146.x

Fischer, C. S., & Carroll, G. R. (1988). Telephone and automobile diffusion in the United States, 1902–1937. *American Journal of Sociology, 93*, 1153–1178. doi: 10.2307/2780368

Fisher, T. D. (2013). Gender roles and pressure to be truthful: The bogus pipeline modifies gender differences in sexual but not non-sexual behavior. *Sex Roles, 68*, 401–414. doi: 10.1007/s11199-013-0266-3

Fisher, T. D., & McNulty, J. K. (2008). Neuroticism and marital satisfaction: The mediating role played by the sexual relationship. *Journal of Family Psychology, 22*, 112–122. doi: 10.1037/0893-3200.22.1.112

Fiske, S. T., & Taylor, S. E. (1991). *Social cognition* (2nd ed.). New York: McGraw-Hill.

Fisman, R., Iyengar, S. S., Kamenica, E., & Simonson, I. (2006). Gender differences in mate selection: Evidence from a speed dating experiment. *The Quarterly Journal of Economics, 121*, 673–697. doi: 10.1162/qjec.2006.121.2.673

Flaherty, J. F., & Dusek, J. B. (1980). An investigation of the relationship between psychological androgyny and components of self-concept. *Journal of Personality and Social Psychology, 38*, 984–992. doi: 10.1037/0022-3514.38.6.984

Flanagan, C. (2014, February 19). The dark power of fraternities: A yearlong investigation of Greek houses reveals their endemic, lurid, and sometimes tragic problems – and a sophisticated system for shifting the blame. *The Atlantic, 313*(2), 72–91.

Flay, B. R., Biglan, A., Boruch, R. F., Castro, F. G. l., Gottfredson, D., Kellam, S., … Ji, P. (2005). Standards of evidence: Criteria for efficacy, effectiveness and dissemination. *Prevention Science, 6*, 151–175. doi: 10.1007/s11121-005-5553-y

Fletcher, G. J. O., & Fincham, F. D. (Eds.). (1991). *Cognition in close relationships*. Hillsdale, NJ: Lawrence Erlbaum.

Fletcher, G. J. O., & Kerr, P. S. G. (2010). Through the eyes of love: Reality and illusion in intimate relationships. *Psychological Bulletin, 136*, 627–658. doi: 10.1037/a0019792

Fletcher, G. J. O., & Simpson, J. A. (2001). Ideal standards in close relationships. In J. P. Forgas, K. D. Williams, & L. Wheeler (Eds.), *The social mind: Cognitive and motivational aspects of interpersonal behavior* (pp. 257–273). New York: Cambridge University Press.

Fletcher, G. J. O., Simpson, J. A., & Thomas, G. (2000). Ideals, perceptions, and evaluations in early relationship development. *Journal of Personality and Social Psychology, 79,* 933–940. doi: 10.1037/0022-3514.79.6.933

Foran, H. M., & O'Leary, K. D. (2008). Alcohol and intimate partner violence: A meta-analytic review. *Clinical Psychology Review, 28,* 1222–1234. doi: 10.1016/j.cpr.2008.05.001

Forthofer, M. S., Markman, H. J., Cox, M., Stanley, S., & Kessler, R. C. (1996). Associations between marital distress and work loss in a national sample. *Journal of Marriage and the Family, 58,* 597–605. doi: 10.2307/353720

Fossett, M. A., & Kiecolt, K. J. (1993). Mate availability and family structure among African Americans in U.S. metropolitan areas. *Journal of Marriage and the Family, 55,* 288–302. doi: 10.2307/352802

Foster, L. (1981). *Religion and sexuality: Three American communal experiments of the nineteenth century.* New York: Oxford University Press.

Fredrickson, B. L. (2001). The role of positive emotions in positive psychology: The broaden-and-build theory of positive emotions. *American Psychologist, 56,* 218–226. doi: 10.1037/0003-066x.56.3.218

Friedman, L. J. (1962). *Virgin wives: A study of unconsummated marriages.* Springfield, IL: Charles C. Thomas

Fry, R. (2013). *A rising share of young adults live in their parents' home: A record 21.6 million in 2012* (Social & Demographic Trends report). Washington, DC: Pew Research Center.

Frye, M. (1990). Lesbian "sex." In J. Allen (Ed.), *Lesbian philosophies and cultures* (pp. 46–54). Albany, NY: State University of New York Press.

Furman, W., & Collins, W. A. (2009). Adolescent romantic relationships and experiences. In K. H. Rubin, W. M. Bukowski, & B. Laursen (Eds.), *Handbook of peer interactions, relationships, and groups* (pp. 341–360). New York: Guilford.

Furman, W., & Hand, L. S. (2006). The slippery nature of romantic relationships: Issues in definition and differentiation. In A. C. Crouter & A. Booth (Eds.), *Romance and sex in adolescence and emerging adulthood: Risks and opportunities* (pp. 171–178). Mahwah, NJ: Lawrence Erlbaum.

Furman, W., Ho, M. J., & Low, S. M. (2007). The rocky road of adolescent romantic experience: Dating and adjustment. In R. C. M. E. Engels, M. Kerr, & H. Stattin (Eds.), *Friends, lovers and groups: Key relationships in adolescence* (pp. 93–104). New York: Wiley.

Furman, W., & Shaffer, L. (2003). The role of romantic relationships in adolescent development. In P. Florsheim (Ed.), *Adolescent romantic relations and sexual behavior: Theory, research, and practical implications* (pp. 3–22). Mahwah, NJ: Lawrence Erlbaum.

Gable, S. L., Gonzaga, G. C., & Strachman, A. (2006). Will you be there for me when things go right? Supportive responses to positive event disclosures.

Journal of Personality and Social Psychology, *91*, 904–917. doi: 10.1037/0022-3514.91.5.904

Gable, S. L., Gosnell, C. L., Maisel, N. C., & Strachman, A. (2012). Safely testing the alarm: Close others' responses to personal positive events. *Journal of Personality and Social Psychology*, *103*, 963–981. doi: 10.1037/a0029488

Gable, S. L., Reis, H. T., Impett, E. A., & Asher, E. R. (2004). What do you do when things go right? The intrapersonal and interpersonal benefits of sharing positive events. *Journal of Personality and Social Psychology*, *87*, 228–245. doi: 10.1037/0022-3514.87.2.228

Gallup. (2014). Gay and lesbian rights. Retrieved March 5, 2014, from http://www.gallup.com/poll/1651/Gay-Lesbian-Rights.aspx

Garcia, J. R., & Reiber, C. (2008). Hook-up behavior: A biopsychosocial perspective. *The Journal of Social, Evolutionary, and Cultural Psychology*, *2*, 192–208.

Garcia-Marques, T., Mackie, D. M., Claypool, H. M., & Garcia-Marques, L. (2013). Once more with feeling! Familiarity and positivity as integral consequences of previous exposure. In C. Unkelbach & R. Greifeneder (Eds.), *The experience of thinking: How the fluency of mental processes influences cognition and behaviour*. (pp. 50–69). New York: Psychology Press.

Gardner, K. A., & Cutrona, C. E. (2004). Social support communication in families. In A. L. Vangelisti (Ed.), *Handbook of Family Communication*. Mahwah, NJ: Lawrence Erlbaum.

Gartrell, N., & Bos, H. (2010). US National Longitudinal Lesbian Family Study: Psychological adjustment of 17-year-old adolescents. *Pediatrics*, *126*, 28–36. doi: 10.1542/peds.2009-3153

Gates, G. J., et al. (2012). Letter to the editors and advisory editors of *Social Science Research*. *Social Science Research*, *41*, 1350–1351. doi: 10.1016/j.ssresearch.2012.08.008

Gaunt, R. (2006). Couple similarity and marital satisfaction: Are similar spouses happier? *Journal of Personality*, *74*, 1401–1420. doi: 10.1111/j.1467-6494.2006.00414.x

GenePartner. (2013). About GenePartner. Retrieved June 3, 2013, from http://www.genepartner.com/index.php/aboutgenepartner

Gibson-Davis, C., & Rackin, H. (2014). Marriage or carriage? Trends in union context and birth type by education. *Journal of Marriage and Family*, *76*, 506–519. doi: 10.1111/jomf.12109

Gindin, L. R., & Resnicoff, D. (2002). Unconsummated marriages: A separate and different clinical entity. *Journal of Sex & Marital Therapy*, *28*, 85–99. doi: 10.1080/009262302525851221

Giordano, P. C., Manning, W. D., & Longmore, M. A. (2005). The romantic relationships of African-American and white adolescents. *The Sociological Quarterly*, *46*, 545–568. doi: 10.1111/j.1533-8525.2005.00026.x

Girme, Y. U., Overall, N. C., & Simpson, J. A. (2013). When visibility matters: Short-term Versus long-term costs and benefits of visible and invisible support. *Personality and Social Psychology Bulletin*, *39*, 1441–1454. doi: 10.1177/0146167213497802

Givens, D. B. (1978). The nonverbal basis of attraction: Flirtation, courtship, and seduction. *Psychiatry: Journal for the Study of Interpersonal Processes, 41*, 346–359.

Givens, D. B. (1983). *Love signals: How to attract a mate.* New York: Crown Publishers.

Glass, L. (1992). *He says, she says: Closing the communication gap between the sexes.* New York: Putnam.

Gleason, M. E. J., Iida, M., Bolger, N., & Shrout, P. E. (2003). Daily supportive equity in close relationships. *Personality & Social Psychology Bulletin, 29*, 1036–1045. doi: 10.1177/0146167203253473

Goffman, E. (1959). *The presentation of self in everyday life.* Garden City, NY: Doubleday.

Goldberg, A. E., Smith, J. Z., & Kashy, D. A. (2010). Preadoptive factors predicting lesbian, gay, and heterosexual couples' relationship quality across the transition to adoptive parenthood. *Journal of Family Psychology, 24*, 221–232. doi: 10.1037/a0019615

Goldner, V. (2004). Attachment and Eros: Opposed or synergistic? *Psychoanalytic Dialogues, 14*, 381–396. doi: 10.1080/10481881409348793

Gottman, J. M. (1979). *Marital interactions: Experimental investigations.* New York: Academic Press.

Gottman, J. M. (1994). *What predicts divorce: The relationship between marital processes and marital outcomes.* Hillsdale, NJ: Erlbaum.

Gottman, J. M., & Levenson, R. W. (1999). Rebound from marital conflict and divorce prediction. *Family Process, 38*, 287–292. doi: 10.1111/j.1545-5300.1999.00287.x

Gould, M. S., Fisher, P., Parides, M., Flory, M., & Shaffer, D. (1996). Psychosocial risk factors of child and adolescent completed suicide. *Archives of General Psychiatry, 53*, 1155–1162. doi: 10.1001/archpsyc.1996.01830120095016

Grammer, K. (1990). Strangers meet: Laughter and nonverbal signs of interest in opposite-sex encounters. *Journal of Nonverbal Behavior, 14*, 209–236. doi: 10.1007/bf00989317

Gray, J. (1992). *Men are from Mars, women are from Venus: A practical guide for improving communication and getting what you want in your relationships.* New York: HarperCollins.

Green, B. L., & Kenrick, D. T. (1994). The attractiveness of gender-typed traits at different relationship levels: Androgynous characteristics may be desirable after all. *Personality and Social Psychology Bulletin, 20*, 244–253. doi: 10.1177/0146167294203002

Grello, C. M., Welsh, D. P., Harper, M. S., & Dickson, J. W. (2003). Dating and sexual relationship trajectories and adolescent functioning. *Adolescent & Family Health, 3*, 103–112.

Grossman, S. (2013, January 25). Woman sues Match.com after date tries to murder her. *Time.* Retrieved January 29, 2013 from http://newsfeed.time.com/2013/01/25/woman-sues-match-com-after-date-tries-to-murder-her/

Guastello, D. D., & Guastello, S. J. (2003). Androgyny, gender role behavior, and emotional intelligence among college students and their parents. *Sex Roles, 49*, 663–673. doi: 10.1023/B:SERS.0000003136.67714.04

Gunraj, D. N., Drumm-Hewitt, A. M., Dashow, E. M., Upadhyay, S. S. N., & Klin, C. M. (2016). Texting insincerely: The role of the period in text messaging. *Computers in Human Behavior, 55, Part B*, 1067–1075. doi: http://dx.doi.org/10.1016/j.chb.2015.11.003

Guzman, L., Caal, S., Hickman, S., Golub, E., & Ramos, M. (2013). *When sex and dating are the same: Latinos' attitudes on teen parenthood and contraception* (Research Brief 49). Bethesda, MD: Child Trends.

Haase, C. M., Saslow, L. R., Bloch, L., Saturn, S. R., Casey, J. J., Seider, B. H., ... Levenson, R. W. (2013). The 5-HTTLPR polymorphism in the serotonin transporter gene moderates the association between emotional behavior and changes in marital satisfaction over time. *Emotion, 13*, 1068–1079. doi: 10.1037/a0033761

Hahlweg, K., Markman, H. J., Thurmaier, F., Engl, J., & Eckert, V. (1998). Prevention of marital distress: Results of a German prospective longitudinal study. *Journal of Family Psychology, 12*, 543–556. doi: 10.1037/0893-3200.12.4.543

Hahlweg, K., Reisner, L., Kohli, G., Vollmer, M., Schindler, L., & Revenstorf, D. (1984). Development and validity of a new system to analyze interpersonal communication: Kategoriensystem für Partnerschaftliche Interaktion. In K. Hahlweg & N. S. Jacobson (Eds.), *Marital interaction: Analysis and modification* (pp. 182–198). New York: Guilford.

Halford, W. K., Sanders, M. R., & Behrens, B. C. (2001). Can skills training prevent relationship problems in at-risk couples? Four-year effects of a behavioral relationship education program. *Journal of Family Psychology, 15*, 750–768. doi: 10.1037/0893-3200.15.4.750

Hall, J. A., Xing, C., & Brooks, S. (2014). Accurately detecting flirting: Error management theory, the traditional sexual script, and flirting base rate. *Communication Research*, advanced online version. doi: 10.1177/0093650214534972

Hamer, D. H., Hu, S., Magnuson, V. L., Hu, N., & Pattatucci, A. M. (1993). A linkage between DNA markers on the X chromosome and male sexual orientation. *Science, 261*, 321–327. doi: 10.1126/science.8332896

Hamilton, L., & Armstrong, E. A. (2009). Gendered sexuality in young adulthood: Double binds and flawed options. *Gender & Society, 23*, 589–616. doi: 10.1177/0891243209345829

Hampton, K., Sessions Goulet, L., Her, E. J., & Rainie, L. (2009). *Social isolation and new technology* (Pew Internet & American Life Project). Washington, DC: Pew Research Center.

Harden, K. P. (2014). A sex-positive framework for research on adolescent sexuality. *Perspectives on Psychological Science, 9*, 455–469. doi: 10.1177/1745691614535934

Haring-Hidore, M., Stock, W. A., Okun, M. A., & Witter, R. A. (1985). Marital status and subjective well-being: A research synthesis. *Journal of Marriage and The Family*, 947–953. doi: 10.2307/352338

Harper, M. S., Dickson, J. W., & Welsh, D. P. (2006). Self-silencing and rejection sensitivity in adolescent romantic relationships. *Journal of Youth and Adolescence, 35*, 459–467. doi: 10.1007/s10964-006-9048-3

Harper, M. S., & Welsh, D. P. (2007). Keeping quiet: Self-silencing and its association with relational and individual functioning among adolescent romantic couples. *Journal of Social and Personal Relationships, 24*, 99–116. doi: 10.1177/0265407507072601

Harvey, S. (2009). *Act like a lady, think like a man: What men really think about love, relationships, intimacy, and commitment*. New York: Amistad.

Haugaard, J. J., & Seri, L. G. (2003). Stalking and other forms of intrusive contact after the dissolution of adolescent dating or romantic relationships. *Violence and Victims, 18*, 279–297. doi: 10.1891/vivi.2003.18.3.279

Hawkins, A. J. (2014). Continuing the important debate on government-supported healthy marriages and relationships initiatives: A brief response to Johnson's (2014) comment. *Family Relations, 63*, 305–308. doi: 10.1111/fare.12059

Hawkins, A. J., Amato, P. R., & Kinghorn, A. (2013). Are government-supported Healthy Marriage Initiatives affecting family demographics? A state-level analysis. *Family Relations, 62*, 501–513. doi: 10.1111/fare.12009

Hawkins, A. J., Blanchard, V. L., Baldwin, S. A., & Fawcett, E. B. (2008). Does marriage and relationship education work? A meta-analytic study. *Journal of Consulting and Clinical Psychology, 76*, 723–734. doi: 10.1037/a0012584

Hawkins, A. J., Stanley, S. M., Cowan, P. A., Fincham, F. D., Beach, S. R. H., Cowan, C. P., ... Daire, A. P. (2013). A more optimistic perspective on government-supported marriage and relationship education programs for lower income couples: Response to Johnson (2012). *American Psychologist, 68*, 110-111. doi: 10.1037/a0031792

Hayden, R. (1975). *Angle of ascent: New and selected poems*. New York: Liveright.

Hayford, S. R., Guzzo, K. B., & Smock, P. J. (2014). The decoupling of marriage and parenthood? Trends in the timing of marital first births, 1945–2002. *Journal of Marriage and Family, 76*, 520–538. doi: 10.1111/jomf.12114

Headey, B., & Wearing, A. (1989). Personality, life events, and subjective well-being: Toward a dynamic equilibrium model. *Journal of Personality and Social Psychology, 57*, 731–739. doi: 10.1037/0022-3514.57.4.731

Heath, M. (2012). *One marriage under God: The campaign to promote marriage in America*. New York: New York University Press.

Heaton, T. B., & Pratt, E. L. (1990). The effects of religious homogamy on marital satisfaction and stability. *Journal of Family Issues, 11*, 191–207. doi: 10.1177/019251390011002005

Heavey, C. L., Layne, C., & Christensen, A. (1993). Gender and conflict structure in marital interaction: A replication and extension. *Journal of Consulting and Clinical Psychology, 61*, 16–27. doi: 10.1037/0022-006X.61.1.16

Hedges, L. V., & Nowell, A. (1995). Sex differences in mental test scores, variability, and numbers of high-scoring individuals. *Science, 269*, 41–45. doi: 10.1126/science.7604277

Heidemann, B., Suhomlinova, O., & O'Rand, A. M. (1998). Economic independence, economic status, and empty nest in midlife marital disruption. *Journal of Marriage and The Family, 60*, 219–231. doi: 10.2307/353453

Heider, F. (1958). *The psychology of interpersonal relations*. New York: John Wiley & Sons.

Heino, R. D., Ellison, N. B., & Gibbs, J. L. (2010). Relationshopping: Investigating the market metaphor in online dating. *Journal of Social and Personal Relationships, 27*, 427–447. doi: 10.1177/0265407510361614

Helgeson, V. S. (1993). Two important distinctions in social support: Kind of support and perceived versus received. *Journal of Applied Social Psychology, 23*, 825–845. doi: 10.1111/j.1559-1816.1993.tb01008.x

Hendrick, C., & Brown, S. R. (1971). Introversion, extraversion, and interpersonal attraction. *Journal of Personality and Social Psychology, 20*, 31–36. doi: 10.1037/h0031699

Hendrix, H. (2004). Do opposites attract? Retrieved June 4, 2013, from http://www.beliefnet.com/Love-Family/Relationships/2004/07/Do-Opposites-Attract.aspx

Henry, J., Helm, H. W., & Cruz, N. (2013). Mate selection: Gender and generational differences. *North American Journal of Psychology, 15*, 63–70.

Henry J. Kaiser Family Foundation. (2001). *Inside-OUT: A report on the experiences of lesbians, gays and bisexuals in america and the public's views on issues and policies related to sexual orientation*. Menlo Park, CA: The Henry J. Kaiser Family Foundation.

Herek, G. M. (2009). Hate crimes and stigma-related experiences among sexual minority adults in the United States: Prevalence estimates from a national probability sample. *Journal of Interpersonal Violence, 24*, 54–74. doi: 10.1177/0886260508316477

Heyman, R. E. (2001). Observation of couple conflicts: Clinical assessment applications, stubborn truths, and shaky foundations. *Psychological Assessment, 13*, 5–35. doi: 10.1037/1040-3590.13.1.5

Heyman, R. E., & Slep, A. M. S. (2001). The hazards of predicting divorce without crossvalidation. *Journal of Marriage and Family, 63*, 473–479. doi: 10.1111/j.1741-3737.2001.00473.x

Hiekel, N., & Castro-Martín, T. (2014). Grasping the diversity of cohabitation: Fertility intentions among cohabiters across Europe. *Journal of Marriage and Family, 76*, 489–505. doi: 10.1111/jomf.12112

Hill, C. T., & Peplau, L. A. (1998). Premarital prediction of relationship outcomes: A 15-year follow-up of the Boston Couples Study. In T. N. Bradbury (Ed.), *The developmental course of marital dysfunction* (pp. 237–278). New York: Cambridge University Press.

Hill, R. (1945). Campus values in mate selection. *Journal of Home Economics, 37*, 554–558.

Hill, R. (1949). *Families under stress*. New York: Harper.

Hillebrand, R. (2008). The Oneida Community. *New York History Net*. Retrieved August 1, 2013, from http://www.nyhistory.com/central/oneida.htm

Hills, J. M., & Johnson, M. D. (2000, April). *Examining the construct validity of a behavioral coding system for marital interactions*. Paper presented at the Eastern Psychological Association, Washington, DC.

Hilpert, P., Bodenmann, G., Nussbeck, F. W., & Bradbury, T. N. (2013). Predicting relationship satisfaction in distressed and non-distressed couples based on a stratified sample: A matter of conflict, positivity, or support? *Family Science*, 110–120. doi: 10.1080/19424620.2013.830633

Hite, S. (2004). *The Hite Report: A nationwide study of female sexuality*. New York: Seven Stories Press.

Hitlin, P., Jurkowitz, M., & Mitchell, A. (2013). *News coverage conveys strong momentum for same-sex marriage* (Pew Research Journalism Project). Retrieved October 19, 2014, from http://www.journalism.org/2013/06/17/news-coverage-conveys-strong-momentum/

Hoekstra-Weebers, J. E. H. M., Jaspers, J. P. C., Kamps, W. A., & Klip, E. C. (1998). Marital dissatisfaction, psychological distress, and the coping of parents of pediatric cancer patients. *Journal of Marriage and Family*, 60, 1012–1021. doi: 10.2307/353642

Holahan, C. J., & Moos, R. H. (1990). Life stressors, resistance factors, and improved psychological functioning: An extension of the stress resistance paradigm. *Journal of Personality and Social Psychology*, 58, 909–917. doi: 10.1037/0022-3514.58.5.909

Holtzworth-Munroe, A., Beatty, S. B., & Anglin, K. (1995). The assessment and treatment of marital violence: An introduction for the marital therapist. In N. S. Jacobson & A. S. Gurman (Eds.), *Clinical handbook of couples therapy* (pp. 317–339). New York: Guilford Press.

Holtzworth-Munroe, A., Clements, K., & Farris, C. (2005). Working with couples who have experienced physical aggression. In M. Harway (Ed.), *Handbook of couples therapy* (pp. 289–312). Hoboken, NJ: Wiley.

Holtzworth-Munroe, A., Markman, H., Daniel O'Leary, K., Neidig, P., Leber, D., Heyman, R. E., ... Smutzler, N. (1995). The need for marital violence prevention efforts: A behavioral–cognitive secondary prevention program for engaged and newly married couples. *Applied and Preventive Psychology*, 4, 77–88. doi: 10.1016/S0962-1849(05)80081-2

Horney, K. (1945). *Our inner conflicts*. New York: Norton.

Houts, R. M., Robins, E., & Huston, T. L. (1996). Compatibility and the development of premarital relationships. *Journal of Marriage and the Family*, 58, 7–20. doi: 10.2307/353373

Howe, G. W., Levy, M. L., & Caplan, R. D. (2004). Job loss and depressive symptoms in couples: Common stressors, stress transmission, or relationship disruption? *Journal of Family Psychology*, 18, 639–650. doi: 10.1037/0893-3200.18.4.639

Hrdy, S. B. (1999). *The woman that never evolved: With a new preface and bibliographical Updates* (Revised ed.). Cambridge, MA: Harvard University Press.

Hrdy, S. B. (2008). *Mothers and others: The evolutionary origins of mutual understanding*. Cambridge, MA: Harvard University Press.

Hsee, C. K., & Zhang, J. (2010). General evaluability theory. *Perspectives on Psychological Science*, 5, 343–355. doi: 10.1177/1745691610374586

Hsueh, J., Alderson, D. P., Lundquist, E., Michalopoulos, C., Gubits, D., Fein, D., & Knox, V. (2012). *The Supporting Healthy Marriage Evaluation: Early impacts on low-income families* (OPRE Report #2012-11). Washington, DC: Office of Planning, Research and Evaluation, Administration for Children and Families, U.S. Department of Health and Human Services.

Huebner, D. M., Mandic, C. G., Mackaronis, J. E., Beougher, S. C., & Hoff, C. C. (2012). The impact of parenting on gay male couples' relationships, sexuality, and HIV risk. *Couple and Family Psychology: Research and Practice, 1*, 106–119. doi: 10.1037/a0028687

Huston, T. L., Caughlin, J. P., Houts, R. M., Smith, S. E., & George, L. J. (2001). The connubial crucible: Newlywed years as predictors of marital delight, distress, and divorce. *Journal of Personality and Social Psychology, 80*, 237–252. doi: 10.1037/0022-3514.80.2.237

Huston, T. L., & Chorost, A. F. (1994). Behavioral buffers on the effect of negativity on marital satisfaction: A longitudinal view. *Personal Relationships, 1*, 223–239. doi: 10.1111/j.1475-6811.1994.tb00063.x

Hyde, J. S. (2005). The gender similarities hypothesis. *American Psychologist, 60*, 581–592. doi: 10.1037/0003-066x.60.6.581

Hyde, J. S. (2014). Gender similarities and differences. *Annual Review of Psychology, 65*, 373–398. doi: 10.1146/annurev-psych-010213-115057

Hyde, J. S., Lindberg, S. M., Linn, M. C., Ellis, A. B., & Williams, C. C. (2008). Gender similarities characterize math performance. *Science, 321*, 494–495. doi: 10.2307/20054571

Hyde, J. S., & Linn, M. C. (1988). Gender differences in verbal ability: A meta-analysis. *Psychological Bulletin, 104*, 53–69. doi: 10.1037/0033-2909.104.1.53

Iyengar, S. S., Simonson, I., Fisman, R., & Mogilner, C. (2005, January). *I know what I want but can I find it? Examining the dynamic relationship between stated and revealed preferences.* Paper presented at the Society for Personality and Social Psychology, New Orleans.

Jacobson, N. S. (1991). Behavioral versus insight-oriented marital therapy: Labels can be misleading. *Journal of Consulting and Clinical Psychology, 59*, 142–145. doi: 10.1037/0022-006X.59.1.142

Jacobson, N. S., & Christensen, A. (1996). *Integrative couple therapy: Promoting acceptance and change.* New York: Norton.

Jacobson, N. S., Follette, W. C., Revenstorf, D., Baucom, D. H., Hahlweg, K., & Margolin, G. (1984). Variability in outcome and clinical significance of behavioral marital therapy: A reanalysis of outcome data. *Journal of Consulting and Clinical Psychology, 52*, 497–504. doi: 10.1037/0022-006X.52.4.497

Jacobson, N. S., & Margolin, G. (1979). *Marital therapy: Strategies based on social learning and behavior exchange principles.* New York: Brunner/Mazel.

Jacobson, N. S., Schmaling, K. B., & Holtzworth-Munroe, A. (1987). Component analysis of behavioral marital therapy: 2-year follow-up and prediction of relapse. *Journal of Marital and Family Therapy, 13*, 187–195. doi: 10.1111/j.1752-0606.1987.tb00696.x

James, W. M. (1947). *John Ruskin and Effie Gray.* New York: C. Scribner's Sons.

Jencks, C. (1992). *Rethinking social policy: Race, poverty and the underclass.* Cambridge, MA: Harvard University Press.

Jiang, L., Bazarova, N. N., & Hancock, J. T. (2011). The disclosure–intimacy link in Computer-mediated communication: An attributional extension of the hyperpersonal model. *Human Communication Research, 37,* 58–77. doi: 10.1111/j.1468-2958.2010.01393.x

Joannides, P. (2012). *Guide to getting it on: A book about the wonders of sex* (7th ed.). Waldport, OR: Goofy Foot Press.

Johnson, B., et al. (2012). Letter to the Editor. *Social Science Research, 41,* 1352–1353. doi: 10.1016/j.ssresearch.2012.08.009

Johnson, M. D. (2002). The observation of specific affect in marital interactions: Psychometric properties of a coding system and a rating system. *Psychological Assessment, 14,* 423–438. doi: 10.1037//1040-3590.14.4.423

Johnson, M. D. (2012). Healthy marriage initiatives: On the need for empiricism in policy implementation. *American Psychologist, 67,* 296–308. doi: 10.1037/a0027743

Johnson, M. D. (2013). Optimistic or quixotic? More data on marriage and relationship education programs for lower income couples. *American Psychologist, 68,* 111–112. doi: 10.1037/a0031793

Johnson, M. D. (2014a). Government-supported healthy marriage initiatives are not associated with changes in family demographics: A comment on Hawkins, Amato, and Kinghorn (2013). *Family Relations, 63,* 300–304. doi: 10.1111/fare.12060

Johnson, M. D. (2014b, February 14). US poor need practical assistance – not marriage classes. Opinion, *Christian Science Monitor.* Retrieved February 14, 2014, from http://www.csmonitor.com/Commentary/Opinion/2014/0214/US-poor-need-practical-assistance-not-marriage-classes

Johnson, M. D. (2015). Making marriage (and other relationships) work. In S. J. Lynn, W. O'Donohue, & S. O. Lilienfeld (Eds.), *Health, happiness, and well-being: Better living through psychological science* (pp. 318–340). Thousand Oaks, CA: Sage.

Johnson, M. D., & Bradbury, T. N. (1998). Divorce. In H. S. Friedman (Ed.), *Encyclopedia of Mental Health* (Vol. 1, pp. 777–786). San Diego, CA: Academic Press.

Johnson, M. D., & Bradbury, T. N. (1999). Marital satisfaction and topographical assessment of marital interaction: A longitudinal analysis of newlywed couples. *Personal Relationships, 6,* 19–40. doi: 10.1111/j.1475-6811.1999.tb00209.x

Johnson, M. D., & Bradbury, T. N. (2015). Contributions of social learning theory to the promotion of healthy relationships: Asset or liability? *Journal of Family Theory & Review, 7,* 13–27. doi: 10.1111/jftr. 12057.

Johnson, M. D., Cohan, C. L., Davila, J., Lawrence, E., Rogge, R. D., Kamey, B. R., ... Bradbury, T. N. (2005). Problem-solving skills and affective expressions as predictors of change in marital satisfaction. *Journal of Consulting and Clinical Psychology, 73,* 15–27. doi: 10.1037/0022-006x.73.1.15

Johnson, M. P. (1973). Commitment: A conceptual structure and empirical application. *The Sociological Quarterly, 14,* 395–406. doi: 10.2307/4105686

Johnson, M. P. (1995). Patriarchal terrorism and common couple violence: Two forms of violence against women. *Journal of Marriage & the Family, 57*, 283–294. doi: 10.2307/353683

Johnson, M. P. (2008). *A typology of domestic violence: Intimate terrorism, violent resistance, and situational couple violence.* Hanover, NH: University Press of New England.

Johnson, S. M., & Wittenborn, A. K. (2012). New research findings on emotionally focused therapy: Introduction to special section. *Journal of Marital and Family Therapy, 38*, 18–22. doi: 10.1111/j.1752-0606.2012.00292.x

Johnston, L. D., Bachman, J. G., & O'Malley, P. M. (2013). *Monitoring the future: Questionnaire responses from the nation's high school seniors* (Vol. 2011). Ann Arbor, MI: University of Michigan.

Jonason, P. K., & Li, N. P. (2013). Playing hard-to-get: Manipulating one's perceived availability as a mate. *European Journal of Personality, 27*, 458–469. doi: 10.1002/per.1881

Jonason, P. K., Li, N. P., & Madson, L. (2012). It is not all about the Benjamins: Understanding preferences for mates with resources. *Personality and Individual Differences, 52*, 306–310. doi: 10.1016/j.paid.2011.10.032

Jones, C. (2010, January 15). Avoiding Mr Wrong on the net. *The Mirror*, pp. Features 32–33.

Jones, D. A. (1996). Discrimination against same-sex couples in hotel reservation policies. *Journal of Homosexuality, 31*, 153–159. doi: 10.1300/J082v31n01_09

Joost, H., & Schulman, A. (Directors), & Joost, H., Schulman, A., Jarecki, A., & Smerling, M. (Producers). (2010). *Catfish* [Motion picture]. USA: Supermarché & Hit The Ground Running Films.

Jose, A., & O'Leary, K. D. (2009). Prevalence of partner aggression in representative and clinic samples. In K. D. O'Leary & E. M. Woodin (Eds.), *Psychological and physical aggression in couples: Causes and interventions* (pp. 15–35). Washington, DC: American Psychological Association.

Jose, A., O'Leary, K. D., & Moyer, A. (2010). Does premarital cohabitation predict subsequent marital stability and marital quality? A meta-analysis. *Journal of Marriage and Family, 72*, 105–116. doi: 10.1111/j.1741-3737.2009.00686.x

Kahneman, D. (2003). Maps of bounded rationality: A perspective on intuitive judgment and choice (Prize Lecture, December 8, 2002). In T. Frängsmyr (Ed.), *Les Prix Nobel 2002* (pp. 449–489). Stockholm, Sweden: The Nobel Foundation.

Kaiser, A., Hahlweg, K., Fehm-Wolfsdorf, G., & Groth, T. (1998). The efficacy of a compact psychoeducational group training program for married couples. *Journal of Consulting and Clinical Psychology, 66*, 753–760. doi: 10.1037/0022-006X.66.5.753

Karney, B. R., & Bradbury, T. N. (1995). The longitudinal course of marital quality and stability: A review of theory, methods, and research. *Psychological Bulletin, 118*, 3–34. doi: 10.1037/0033-2909.118.1.3

Karney, B. R., & Bradbury, T. N. (1997). Neuroticism, marital interaction, and the trajectory of marital satisfaction. *Journal of Personality and Social Psychology, 72*, 1075–1092. doi: 10.1037/0022-3514.72.5.1075

Karney, B. R., & Bradbury, T. N. (2000). Attributions in marriage: State or trait? A growth curve analysis. *Journal of Personality and Social Psychology, 78,* 295–309. doi: 10.1037/0022-3514.78.2.295

Karney, B. R., Bradbury, T. N., Fincham, F. D., & Sullivan, K. T. (1994). The role of negative affectivity in the association between attributions and marital satisfaction. *Journal of Personality and Social Psychology, 66,* 413–424. doi: 10.1037/0022-3514.66.2.413

Karney, B. R., & Crown, J. S. (2007). *Families under stress: An assessment of data, theory, and research on marriage and divorce in the military.* Santa Monica, CA: Rand.

Karney, B. R., & Frye, N. E. (2002). "But we've been getting better lately": Comparing prospective and retrospective views of relationship development. *Journal of Personality and Social Psychology, 82,* 222–238. doi: 10.1037/0022-3514.82.2.222

Kaslow, F., & Robison, J. A. (1996). Long-term satisfying marriages: Perceptions of contributing factors. *American Journal of Family Therapy, 24,* 153–170.

Katie, B., & Katz, M. (2005). *I need your love – is that true?: How to stop seeking love, approval, and appreciation and start finding them instead.* New York: Harmony Books.

Katie, B., & Mitchell, S. (2002). *Loving what is: Four questions that can change your life.* New York: Harmony Books.

Kelley, H. H. (1971). *Attribution in social interaction.* Morristown, NJ: General Learning Press.

Kelley, H. H., Berscheid, E., Christensen, A., Harvey, J. H., Huston, T. L., Levinger, G., ... Peterson, D. R. (1983). Analyzing close relationships. In H. H. Kelley, E. Berscheid, A. Christensen, J. H. Harvey, T. L. Huston, G. Levinger, ... D. R. Peterson (Eds.), *Close relationships* (pp. 20–67). New York: W. H. Freeman.

Kelly, E. L., & Conley, J. J. (1987). Personality and compatibility: A prospective analysis of marital stability and marital satisfaction. *Journal of Personality and Social Psychology, 52,* 27–40. doi: 10.1037/0022-3514.52.1.27

Kendon, A. (1975). Some functions of the face in a kissing round. *Semiotica, 15,* 299–334. doi: 10.1515/semi.1975.15.4.299

Kendon, A., Harris, R. M., & Key, M. R. (Eds.). (1975). *Organization of behavior in face-to-face interaction.* The Hague: Mouton.

Kenny, D. A., Mohr, C. D., & Levesque, M. J. (2001). A social relations variance partitioning of dyadic behavior. *Psychological Bulletin, 127,* 128–141. doi: 10.1037/0033-2909.127.1.128

Kiesler, S., Siegel, J., & McGuire, T. W. (1984). Social psychological aspects of computer-mediated communication. *American Psychologist, 39,* 1123–1134. doi: 10.1037/0003-066X.39.10.1123

Kim, H. K., Capaldi, D. M., & Crosby, L. (2007). Generalizability of Gottman and colleagues' affective process models of couples' relationship outcomes. *Journal of Marriage and Family, 69,* 55–72. doi: 10.1111/ j.1467-9507.1997. tb00101.x

Kinsey, A. C. (1953). *Sexual behavior in the human female.* Philadelphia: Saunders.

Kitzinger, C. (1987). *The social construction of lesbianism*. Newbury Park, CA: Sage.

Klarman, M. J. (2013). *From the closet to the altar: Courts, backlash, and the struggle for same-sex marriage*. New York: Oxford University Press.

Klaw, S. (1993). *Without sin: The life and death of the Oneida community*. New York: Allen Lane.

Kleinke, C. L., Meeker, F. B., & Staneski, R. A. (1986). Preference for opening lines: Comparing ratings by men and women. *Sex Roles, 15*, 585–600. doi: 10.1007/bf00288216

Kline, G. H., Stanley, S. M., Markman, H. J., Olmos-Gallo, P. A., St. Peters, M., Whitton, S. W., & Prado, L. M. (2004). Timing is everything: Pre-engagement cohabitation and increased risk for poor marital outcomes. *Journal of Family Psychology, 18*, 311–318. doi: 10.1037/0893-3200.18.2.311

Kling, K. C., Hyde, J. S., Showers, C. J., & Buswell, B. N. (1999). Gender differences in self-esteem: A meta-analysis. *Psychological Bulletin, 125*, 470–500. doi: 10.1037/0033-2909.125.4.470

Klohnen, E. C., & Luo, S. (2003). Interpersonal attraction and personality: What is attractive – self similarity, ideal similarity, complementarity or attachment security? *Journal of Personality and Social Psychology, 85*, 709–722. doi: 10.1037/0022-3514.85.4.709

Klohnen, E. C., & Mendelsohn, G. A. (1998). Partner selection for personality characteristics: A couple-centered approach. *Personality and Social Psychology Bulletin, 24*, 268–278. doi: 10.1177/0146167298243004

Kluwer, E. S., & Johnson, M. D. (2007). Conflict frequency and relationship quality across the transition to parenthood. *Journal of Marriage and Family, 69*, 1089–1106. doi: 10.1111/j.1741-3737.2007.00434.x

Kornblum, J. (2005, May 18). eHarmony: Heart and soul. *USA Today*. Retrieved June 3, 2013, from http://usatoday30.usatoday.com/life/people/2005-05-18-eharmony_x.htm?POE=LIFISVA#

Kreider, R. M., & Ellis, R. (2011). *Number, timing, and duration of marriages and divorces: 2009* (P70-125). Washington, DC: U.S. Department of Commerce, U.S. Census Bureau. Retrieved January 14, 2014, from http://www.census.gov/prod/2011pubs/p70-125.pdf.

Kring, A. M., & Gordon, A. H. (1998). Sex differences in emotion: Expression, experience, and physiology. *Journal of Personality and Social Psychology, 74*, 686–703. doi: 10.1037/0022-3514.74.3.686

Kuhle, B. X., & Radtke, S. (2013). Born both ways: The alloparenting hypothesis for sexual fluidity in women. *Evolutionary Psychology, 11*, 304–323.

Kurdek, L. A. (1991). Sexuality in homosexual and heterosexual couples. In K. McKinney & S. Sprecher (Eds.), *Sexuality in close relationships* (pp. 177–191). Hillsdale, NJ: Lawrence Erlbaum.

Kurdek, L. A. (1994). The nature and correlates of relationship quality in gay, lesbian, and heterosexual cohabiting couples: A test of the individual difference, interdependence, and discrepancy models. In B. Greene & G. M. Herek (Eds.), *Lesbian and gay psychology: Theory, research, and clinical applications*. (pp. 133–155). Thousand Oaks, CA: Sage.

Kurdek, L. A. (1997). Adjustment to relationship dissolution in gay, lesbian, and heterosexual partners. *Personal Relationships, 4,* 145–161. doi: 10.1111/j.1475-6811.1997.tb00136.x

Kurdek, L. A. (1998a). The nature and predictors of the trajectory of change in marital quality over the first 4 years of marriage for first-married husbands and wives. *Journal of Family Psychology, 12,* 494–510. doi: 10.1037/0893-3200.12.4.494

Kurdek, L. A. (1998b). Relationship outcomes and their predictors: Longitudinal evidence from heterosexual married, gay cohabiting, and lesbian cohabiting couples. *Journal of Marriage and the Family, 60,* 553–568. doi: 10.2307/353528

Kurdek, L. A. (1999). The nature and predictors of the trajectory of change in marital quality for husbands and wives over the first 10 years of marriage. *Developmental Psychology, 35,* 1283–1296. doi: 10.1037/0012-1649.35.5.1283

Kurdek, L. A. (2001). Differences between heterosexual-nonparent couples and gay, lesbian, and heterosexual-parent couples. *Journal of Family Issues, 22,* 727–754. doi: 10.1177/019251301022006004

Kurdek, L. A. (2004). Are gay and lesbian cohabiting couples really different from heterosexual married couples? *Journal of Marriage and Family, 66,* 880–900. doi: 10.1111/j.0022-2445.2004.00060.x

Kurdek, L. A. (2005). What do we know about gay and lesbian couples? *Current Directions in Psychological Science, 14,* 251–254. doi: 10.1111/j.0963-7214.2005.00375.x

Kurdek, L. A. (2006). Differences between partners from heterosexual, gay, and lesbian cohabiting couples. *Journal of Marriage and Family, 68,* 509–528. doi: 10.1111/j.1741-3737.2006.00268.x

Kurdek, L. A. (2008). Change in relationship quality for partners from lesbian, gay male, and heterosexual couples. *Journal of Family Psychology, 22,* 701–711. doi: 10.1037/0893-3200.22.5.701

Kurzban, R., & Weeden, J. (2005). HurryDate: Mate preferences in action. *Evolution and Human Behavior, 26,* 227–244. doi: 10.1016/j.evolhumbehav.2004.08.012

LaHaye, T. F. (1998). *Opposites attract: I love you, but why are we so different?* Eugene, OR: Harvest House.

Langer, A., Lawrence, E., & Barry, R. A. (2008). Using a vulnerability-stress-adaptation framework to predict physical aggression trajectories in newlywed marriage. *Journal of Consulting and Clinical Psychology, 76,* 756–768. doi: 10.1037/a0013254

Langer, L. M., Zimmerman, R. S., & Katz, J. A. (1995). Virgins' expectations and nonvirgins' reports: How adolescents feel about themselves. *Journal of Adolescent Research, 10,* 291–306. doi: 10.1177/0743554895102006

Langhinrichsen-Rohling, J., Snarr, J. D., Slep, A. M. S., Heyman, R. E., & Foran, H. M. (2011). Risk for suicidal ideation in the U.S. Air Force: An ecological perspective. *Journal of Consulting and Clinical Psychology, 79,* 600–612. doi: 10.1037/a0024631

Langston, C. A. (1994). Capitalizing on and coping with daily-life events: Expressive responses to positive events. *Journal of Personality and Social Psychology, 67*, 1112–1125. doi: 10.1037/0022-3514.67.6.1112

Laqueur, T. (1990). *Making sex: Body and gender from the Greeks to Freud.* Cambridge, MA: Harvard University Press.

Larsen, A. S., & Olson, D. H. (1989). Predicting marital satisfaction using PREPARE: A replication study. *Journal of Marital and Family Therapy, 15*, 311–322. doi: 10.1111/j.1752-0606.1989.tb00812.x

Laumann, E. O., Gagnon, J. H., Michael, R. T., & Michaels, S. (1994). *The social organization of sexuality: Sexual practices in the United States.* Chicago: University of Chicago Press.

Laurenceau, J.-P., Stanley, S. M., Olmos-Gallo, P. A., Baucom, B., & Markman, H. J. (2004). Community-based prevention of marital dysfunction: Multilevel modeling of a randomized effectiveness study. *Journal of Consulting and Clinical Psychology, 72*, 933–943. doi: 10.1037/0022-006X.72.6.933

Lavner, J. A., Waterman, J., & Peplau, L. A. (2012). Can gay and lesbian parents promote healthy development in high-risk children adopted from foster care? *American Journal of Orthopsychiatry, 82*, 465–472. doi: 10.1111/j.1939-0025. 2012.01176.x

Lawrence, A. A., Latty, E. M., Chivers, M. L., & Bailey, J. M. (2005). Measurement of sexual arousal in postoperative male-to-female transsexuals using vaginal photoplethysmography. *Archives of Sexual Behavior, 34*, 135–145. doi: 10.1007/s10508-005-1792-z

Lawrence, E., Pederson, A., Bunde, M., Barry, R. A., Brock, R. L., Fazio, E., ... Dzankovic, S. (2008). Objective ratings of relationship skills across multiple domains as predictors of marital satisfaction trajectories. *Journal of Social and Personal Relationships, 25*, 445–466. doi: 10.1177/0265407508090868

Lawrence, E., Rothman, A. D., Cobb, R. J., Rothman, M. T., & Bradbury, T. N. (2008). Marital satisfaction across the transition to parenthood. *Journal of Family Psychology, 22*, 41–50. doi: 10.1037/0893-3200.22.1.41

Le, B., Dove, N. L., Agnew, C. R., Korn, M. S., & Mutso, A. A. (2010). Predicting nonmarital romantic relationship dissolution: A meta-analytic synthesis. *Personal Relationships, 17*, 377–390. doi: 10.1111/j.1475-6811.2010. 01285.x

Leaper, C., & Robnett, R. D. (2011). Women are more likely than men to use tentative language, aren't they? A meta-analysis testing for gender differences and moderators. *Psychology of Women Quarterly, 35*, 129–142. doi: 10.1177/0361684310392728

Lebow, J. L., Chambers, A. L., Christensen, A., & Johnson, S. M. (2012). Research on the treatment of couple distress. *Journal of Marital and Family Therapy, 38*, 145–168. doi: 10.1111/j.1752-0606.2011.00249.x

Ledbetter, A. M. (2008). Chronemic cues and sex differences in relational e-mail. *Social Science Computer Review, 26*, 466–482. doi: 10.1177/0894439308314812

Leigh, J. P., & Lust, J. (1988). Determinants of employee tardiness. *Work & Occupations, 15*, 78–95.

LeMasters, E. E. (1957). Parenthood as crisis. *Marriage and Family Living, 19*, 352–355. doi: 10.2307/347802

Lenton, A. P., Fasolo, B., & Todd, P. M. (2008). "Shopping" for a mate: Expected versus experienced preferences in online mate choice. *IEEE Transactions on Professional Communication, 51*, 169–182. doi: 10.1109/TPC.2008.2000342

Lenton, A. P., Fasolo, B., & Todd, P. M. (2009). The relationship between number of potential mates and mating skew in humans. *Animal Behaviour, 77*, 55–60. doi: 10.1016/j.anbehav.2008.08.025

Lenton, A. P., & Francesconi, M. (2010). How humans cognitively manage an abundance of mate options. *Psychological Science, 21*, 528–533. doi: 10.1177/0956797610364958

Lenton, A. P., & Stewart, A. (2008). Changing her ways: The number of options and mate-standard strength impact mate choice strategy and satisfaction. *Judgment and Decision Making, 3*, 501–511. doi: 10.1037/0003-066x.55.1.79

Lenzenweger, M. F., Johnson, M. D., & Willett, J. B. (2004). Individual growth curve analysis illuminates stability and change in personality disorder features: The Longitudinal Study of Personality Disorders. *Archives of General Psychiatry, 61*, 1015–1024. doi: 10.1001/archpsyc.61.10.1015

Lepore, J. (2010, March 29). The rise of marriage therapy, and other dreams of human betterment. *The New Yorker.*

Levinger, G. (1976). A social psychological perspective on marital dissolution. *Journal of Social Issues, 32*, 21–47.

Levinger, G. (1986). Compatibility in relationships. *Social Science, 71*, 173–177.

Levy, A. (2005). *Female chauvinist pigs: Women and the rise of raunch culture.* New York: Free Press.

Lewandowski, G. W., Ciarocco, N. J., Pettenato, M., & Stephan, J. (2012). Pick me up: Ego depletion and receptivity to relationship initiation. *Journal of Social and Personal Relationships, 29*, 1071–1084. doi: 10.1177/0265407512449401

Lewd and Lascivious Behavior, XLVI Chapter 798, 2013 Florida Statutes § 02 (1868).

Lewd and Lascivious Cohabitation and Gross Lewdness, XLVIII Chapter 750, The Michigan Penal Code § 335 (1931).

Lichter, D. T., McLaughlin, D. K., & Ribar, D. C. (1997). Welfare and the rise in female-headed families. *American Journal of Sociology, 103*, 112–143. doi: 10.1086/231173

Liefbroer, A., & Dourleijn, E. (2006). Unmarried cohabitation and union stability: Testing the role of diffusion using data from 16 European countries. *Demography, 43*, 203–221. doi: 10.1353/dem.2006.0018

Lilienfeld, S. O., Lynn, S. J., Ruscio, J., & Beyerstein, B. L. (2009). *50 Great Myths of Popular Psychology: Shattering Widespread Misconceptions about Human Behavior.* Chichester, UK: Wiley Blackwell.

Lindau, S. T., Laumann, E. O., & Levinson, W. (2007). Sexuality and health among older adults in the United States: Reply. *The New England Journal of Medicine, 357*, 2732–2733.

Lindau, S. T., Schumm, L. P., Laumann, E. O., Levinson, W., O'Muircheartaigh, C. A., & Waite, L. J. (2007). A study of sexuality and health among older adults in the United States. *The New England Journal of Medicine, 357*, 762–775.

Lindberg, S. M., Hyde, J. S., Petersen, J. L., & Linn, M. C. (2010). New trends in gender and mathematics performance: A meta-analysis. *Psychological Bulletin, 136*, 1123–1135. doi: 10.1037/a0021276 & 10.1037/a0021276.supp (Supplemental)

Lipka, M. (2014). *Young U.S. Catholics overwhelmingly accepting of homosexuality* (Pew Research Center Fact-Tank). Retrieved October 19, 2014, from http://www.pewresearch.org/fact-tank/2014/10/16/young-u-s-catholics-overwhelmingly-accepting-of-homosexuality/

Lippa, R. A. (2009). Sex differences in sex drive, sociosexuality, and height across 53 nations: Testing evolutionary and social structural theories. *Archives of Sexual Behavior, 38*, 631–651.

Loudon, A. (2013, February 26). Has technology killed romance? [Web publication]. *The Independent*. Retrieved 22 May, 2013, from http://www.independent.co.uk/life-style/dating/advice/has-technology-killed-romance-8511647.html.

Lucas, R. E. (2005). Time does not heal all wounds: A longitudinal study of reaction and adaptation to divorce. *Psychological Science, 16*, 945–950. doi: 10.1111/j.1467-9280.2005.01642.x

Lundquist, E., Hsueh, J., Lowenstein, A. E., Faucetta, K., Gubits, D., Michalopoulos, C., & Knox, V. (2014). *A family-strengthening program for low-income families: Final impacts from the Supporting Healthy Marriage Evaluation* (OPRE Report 2014-09A). Washington, DC: Office of Planning, Research and Evaluation, Administration for Children and Families, U.S. Department of Health and Human Services.

Luo, S., Chen, H., Yue, G., Zhang, G., Zhaoyang, R., & Xu, D. (2008). Predicting marital satisfaction from self, partner, and couple characteristics: Is it me, you, or us? *Journal of Personality, 76*, 1231–1265. doi: 10.1111/j.1467-6494.2008.00520.x

Lutyens, M. (1972). *The Ruskins and the Grays*. London: John Murray.

Lye, D. N., & Biblarz, T. J. (1993). The effects of attitudes toward family life and gender roles on marital satisfaction. *Journal of Family Issues, 14*, 157–188. doi: 10.1177/019251393014002002

MacDermid, S. M., Huston, T. L., & McHale, S. M. (1990). Changes in marriage associated with the transition to parenthood: Individual differences as a function of sex-role attitudes and changes in the division of household labor. *Journal of Marriage and The Family, 52*, 475–486. doi: 10.2307/353041

Macfadden, B. (1916). *Manhood and marriage*. New York: Macfadden Publications.

Maddox, B. (2009). *George Eliot: Novelist, lover, wife*. London: HarperPress.

Maisel, N. C., & Gable, S. L. (2009). The paradox of received social support: The importance of responsiveness. *Psychological Science, 20*, 928–932. doi: 10.1111/j.1467-9280.2009.02388.x

Malouff, J. M., Thorsteinsson, E. B., Schutte, N. S., Bhullar, N., & Rooke, S. E. (2010). The Five-Factor Model of personality and relationship satisfaction of intimate partners: A meta-analysis. *Journal of Research in Personality, 44*, 124–127. doi: 10.1016/j.jrp.2009.09.004

Mancini, A. D., Bonanno, G. A., & Clark, A. E. (2011). Stepping off the hedonic treadmill: Individual differences in response to major life events. *Journal of Individual Differences, 32*, 144–152. doi: 10.1027/1614-0001/a000047

Manjoo, F. (2009). You have no friends: Everyone else is on Facebook. Why aren't you? *Slate.* Retrieved May 23, 2013, from Slate.com website: http://www.slate.com/articles/technology/technology/2009/01/you_have_no_friends.html

Mann, J. (2014, September 28). British sex survey 2014: "The nation has lost some of its sexual swagger," *The Gaurdian.* Retrieved November 2, 2014, from http://www.theguardian.com/lifeandstyle/2014/sep/28/british-sex-survey-2014-nation-lost-sexual-swagger

Manning, W. D. (2013). Trends in cohabitation: Over twenty years of change, 1987–2010. Bowling Green, OH: National Center for Family & Marriage Research.

Manning, W. D., & Cohen, J. A. (2012). Premarital cohabitation and marital dissolution: An examination of recent marriages. *Journal of Marriage and Family, 74*, 377–387. doi: 10.1111/j.1741-3737.2012.00960.x

Manning, W. D., & Smock, P. J. (2005). Measuring and modeling cohabitation: New perspectives from qualitative data. *Journal of Marriage and Family, 67*, 989–1002. doi: 10.1111/j.1741-3737.2005.00189.x

Marie Claire. (2014). Marie Claire's hottest and sexiest men. Retrieved May 14, 2014, from http://www.marieclaire.co.uk/celebrity/pictures/35738/0/hottest-and-sexiest-men.html

Markey, P. M., Lowmaster, S., & Eichler, W. (2010). A real-time assessment of interpersonal complementarity. *Personal Relationships, 17*, 13–25. doi: 10.1111/j.1475-6811.2010.01249.x

Markey, P. M., & Markey, C. N. (2007). Romantic ideals, romantic obtainment, and relationship experiences. *Journal of Social and Personal Relationships, 24*, 517–533. doi: 10.1177/0265407507079241

Markman, H. J. (1979). Application of a behavioral model of marriage in predicting relationship satisfaction of couples planning marriage. *Journal of Consulting and Clinical Psychology, 47*, 743–749. doi: 10.1037/0022-006X.47.4.743

Markman, H. J. (1981). Prediction of marital distress: A 5-year follow up. *Journal of Consulting and Clinical Psychology,49*,760–762. doi:10.1037/0022-006X.49.5.760

Markman, H. J., & Floyd, F. (1980). Possibilities for the prevention of marital discord: A behavioral perspective. *American Journal of Family Therapy, 8*, 29–48. doi: 10.1080/01926188008250355

Markman, H. J., Floyd, F. J., Stanley, S. M., & Storaasli, R. D. (1988). Prevention of marital distress: A longitudinal investigation. *Journal of Consulting and Clinical Psychology, 56*, 210–217. doi: 10.1037/0022-006X.56.2.210

Markman, H. J., Renick, M. J., Floyd, F., Stanley, S., & Clements, M. (1993). Preventing marital distress through communication and conflict management training: A 4- and 5-year follow-up. *Journal of Consulting and Clinical Psychology, 61*, 70–77. doi: 10.1037/0022-006X.61.1.70

Markman, H. J., Rhoades, G. K., Stanley, S. M., & Peterson, K. M. (2013). A randomized clinical trial of the effectiveness of premarital intervention: Moderators of divorce outcomes. *Journal of Family Psychology, 27*, 165–172. doi: 10.1037/a0031134

Markman, H. J., Stanley, S., & Blumberg, S. L. (1994). *Fighting for your marriage.* San Francisco: Jossey-Bass.

Marks, L. (2012). Same-sex parenting and children's outcomes: A closer examination of the American psychological association's brief on lesbian and gay parenting. *Social Science Research, 41*, 735–751. doi: 10.1016/j.ssresearch. 2012.03.006

Martin, J. A., Hamilton, B. E., Osterman, M. J. K., Curtin, S. C., & Mathews, T. J. (2013). *Births: Final data for 2012* (National Vital Statistics Reports, 62). Hyattsville, MD: National Center for Health Statistics.

Martin, S. P., & Parashar, S. (2006). Women's changing attitudes toward divorce, 1974–2002: Evidence for an educational crossover. *Journal of Marriage and Family, 68*, 29–40. doi: 10.2307/3600354

Martinez, G. M., Chandra, A., Abma, J. C., Jones, J., & Mosher, W. D. (2006). *Fertility, contraception, and fatherhood: Data on men and women from Cycle 6 (2002) of the National Survey of Family Growth* (PHS2006-1978). Washington, DC: U.S. Department of Health and Human Services, National Center for Health Statistics.

Match.com LLC. (2012). chemistry.com. Retrieved October 9, 2012, from http://www.chemistry.com/

Matrimonial Causes Act § 12 (1973).

Matthiessen, C. (2008). Love and marriage (and caregiving): Caring.com's marriage survey. *Caring.com.* Retrieved November 2, 2014, from https://www.caring.com/articles/love-and-marriage-when-caregiving

Mattson, R. E., Frame, L. E., & Johnson, M. D. (2011). Premarital affect as a predictor of postnuptial marital satisfaction. *Personal Relationships, 18*, 532–546. doi: 10.1111/j.1475-6811.2010.01315.x

Mayhall, J., & Mayhall, C. (1990). *Opposites attack: Turning your differences into opportunities.* Colorado Springs, CO: NavPress.

Mazelis, J. M., & Mykyta, L. (2011). Relationship status and activated kin support: The role of need and norms. *Journal of Marriage and Family, 73*, 430–445. doi: 10.1111/j.1741-3737.2010.00816.x

McCarthy, B. W. (2001). Integrating sex therapy strategies and techniques into marital therapy. *Journal of Family Psychotherapy, 12*, 45–53. doi: 10.1300/J085v12n03_03

McCarthy, B. W., & McCarthy, E. J. (2003). *Rekindling desire: A step-by-step program to help low-sex and no-sex marriages.* New York: Brunner-Routledge.

McCarthy, E. (2009, April 24). On dating by Ellen McCarthy: Shared qualities for a successful relationship. *Washington Post.*

McClintock, M. K., & Anisko, J. J. (1982). Group mating among Norway rats: I. Sex differences in the pattern and neuroendocrine consequences of copulation. *Animal Behaviour, 30*, 398–409. doi: 10.1016/S0003-3472(82)80051-1

McCormick, N. B., & Jones, A. J. (1989). Gender differences in nonverbal flirtation. *Journal of Sex Education & Therapy, 15*, 271–282.

McCrae, R. R., & Costa, P. T., Jr. (1997). Personality trait structure as a human universal. *American Psychologist, 52*, 509–516. doi: 10.1037/0003-066x. 52.5.509

McCubbin, H. I., & Patterson, J. M. (1982). Family adaptations to crises. In H. I. McCubbin, A. E. Cauble, & J. M. Patterson (Eds.), *Family stress, coping, and social support* (pp. 26–47). Springfield, IL: Charles C. Thomas.

McFadden, R. D. (2011, March 1). Rev. Peter J. Gomes is dead at 68: A leading voice against intolerance. *The New York Times*, p. A23. Retrieved June 21, 2013, from http://www.nytimes.com/2011/03/02/us/02gomes.html

McGinnis, S. L. (2003). Cohabitating, dating, and perceived costs of marriage: A model of marriage entry. *Journal of Marriage and Family, 65*, 105–116. doi: 10.1111/j.1741-3737.2003.00105.x

McHale, S. M., & Huston, T. L. (1984). Men and women as parents: Sex role orientations, employment, and parental roles with infants. *Child Development, 55*, 1349–1361. doi: 10.2307/1130005

McKenna, K. Y. A., Green, A. S., & Gleason, M. E. J. (2002). Relationship formation on the Internet: What's the big attraction? *Journal of Social Issues, 58*, 9–31. doi: 10.1111/1540-4560.00246

McLoyd, V. C., Cauce, A. M., Takeuchi, D., & Wilson, L. (2000). Marital processes and parental socialization in families of color: A decade review of research. *Journal of Marriage and the Family, 62*, 1070–1093. doi: 10.1111/j.1741-3737.2000.01070.x

McNulty, J. K., & Russell, V. M. (2010). When "negative" behaviors are positive: A contextual analysis of the long-term effects of problem-solving behaviors on changes in relationship satisfaction. *Journal of Personality and Social Psychology, 98*, 587–604. doi: 10.1037/a0017479

McShall, J. R., & Johnson, M. D. (2015a). The association between relationship distress and psychopathology is consistent across racial and ethnic groups. *Journal of Abnormal Psychology, 124*, 226–231. doi: 10.1037/a0038267

McShall, J. R., & Johnson, M. D. (2015b). The association between relationship quality and physical health across ethnic groups. *Journal of Cross-Cultural Psychology, 46*, 789–804. doi: 10.1177/0022022115587026

Meier, A., & Allen, G. (2008). Intimate relationship development during the transition to adulthood: Differences by social class. *New Directions for Child and Adolescent Development, 2008*, 25–39. doi: 10.1002/cd.207

Meier, A., & Allen, G. (2009). Romantic relationships from adolescence to young adulthood: Evidence from the National Longitudinal Study of Adolescent Health. *The Sociological Quarterly, 50*, 308–335. doi: 10.1111/j.1533-8525.2009.01142.x

Men's Health. (2013). The 100 hottest women of all time. Retrieved May 14, 2014, from http://www.menshealth.com/sex-women/hottest-women-all-time

Meston, C. M., & Buss, D. M. (2009). *Why women have sex*. New York: Henry Holt and Company.

Metz, M. E., & McCarthy, B. W. (2003). *Coping with premature ejaculation: How to overcome PE, please your partner and have great sex.* Oakland, CA: New Harbinger Publications.

Metz, M. E., & McCarthy, B. W. (2004). *Coping with erectile dysfunction: How to regain confidence and enjoy great sex.* Oakland, CA: New Harbinger.

Meyer, J., & Ford, A. (1994, June 23). 911 tape tells of stormy Simpson relationship inquiry: Defendant's ex-wife pleads for help as obscenities are screamed. *Los Angeles Times*, p. 1.

Michie, H. (2006). *Victorian honeymoons: Journeys to the conjugal.* Cambridge: Cambridge University Press.

Miller, G. E., Dopp, J. M., Myers, H. F., Stevens, S. Y., & Fahey, J. L. (1999). Psychosocial predictors of natural killer cell mobilization during marital conflict. *Health Psychology, 18*, 262–271. doi: 10.1037/0278-6133.18.3.262

Miller, J. (2013, October 3). *Men are cats, women are dogs (stand-up comedy).* Retrieved May 4, 2014, from http://youtu.be/r8WNW-Y7xkc

Mitnick, D. M., Heyman, R. E., & Smith Slep, A. M. (2009). Changes in relationship satisfaction across the transition to parenthood: A meta-analysis. *Journal of Family Psychology, 23*, 848–852. doi: 10.1037/a0017004; 10.1037/a0017004. supp (Supplemental)

Moffitt, T. E. (2001). *Sex differences in antisocial behaviour: Conduct disorder, delinquency, and violence in the Dunedin Longitudinal Study.* Cambridge: Cambridge University Press.

Molden, D. C., Lucas, G. M., Finkel, E. J., Kumashiro, M., & Rusbult, C. E. (2009). Perceived support for promotion-focused and prevention-focused goals: Associations with well-being in unmarried and married couples. *Psychological Science, 20*, 787–793. doi: 10.1111/j.1467-9280.2009.02362.x

Monroe, S. M., Rohde, P., Seeley, J. R., & Lewinsohn, P. M. (1999). Life events and depression in adolescence: Relationship loss as a prospective risk factor for first onset of major depressive disorder. *Journal of Abnormal Psychology, 108*, 606–614.

Montoya, R. M., & Horton, R. S. (2013). A meta-analytic investigation of the processes underlying the similarity-attraction effect. *Journal of Social and Personal Relationships, 30*, 64–94. doi: 10.1177/0265407512452989

Montoya, R. M., Horton, R. S., & Kirchner, J. (2008). Is actual similarity necessary for attraction? A meta-analysis of actual and perceived similarity. *Journal of Social and Personal Relationships, 25*, 889–922. doi: 10.1177/0265407508096700

Moore, M. M. (2010). Human nonverbal courtship behavior: A brief historical review. *Journal of Sex Research, 47*, 171–180. doi: 10.1080/00224490903402520

Mosher, W. D., Chandra, A., & Jones, J. (2005). Sexual behavior and selected health measures: Men and women 15–44 years of age, United States, 2002. Advance data from *Vital and Health Statistics*, no 362. Hyattsville, MD: National Center for Health Statistics.

Muehlenhard, C. L., Koralewski, M. A., Andrews, S. L., & Burdick, C. A. (1986). Verbal and nonverbal cues that convey interest in dating: Two studies. *Behavior Therapy, 17*, 404–419. doi: 10.1016/S0005-7894(86)80071-5

Muehlenhard, C. L., & McFall, R. M. (1981). Dating initiation from a woman's perspective. *Behavior Therapy*, *12*, 682–691. doi: 10.1016/S0005-7894(81)80139-6

Murry, V. M., Brown, P. A., Brody, G. H., Cutrona, C. E., & Simons, R. L. (2001). Racial discrimination as a moderator of the links among stress, maternal psychological functioning, and family relationships. *Journal of Marriage and the Family*, *63*, 915–926. doi: 10.1111/j.1741-3737.2001.00915.x

Myers, D. C. (1999). Close relationships and quality of life. In D. Kahneman, E. Diener, & N. Schwarz (Eds.), *Well-being: Foundations of hedonic psychology* (pp. 374–391). New York: Russell Sage Foundation.

Nagoshi, C. T., Johnson, R. C., & Honbo, K. A. (1992). Assortative mating for cognitive abilities, personality, and attitudes: Offspring from the Hawaii Family Study of Cognition. *Personality and Individual Differences*, *13*, 883–891. doi: 10.1016/0191-8869(92)90005-A

Nelson, H. D., Bougatsos, C., & Blazina, I. (2012). Screening women for intimate partner violence: A systematic review to update the US Preventive Services Task Force Recommendation. *Annals of Internal Medicine*, *156*, 796–808. doi: 10.7 326/0003-4819-156-11-201206050-00447

Nepomnyaschy, L., & Teitler, J. (2013). Cyclical cohabitation among unmarried parents in fragile families. *Journal of Marriage and Family*, *75*, 1248–1265. doi: 10.1111/jomf.12064

Newcomb, T. M. (1956). The prediction of interpersonal attraction. *American Psychologist*, *11*, 575–586. doi: 10.1037/h0046141

Newport, F., & Himelfarb, I. (2013). In U.S., record-high say gay, lesbian relations morally OK. Retrieved March 5, 2014, from http://www.gallup.com/poll/162689/record-high-say-gay-lesbian-relations-morally.aspx

Nichols, M. (1987). Lesbian sexuality: Issues and developing theory. In the Boston Lesbian Psychologies Collective (Ed.), *Lesbian psychologies: Explorations and challenges* (pp. 97–125). Urbana: University of Illinois Press.

Nichols, M. (1988). Low sexual desire in lesbian couples. In S. R. Leiblum & R. C. Rosen (Eds.), *Sexual desire disorders* (pp. 387–412). New York: Guilford.

Nisbett, R. E., & Wilson, T. D. (1977). Telling more than we can know: Verbal reports on mental processes. *Psychological Review*, *84*, 231–259. doi: 10.1037/0033-295X.84.3.231

Nock, M. K., Green, J. G., Hwang, I., McLaughlin, K. A., Sampson, N. A., Zaslavsky, A. M., & Kessler, R. C. (2013). Prevalence, correlates, and treatment of lifetime suicidal behavior among adolescents: Results from the National Comorbidity Survey Replication Adolescent Supplement. *JAMA Psychiatry*, *70*, 300–310. doi: 10.1001/2013.jamapsychiatry.55

Nomaguchi, K. M., & Milkie, M. A. (2003). Costs and rewards of children: The effects of becoming a parent on adults' lives. *Journal of Marriage and Family*, *65*, 356–374. doi: 10.1111/j.1741-3737.2003.00356.x

Nomaguchi, K. M., Milkie, M. A., & Bianchi, S. M. (2005). Time strains and psychological well-being: Do dual-earner mothers and fathers differ? *Journal of Family Issues*, *26*, 756–792. doi: 10.1177/0192513x05277524

Obama, B. (2006). *The audacity of hope: Thoughts on reclaiming the American dream.* New York: Crown.

O'Leary, K. D., & Slep, A. M. S. (2012). Prevention of partner violence by focusing on behaviors of both young males and females. *Prevention Science, 13,* 329–339. doi: 10.1007/s11121-011-0237-2

O'Leary, K. D., Slep, A. M. S., & O'Leary, S. G. (2007). Multivariate models of men's and women's partner aggression. *Journal of Consulting and Clinical Psychology, 75,* 752764. doi: 10.1037/0022-006X.75.5.752

O'Leary, K. D., & Woodin, E. M. (Eds.). (2009). *Psychological and physical aggression in couples: Causes and interventions.* Washington, DC: American Psychological Association.

Oliver, M. B., & Hyde, J. S. (1993). Gender differences in sexuality: A meta-analysis. *Psychological Bulletin, 114,* 29–51. doi: 10.1037/0033-2909.114.1.29

Orantia, J. (2013, February 26). iLove to love you, baby. *The Sun Herald,* TV liftout, p. 13.

Osborne, C., Manning, W. D., & Smock, P. J. (2007). Married and cohabiting parents' relationship stability: A focus on race and ethnicity. *Journal of Marriage and Family, 69,* 1345–1366. doi: 10.1111/j.1741-3737.2007.00451.x

Osterhout, R. E., Frame, L. E., & Johnson, M. D. (2011). Maladaptive attributions and dyadic behavior are associated in engaged couples. *Journal of Social and Clinical Psychology, 30,* 787–818. doi: 10.1521/jscp.2011.30.8.787

Oswald, R. F. (2002). Inclusion and belonging in the family rituals of gay and lesbian people. *Journal of Family Psychology, 16,* 428–436. doi: 10.1037/0893-3200.16.4.428

Overall, N. C., Fletcher, G. J. O., & Simpson, J. A. (2006). Regulation processes in intimate relationships: The role of ideal standards. *Journal of Personality and Social Psychology, 91,* 662–685. doi: 10.1037/0022-3514.91.4.662

Overall, N. C., Fletcher, G. J. O., & Simpson, J. A. (2010). Helping each other grow: Romantic partner support, self-improvement, and relationship quality. *Personality and Social Psychology Bulletin, 36,* 1496–1513. doi: 10.1177/0146167210383045

Overall, N. C., Fletcher, G. J. O., Simpson, J. A., & Sibley, C. G. (2009). Regulating partners in intimate relationships: The costs and benefits of different communication strategies. *Journal of Personality and Social Psychology, 96,* 620–639. doi: 10.1037/a0012961

Overall, N. C., Sibley, C. G., & Tan, R. (2011). The costs and benefits of sexism: Resistance to influence during relationship conflict. *Journal of Personality and Social Psychology, 101,* 271–290. doi: 10.1037/a0022727

Owen, J., Rhoades, G. K., & Stanley, S. M. (2013). Sliding versus deciding in relationships: Associations with relationship quality, commitment, and infidelity. *Journal of Couple & Relationship Therapy, 12,* 135–149. doi: 10.1080/15332691.2013.779097

Özdemir, Ö., Şimşek, F., Özkardeş, S., İncesu, C., & Karakoç, B. (2008). The unconsummated marriage: Its frequency and clinical characteristics in a sexual dysfunction clinic. *Journal of Sex & Marital Therapy, 34,* 268–279. doi: 10.1080/00926230701866380

Pallasch, A. M. (2007, May 7). Racy billboard peddles divorce: Head of lawyers' group says it's bad for profession's image, *Chicago Sun–Times*, p. 5.

Pasch, L. A., & Bradbury, T. N. (1998). Social support, conflict, and the development of marital dysfunction. *Journal of Consulting and Clinical Psychology*, 66, 219–230. doi: 10.1037/0022-006X.66.2.219

Pasch, L. A., Bradbury, T. N., & Davila, J. (1997). Gender, negative affectivity, and observed social support behavior in marital interaction. *Personal Relationships*, 4, 361–378. doi: 10.1111/j.1475-6811.1997.tb00151.x

Pate, A. M., & Hamilton, E. E. (1992). Formal and informal deterrents to domestic violence: The Dade County Spouse Assault Experiment. *American Sociological Review*, 57, 691–697. doi: 10.2307/2095922

Patterson, C. J., & Wainright, J. L. (2012). Adolescents with same-sex parents: Findings from the National Longitudinal Study of Adolescent Health. In D. M. Brodzinsky & A. Pertman (Eds.), *Adoption by lesbians and gay men: A new dimension in family diversity* (pp. 85–111). New York: Oxford.

Paumgarten, N. (2011, July 4). Looking for someone: Sex, love, and loneliness on the Internet. *The New Yorker*, 87, 36–49.

Pearce, J. W., LeBow, M. D., & Orchard, J. (1981). Role of spouse involvement in the behavioral treatment of overweight women. *Journal of Consulting and Clinical Psychology*, 49, 236–244. doi: 10.1037/0022-006x.49.2.236

Pearce, M. J., Boergers, J., & Prinstein, M. J. (2002). Adolescent obesity, overt and relational peer victimization, and romantic relationships. *Obesity Research*, 10, 386–393. doi: 10.1038/oby.2002.53

Peplau, L. A., Cochran, S., Rook, K., & Padesky, C. (1978). Loving women: Attachment and autonomy in lesbian relationships. *Journal of Social Issues*, 34, 7–27. doi: 10.1111/j.1540-4560.1978.tb02611.x

Peplau, L. A., & Fingerhut, A. W. (2007). The close relationships of lesbians and gay men. *Annual Review of Psychology*, 58, 405–424. doi: doi:10.1146/annurev.psych.58.110405.085701

Peplau, L. A., Fingerhut, A. W., & Beals, K. P. (2004). Sexuality in the relationships of lesbians and gay men. In J. H. Harvey, A. Wenzel, & S. Sprecher (Eds.), *The handbook of sexuality in close relationships* (pp. 349–369). Mahwah, NJ: Erlbaum

Perel, E. (2006). *Mating in captivity*. New York: HarperCollins.

Perilloux, C., & Kurzban, R. (2014). Do men overperceive women's sexual interest? *PsychologicalScience*, advance online publication. doi: 10.1177/0956797614555727

Perper, T. (1985). *Sex signals: The biology of love*. Philadelphia: ISI Press.

Perper, T. (1989). Theories and observations on sexual selection and female choice in human beings. *Medical Anthropology*, 11, 409–454. doi: 10.1080/01459740.1989.9966006

Perper, T., & Weis, D. L. (1987). Proceptive and rejective strategies of U.S. and Canadian college women. *Journal of Sex Research*, 23, 455–480. doi: 10.1080/00224498709551385

Perrin, A. J., Cohen, P. N., & Caren, N. (2013). Are children of parents who had same-sex relationships disadvantaged? A scientific evaluation of the no-differences hypothesis. *Journal of Gay & Lesbian Mental Health*, 17, 327–336. doi: 10.1080/19359705.2013.772553

Perry-Jenkins, M., Goldberg, A. E., Pierce, C. P., & Sayer, A. G. (2007). Shift work, role overload, and the transition to parenthood. *Journal of Marriage and Family*, 69, 123–138. doi: 10.1111/j.1741-3737.2006.00349.x

Petersen, J. L., & Hyde, J. S. (2010). A meta-analytic review of research on gender differences in sexuality, 1993–2007. *Psychological Bulletin*, 136, 21–38. doi: 10.1037/a0017504 & 10.1037/a0017504.supp (Supplemental)

Peterson, C. D., Baucom, D. H., Elliott, M. J., & Farr, P. A. (1989). The relationship between sex role identity and marital adjustment. *Sex Roles*, 21, 775–787. doi: 10.1007/bf00289808

Pew Research Center. (2003). Religious beliefs underpin opposition to homosexuality. Retrieved October 19, 2014, from http://www.people-press.org/files/legacy-pdf/197.pdf

Pew Research Center. (2013). Changing attitudes on same sex marriage, gay friends and family. Retrieved October 19, 2014, from http://www.people-press.org/2013/06/06/changing-attitudes-on-same-sex-marriage-gay-friends-and-family/

Pew Research Center. (2014). Millennials in adulthood: Detached from institutions, networked with friends. Retrieved October 19, 2014, from http://www.pewsocialtrends.org/files/2014/03/2014-03-07_generations-report-version-for-web.pdf

Pillay, A. P. (1955). Non-consummation of marriage: A clinical study. *International Journal of Sexology*, 8, 131–136.

Platt, J. R. (1964). Strong inference. *Science*, 146, 347–353.

Popenoe, D., & Whitehead, B. D. (2001). *The state of our unions: The social health of marriage in America*. Piscataway, NJ: The National Marriage Project.

Popper, K. R. (1959). *The logic of scientific discovery* (English translation). New York: Basic Books.

Potter, D. (2012). Same-sex parent families and children's academic achievement. *Journal of Marriage and Family*, 74, 556–571. doi: 10.1111/j.1741-3737.2012.00966.x

Prochaska, J., & Prochaska, J. (1978). Twentieth century trends in marriage and marital therapy. In T. J. Paolino & B. S. McCrady (Eds.), *Marriage and marital therapy: Psychoanalytic, behavioral and systems theory perspectives* (pp. 1–24). New York: Brunner/Mazel.

Putnam, R. D. (2000). *Bowling alone: The collapse and revival of American community*. New York: Simon & Schuster.

Radtke, S. (2013). Sexual fluidity in women: How feminist research influenced evolutionary studies of same-sex behavior. *Journal of Social, Evolutionary, and Cultural Psychology*, 7, 336–343. doi: 10.1037/h0099185

Rainie, L., Lenhart, A., Fox, S., Spooner, T., & Horrigan, J. (2000). *Tracking online life: How women use the Internet to cultivate relationships with family and friends* (Pew Internet & American Life Project). Washington, DC: Pew Research Center.

Ramirez, A., & Broneck, K. (2009). "IM me": Instant messaging as relational maintenance and everyday communication. *Journal of Social and Personal Relationships, 26,* 291–314. doi: 10.1177/0265407509106719

Ramirez, A., & Wang, Z. (2008). When online meets offline: An expectancy violations theory perspective on modality switching. *Journal of Communication, 58,* 20–39. doi: 10.1111/j.1460-2466.2007.00372.x

Ramirez, A., & Zhang, S. (2007). When online meets offline: The effect of modality switching on relational communication. *Communication Monographs, 74,* 287–310. doi: 10.1080/03637750701543493

Randall, A. K., & Bodenmann, G. (2009). The role of stress on close relationships and marital satisfaction. *Clinical Psychology Review, 29,* 105–115. doi: 10.1016/j.cpr.2008.10.004

Randles, J. M. (2014). Partnering and parenting in poverty: A qualitative analysis of a relationship skills program for low-income, unmarried families. *Journal of Policy Analysis and Management, 33,* 385–412. doi: 10.1002/pam.21742

Raush, H. L., Barry, W. A., Hertel, R. K., & Swain, M. A. (1974). *Communication conflict and marriage.* Oxford: Jossey-Bass.

Reber, R., Schwarz, N., & Winkielman, P. (2004). Processing fluency and aesthetic pleasure: Is beauty in the perceiver's processing experience? *Personality and Social Psychology Review, 8,* 364–382. doi: 10.1207/s15327957pspr0804_3

Reddicliffe, S. (2010, December 26). Multimedia king? Survey says, "Steve Harvey." *The New York Times,* p. AR1. Retrieved May 4, 2014, from http://www.nytimes.com/2010/12/26/arts/television/26harvey.html

Regan, P. C., & Joshi, A. (2003). Ideal partner preferences among adolescents. *Social Behavior and Personality, 31,* 13–20. doi: 10.2224/sbp.2003.31.1.13

Regan, P. C., Shen, W., De La Peña, E., & Gosset, E. (2007). "Fireworks exploded in my mouth": Affective responses before, during, and after the very first kiss. *International Journal of Sexual Health, 19,* 1–16. doi: 10.1300/J514v19n02_01

Regnerus, M. (2012a). How different are the adult children of parents who have same-sex relationships? Findings from the New Family Structures Study. *Social Science Research, 41,* 752–770. doi: 10.1016/j.ssresearch.2012.03.009

Regnerus, M. (2012b). Q & A with Mark Regnerus about the background of his new study. *Black, White and Gray.* Retrieved March 27, 2014, from http://www.patheos.com/blogs/blackwhiteandgray/2012/06/q-a-with-mark-regnerus-about-the-background-of-his-new-study/

Reis, H. T., Maniaci, M. R., Caprariello, P. A., Eastwick, P. W., & Finkel, E. J. (2011). Familiarity does indeed promote attraction in live interaction. *Journal of Personality and Social Psychology, 101,* 557–570. doi: 10.1037/a0022885

Reis, H. T., & Shaver, P. (1988). Intimacy as an interpersonal process. In S. Duck & D. F. Hay (Eds.), *Handbook of personal relationships: Theory, research and interventions* (pp. 367–389). Oxford: John Wiley & Sons.

Reissing, E. D., Binik, Y. M., Khalifé, S., Cohen, D., & Amsel, R. (2004). Vaginal spasm, pain, and behavior: An empirical investigation of the diagnosis of vaginismus. *Archives of Sexual Behavior, 33,* 5–17. doi: 10.1023/B:ASEB.0000007458.32852.c8

Repetti, R. L. (1989). Effects of daily workload on subsequent behavior during marital interaction: The roles of social withdrawal and spouse support. *Journal of Personality and Social Psychology, 57,* 651–659. doi: 10.1037/0022-3514.57.4.651

Repetti, R. L. (1994). Short-term and long-term processes linking job stressors to father–child interaction. *Social Development, 3,* 1–15. doi: 10.1111/j.1467-9507.1994.tb00020.x

Repetti, R. L., Wang, S.-W., & Saxbe, D. (2009). Bringing it all back home: How outside stressors shape families' everyday lives. *Current Directions in Psychological Science, 18,* 106–111. doi: 10.1111/j.1467-8721.2009.01618.x

Rhoades, G. K., Stanley, S. M., & Markman, H. J. (2009). The pre-engagement cohabitation effect: A replication and extension of previous findings. *Journal of Family Psychology, 23,* 107–111. doi: 10.1037/a0014358

Ribner, D. S., & Rosenbaum, T. Y. (2005). Evaluation and treatment of unconsummated marriages among Orthodox Jewish couples. *Journal of Sex & Marital Therapy, 31,* 341–353. doi: 10.1080/00926230590950244

Rice, R. E., & Love, G. (1987). Electronic emotion: Socioemotional content in a computer-mediated communication network. *Communication Research, 14,* 85–108. doi: 10.1177/009365087014001005

Rick, S. I., Small, D. A., & Finkel, E. J. (2011). Fatal (fiscal) attraction: Spendthrifts and tightwads in marriage. *Journal of Marketing Research, 48,* 228–237. doi: 10.1509/jmkr.48.2.228

Rieger, G., Chivers, M. L., & Bailey, J. M. (2005). Sexual arousal patterns of bisexual men. *Psychological Science, 16,* 579–584. doi: 10.1111/j.1467-9280.2005.01578.x

Rith, K. A., & Diamond, L. M. (2013). Same-sex relationships. In M. A. Fine & F. D. Fincham (Eds.), *Handbook of family theories: A content-based approach* (pp. 123–144). New York: Routledge.

Robertson, C. N. (1970). *Oneida Community: An autobiography, 1851-1876.* Syracuse, NY: Syracuse University Press.

Robinson, A. L., & Chandek, M. S. (2000). The domestic violence arrest decision: Examining demographic, attitudinal, and situational variables. *Crime & Delinquency, 46,* 18–37. doi: 10.1177/0011128700046001002

Rogge, R. D., & Bradbury, T. N. (1999). Till violence does us part: The differing roles of communication and aggression in predicting adverse marital outcomes. *Journal of Consulting and Clinical Psychology, 67,* 340–351. doi: 10.1037/0022-006X.67.3.340

Rogge, R. D., Cobb, R. J., Lawrence, E., Johnson, M. D., & Bradbury, T. N. (2013). Is skills training necessary for the primary prevention of marital distress and dissolution? A 3-year experimental study of three interventions. *Journal of Consulting and Clinical Psychology, 81,* 949–961. doi: 10.1037/a0034209

Rogge, R. D., Cobb, R. M., Johnson, M. D., Lawrence, E., & Bradbury, T. N. (2002). The CARE program: A preventative approach to marital intervention. In A. S. Gurman & N. S. Jacobson (Eds.), *Clinical handbook of couple therapy* (3rd ed., pp. 420–435). New York: Guilford.

Roisman, G. I., Clausell, E., Holland, A., Fortuna, K., & Elieff, C. (2008). Adult romantic relationships as contexts of human development: A multimethod comparison of same-sex couples with opposite-sex dating, engaged, and married dyads. *Developmental Psychology, 44*, 91–101. doi: 10.1037/0012-1649.44.1.91

Rose, S. (2012). Bobmshell: Corruption uncovered in Regnerus anti-gay study scandal. *The New Civil Rights Movement*. Retrieved March 27, 2014, from http://thenewcivilrightsmovement.com/bombshell-corruption-uncovered-in-regnerus-anti-gay-study-scandal/legal-issues/2012/08/29/47670

Rosenbaum, T. Y. (2009). Applying theories of social exchange and symbolic interaction in the treatment of unconsummated marriage/relationship. *Sexual and Relationship Therapy, 24*, 38–46. doi: 10.1080/14681990902718096

Rule, N. O., & Ambady, N. (2010). Democrats and Republicans can be differentiated from their faces. *PLoS ONE, 5*, e8733. doi: 10.1371/journal.pone.0008733

Rusbult, C. E. (1980). Commitment and satisfaction in romantic associations: A test of the investment model. *Journal of Experimental Social Psychology, 16*, 172–186. doi: 10.1016/0022-1031(80)90007-4

Ryan, R. M., Tolani, N., & Brooks-Gunn, J. (2009). Relationship trajectories, parenting stress, and unwed mothers' transition to a new baby. *Parenting, 9*, 160–177. doi: 10.1080/15295190802656844

Sanders, K. M. (2010). *Marital satisfaction Across the transition to parenthood*. Master's thesis, University of Nebraska, Lincoln, NE. Retrieved April 22, 2014, from http://digitalcommons.unl.edu/sociologydiss/2

Sanders, S. A., & Reinisch, J. (1999). Would you say you "had sex" if ...? *Journal of the American Medical Association, 281*, 275–277. doi: 10.1001/jama.281.3.275

Santorum, R. (2005). *It takes a family: Conservatism and the common good*. Wilmington, DE: ISI Books.

Sarason, B. R., Sarason, I. G., & Gurung, R. A. R. (1997). Close personal relationships and health outcomes: A key to the role of social support. In S. Duck (Ed.), *Handbook of personal relationships: Theory, research and interventions* (2nd ed., pp. 547–573). Hoboken, NJ: John Wiley & Sons.

Saroja, K., & Surendra, H. S. (1991). A study of postgraduate students' endogamous preference in mate selection. *Indian Journal of Behaviour, 15*, 1–13.

Sassler, S. (2004). The process of entering into cohabiting unions. *Journal of Marriage and Family, 66*, 491–505. doi: 10.1111/j.1741-3737.2004.00033.x

Sassler, S., Cunningham, A., & Lichter, D. T. (2009). Intergenerational patterns of union formation and relationship quality. *Journal of Family Issues, 30*, 757–786. doi: 10.1177/0192513x09331580

Savin-Williams, R. C. (2005). *The new gay teenager*. Cambridge, MA: Harvard University Press.

Savin-Williams, R. C. (2008). Then and now: Recruitment, definition, diversity, and positive attributes of same-sex populations. *Developmental Psychology, 44*, 135–138. doi: 10.1037/0012-1649.44.1.135

Saxbe, D. E., Repetti, R. L., & Nishina, A. (2008). Marital satisfaction, recovery from work, and diurnal cortisol among men and women. *Health Psychology, 27*, 15–25. doi: 10.1037/0278-6133.27.1.15

Schaefer, J. A., & Moos, R. H. (1992). Life crises and personal growth. In B. N. Carpenter (Ed.), *Personal coping: Theory, research, and application* (pp. 149–170). Westport, CT: Praeger.

Scheibehenne, B., Greifeneder, R., & Todd, P. M. (2010). Can there ever be too many options? A meta-analytic review of choice overload. *Journal of Consumer Research, 37,* 409–425. doi: 10.1086/651235

Schick, V. R., Rima, B. N., & Calabrese, S. K. (2011). Evulvalution: The portrayal of women's external genitalia and physique across time and the current Barbie doll ideals. *The Journal of Sex Research, 48,* 74–81. doi: 10.1080/00224490903308404

Schmeer, K. K. (2011). The child health disadvantage of parental cohabitation. *Journal of Marriage and Family, 73,* 181–193. doi: 10.1111/j.1741-3737.2010.00797.x

Schneider, D. (2011). Wealth and the marital divide. *American Journal of Sociology, 117,* 627–667. doi: 10.1086/661594

Schoebi, D., Way, B. M., Karney, B. R., & Bradbury, T. N. (2012). Genetic moderation of sensitivity to positive and negative affect in marriage. *Emotion, 12,* 208–212. doi: 10.1037/a0026067

Schreurs, K. M. G., & Buunk, B. P. (1996). Closeness, autonomy, equity, and relationship satisfaction in lesbian couples. *Psychology of Women Quarterly, 20,* 577–592. doi: 10.1111/j.1471-6402.1996.tb00323.x

Schroder, M., & Carroll, R. A. (1999). New women: Sexological outcomes of male-to-female gender reassignment surgery. *Journal of Sex Education & Therapy, 24,* 137–146.

Schulz, M. S., Cowan, P. A., Cowan, C. P., & Brennan, R. T. (2004). Coming home upset: Gender, marital satisfaction, and the daily spillover of workday experience into couple interactions. *Journal of Family Psychology, 18,* 250–263. doi: 10.1037/0893-3200.18.1.250

Seccombe, K. (2000). Families in poverty in the 1990s: Trends, causes, consequences, and lessons learned. *Journal of Marriage and the Family, 62,* 1094–1113. doi: 10.1111/j.1741-3737.2000.01094.x

Second Vatican Council. (1966). Pastoral Constitution on the Church in the World of Today (Vol. no. 50: AAS 58 (1966), 1070-1072 [TPS XI, 292-293]). Vatican City: Vatican Printing House.

Seiffge-Krenke, I. (2003). Testing theories of romantic development from adolescence to young adulthood: Evidence of a developmental sequence. *International Journal of Behavioral Development, 27,* 519–531. doi: 10.1080/01650250344000145

Senior, J. (2014). *All joy and no fun: The paradox of modern parenthood.* New York: Ecco.

Shadish, W. R., & Baldwin, S. A. (2005). Effects of behavioral marital therapy: A meta-analysis of randomized controlled trials. *Journal of Consulting and Clinical Psychology, 73,* 6–14. doi: 10.1037/0022-006x.73.1.6

Shapiro, A. F., Gottman, J. M., & Carrére, S. (2000). The baby and the marriage: Identifying factors that buffer against decline in marital satisfaction after the first baby arrives. *Journal of Family Psychology, 14*, 59–70. doi: 10.1037/0893-3200.14.1.59

Shaver, P. R., Papalia, D., Clark, C. L., & Koski, L. R. (1996). Androgyny and attachment security: Two related models of optimal personality. *Personality and Social Psychology Bulletin, 22*, 582–597. doi: 10.1177/0146167296226004

Shaw, G. B. (1920). *Getting married*: New York: Brentano's.

Shelley, M. W. (1831). *Frankenstein, or, The modern Prometheus* (3rd ed., revised, corrected, and illustrated with a new introduction by the author). London: Henry Colburn and Richard Bentley.

Sherkat, D. E. (2012). The editorial process and politicized scholarship: Monday morning editorial quarterbacking and a call for scientific vigilance. *Social Science Research, 41*, 1346–1349. doi: 10.1016/j.ssresearch.2012.08.007

Sherman, L., & Harris, H. (2013). Increased homicide victimization of suspects arrested for domestic assault: A 23-year follow-up of the Milwaukee Domestic Violence Experiment (MilDVE). *Journal of Experimental Criminology, 9*, 491–514. doi: 10.1007/s11292-013-9193-0

Simon, H. A. (1956). Rational choice and the structure of the environment. *Psychological Review, 63*, 129–138. doi: 10.1037/h0042769

Simpson, J. A., Rholes, W. S., & Nelligan, J. S. (1992). Support seeking and support giving within couples in an anxiety-provoking situation: The role of attachment styles. *Journal of Personality and Social Psychology, 62*, 434–446. doi: 10.1037/0022-3514.62.3.434

Skinner, B. F. (1974). *About behaviorism*. New York: Knopf.

Slatcher, R. B., Vazire, S., & Pennebaker, J. W. (2008). Am "I" more important than "we"? Couples' word use in instant messages. *Personal Relationships, 15*, 407–424. doi: 10.1111/j.1475-6811.2008.00207.x

Slep, A. M. S., & O'Leary, S. G. (2005). Parent and partner violence in families with young children: Rates, patterns, and connections. *Journal of Consulting and Clinical Psychology, 73*, 435–444. doi: 10.1037/0022-006x.73.3.435

Smith, D. A., Vivian, D., & O'Leary, K. D. (1990). Longitudinal prediction of marital discord from premarital expressions of affect. *Journal of Consulting and Clinical Psychology, 58*, 790–798. doi: 10.1037/0022-006X.58.6.790

Smock, P. J., Manning, W. D., & Gupta, S. (1999). The effect of marriage and divorce on women's economic well-being. *American Sociological Review, 64*, 794–812. doi: 10.2307/2657403

Snyder, D. K., & Wills, R. M. (1989). Behavioral versus insight-oriented marital therapy: Effects on individual and interspousal functioning. *Journal of Consulting and Clinical Psychology, 57*, 39–46. doi: 10.1037/0022-006X.57.1.39

Snyder, D. K., Wills, R. M., & Grady-Fletcher, A. (1991a). Long-term effectiveness of behavioral versus insight-oriented marital therapy: A 4-year follow-up study. *Journal of Consulting and Clinical Psychology, 59*, 138–131. doi: 10.1037/0022-006X.59.1.138

Snyder, D. K., Wills, R. M., & Grady-Fletcher, A. (1991b). Risks and challenges of long-term psychotherapy outcome research: Reply to Jacobson. *Journal of Consulting and Clinical Psychology, 59*, 146–149. doi: 10.1037/0022-006X.59.1.146

Solomon, S. E., Rothblum, E. D., & Balsam, K. F. (2005). Money, housework, sex, and conflict: Same-sex couples in civil unions, those not in civil unions, and heterosexual married siblings. *Sex Roles, 52,* 561–575. doi: 10.1007/s11199-005-3725-7

Soons, J. P. M., & Kalmijn, M. (2009). Is marriage more than cohabitation? Well-being differences in 30 European countries. *Journal of Marriage and Family, 71,* 1141–1157. doi: 10.1111/j.1741-3737.2009.00660.x

South, S. C., Turkheimer, E., & Oltmanns, T. F. (2008). Personality disorder symptoms and marital functioning. *Journal of Consulting and Clinical Psychology, 76,* 769–780. doi: 10.1037/a0013346

South, S. J., & Lloyd, K. M. (1992). Marriage opportunities and family formation: Further implications of imbalanced sex ratios. *Journal of Marriage and the Family, 54,* 440–451. doi: 10.2307/353075

Sprecher, S., & Cate, R. M. (2004). Sexual satisfaction and sexual expression as predictors of relationship satisfaction and stability. In J. H. Harvey, A. Wenzel, & S. Sprecher (Eds.), *The handbook of sexuality in close relationships* (pp. 235–256). Mahwah, NJ: Lawrence Erlbaum.

Stafford, L., Kline, S. L., & Rankin, C. T. (2004). Married individuals, cohabiters, and cohabiters who marry: A longitudinal study of relational and individual well-being. *Journal of Social and Personal Relationships, 21,* 231–248. doi: 10.1177/0265407504041385

Stanley, S. M., Allen, E. S., Markman, H. J., Rhoades, G. K., & Prentice, D. L. (2010). Decreasing divorce in U.S. army couples: Results from a randomized controlled trial using PREP for strong bonds. *Journal of Couple & Relationship Therapy, 9,* 149–160. doi: 10.1080/15332691003694901

Stanley, S. M., Allen, E. S., Markman, H. J., Saiz, C. C., Bloomstrom, G., Thomas, R., ... Bailey, A. E. (2005). Dissemination and evaluation of marriage education in the Army. *Family Process, 44,* 187–201. doi: 10.1111/j.1545-5300.2005.00053.x

Stanley, S. M., & Markman, H. J. (1992). Assessing commitment in personal relationships. *Journal of Marriage and the Family, 54,* 595–608. doi: 10.2307/353245

Stanley, S. M., Markman, H. J., Prado, L. M., Olmos Gallo, P. A., Tonelli, L., St Peters, M., ... Whitton, S. W. (2001). Community-based premarital prevention: Clergy and lay leaders on the front lines. *Family Relations, 50,* 67–76. doi: 10.1111/j.1741-3729.2001.00067.x

Stanley, S. M., Rhoades, G. K., Amato, P. R., Markman, H. J., & Johnson, C. A. (2010). The timing of cohabitation and engagement: Impact on first and second marriages. *Journal of Marriage and Family, 72,* 906–918. doi: 10.1111/j.1741-3737.2010.00738.x

Stanley, S. M., Rhoades, G. K., & Markman, H. J. (2006). Sliding versus deciding: Inertia and the premarital cohabitation effect. *Family Relations, 55,* 499–509. doi: 10.1111/j.1741-3729.2006.00418.x

Stanley, S. M., Whitton, S. W., & Markman, H. J. (2004). Maybe I do: Interpersonal commitment and premarital or nonmarital cohabitation. *Journal of Family Issues, 25,* 496–519. doi: 10.1177/0192513x03257797

Stepp, L. S. (2007). *Unhooked: How young women pursue sex, delay love and lose at both*. New York: Penguin.

Stevenson, R. L. (1908). Talk and talkers II. In R. L. Stevenson (Ed.), Memories and portraits (pp. 169–190). New York: Charles Scribner's Sons.

Stewart, S., Stinnett, H., & Rosenfeld, L. B. (2000). Sex differences in desired characteristics of short-term and long-term relationship partners. *Journal of Social and Personal Relationships*, *17*, 843–853. doi: 10.1177/0265407500176008

Stith, S., Green, N., Smith, D., & Ward, D. (2008). Marital satisfaction and marital discord as risk markers for intimate partner violence: A meta-analytic review. *Journal of Family Violence*, *23*, 149–160. doi: 10.1007/s10896-007-9137-4

Story, L. B., & Bradbury, T. N. (2004). Understanding marriage and stress: Essential questions and challenges. *Clinical Psychology Review*, *23*, 1139–1162. doi: 10.1016/j.cpr.2003.10.002

Story, L. B., & Repetti, R. L. (2006). Daily occupational stressors and marital behavior. *Journal of Family Psychology*, *20*, 690–700. doi: 10.1037/0893-3200.20.4.690

Straus, M. A. (1979). Measuring intrafamily conflict and violence: The conflict tactics (CT) scales. *Journal of Marriage and the Family*, *41*, 75–88. doi: 10.2307/351733

Straus, M. A., & Gelles, R. J. (1986). Societal change and change in family violence from 1975 to 1985 as revealed by two national surveys. *Journal of Marriage and the Family*, *48*, 465–479. doi: 10.2307/352033

Strauss, N. (2007). *Rules of the game* (1st ed.). New York: Harper.

Stuart, R. B. (1969). Operant-interpersonal treatment for marital discord. *Journal of Consulting and Clinical Psychology*, *33*, 675–682. doi: 10.1037/h0028475

Stuart, R. B. (1980). *Helping couples change: A social learning approach to marital therapy*. New York: Guilford.

Suh, E., Diener, E., & Fujita, F. (1996). Events and subjective well-being: Only recent events matter. *Journal of Personality and Social Psychology*, *70*, 1091–1102. doi: 10.1037/0022-3514.70.5.1091

Sullivan, K. T., & Davila, J. (Eds.). (2010). *Support processes in intimate relationships*. New York: Oxford University Press.

Sullivan, K. T., Pasch, L. A., Johnson, M. D., & Bradbury, T. N. (2010). Social support, problem solving, and the longitudinal course of newlywed marriage. *Journal of Personality and Social Psychology*, *98*, 631–644. doi: 10.1037/a0017578

Suschinsky, K. D., Lalumière, M. L., & Chivers, M. L. (2009). Sex differences in patterns of genital sexual arousal: Measurement artifacts or true phenomena? *Archives of Sexual Behavior*, *38*, 559–573. doi: 10.1007/s10508-008-9339-8

Swan, S. C., & Snow, D. L. (2002). A typology of women's use of violence in intimate relationships. *Violence Against Women*, *8*, 286–319. doi: 10.1177/10778010222183071

Swarns, R. L. (2012, October 25). Seeking love? Find strength in numbers. *The New York Times*, p. E1.

Tach, L., & Halpern-Meekin, S. (2009). How does premarital cohabitation affect trajectories of marital quality? *Journal of Marriage and Family, 71*, 298–317. doi: 10.1111/j.1741-3737.2009.00600.x

Tambling, R. B. (2012). A literature review of therapeutic expectancy effects. *Contemporary Family Therapy: An International Journal, 34*, 402–415. doi: 10.1007/s10591-012-9201-y

Tambling, R. B., & Johnson, L. N. (2010). Client expectations about couple therapy. *American Journal of Family Therapy, 38*, 322–333. doi: 10.1080/01926187.2010.493465

Tannen, D. (1990). *You just don't understand: Women and men in conversation.* New York: Ballantine.

Taylor, K. (2013). She can play that game, too. *The New York Times*, pp. 1, 6, & 7.

Taylor, S. E., & Brown, J. D. (1988). Illusion and well-being: A social psychological perspective on mental health. *Psychological Bulletin, 103*, 193–210. doi: 10.1037/0033-2909.103.2.193

Terman, L. M. (1938). *Psychological factors in marital happiness.* New York: McGraw-Hill.

Tesch, B., Bekerian, D., English, P., & Harrington, E. (2010). Same-sex domestic violence: Why victims are more at risk. *International Journal of Police Science & Management, 12*, 526–535. doi: 10.1350/ijps.2010.12.4.204

Testa, M., Astone, N. M., Krogh, M., & Neckerman, K. M. (1993). Employment and marriage among inner-city fathers. In W. J. Wilson (Ed.), *The ghetto underclass: Social science perspectives* (updated ed., pp. 96–108). Thousand Oaks, CA: Sage.

Thibaut, J. W., & Kelley, H. H. (1959). *The social psychology of groups.* New York: Wiley.

Thomas, J. R., & French, K. E. (1985). Gender differences across age in motor performance: A meta-analysis. *Psychological Bulletin, 98*, 260–282. doi: 10.1037/0033-2909.98.2.260

Thorndike, E. L. (1914). *Educational psychology* (Vol. 3). New York: Teachers College, Columbia University.

Thornhill, R., & Gangestad, S. W. (2008). *The evolutionary biology of human female sexuality.* New York: Oxford University Press.

Thornton, A., Axinn, W. G., & Hill, D. H. (1992). Reciprocal effects of religiosity, cohabitation, and marriage. *American Journal of Sociology, 98*, 628–651. doi: 10.1086/230051

Thornton, A., & Young-DeMarco, L. (2001). Four decades of trends in attitudes toward family issues in the United States: The 1960s through the 1990s. *Journal of Marriage and Family, 63*, 1009–1037. doi: 10.1111/j.1741-3737.2001.01009.x

Till, A., & Freedman, E. M. (1978). Complementarity versus similarity of traits operating in the choice of marriage and dating partners. *The Journal of Social Psychology, 105*, 147–148.

Trail, T. E., Goff, P. A., Bradbury, T. N., & Karney, B. R. (2012). The costs of racism for marriage: How racial discrimination hurts, and ethnic identity protects, newlywed marriages among Latinos. *Personality and Social Psychology Bulletin, 38*, 454–465. doi: 10.1177/0146167211429450

Trail, T. E., & Karney, B. R. (2012). What's (not) wrong with low-income marriages. *Journal of Marriage and Family, 74*, 413–427. doi: 10.1111/j.1741-3737.2012.00977.x

Trillingsgaard, T., Baucom, K. J. W., Heyman, R. E., & Elklit, A. (2012). Relationship interventions during the transition to parenthood: Issues of timing and efficacy. *Family Relations, 61*, 770–783. doi: 10.1037/0022-006x.56.2.210.

Tversky, A. (1972). Elimination by aspects: A theory of choice. *Psychological Review, 79*, 281–299. doi: 10.1037/h0032955

Tversky, A., & Kahneman, D. (1974). Judgment under uncertainty: Heuristics and biases. *Science, 185*, 1124–1131. doi: 10.2307/1738360

Twenge, J. M., Campbell, W. K., & Foster, C. A. (2003). Parenthood and marital satisfaction: A meta-analytic review. *Journal of Marriage and Family, 65*, 574–583. doi: 10.1111/j.1741-3737.2003.00574.x

U.S. Census Bureau. (2013a). *America's families and living arrangements: 2013: Unmarried couples* (UC table series). Retrieved January 14, 2014, from http://www.census.gov/hhes/families/data/cps2013UC.html

U.S. Census Bureau. (2013b). *Percent childless and births per 1,000 women in the last 12 months: Selected years, 1976 to 2010.* Washington, DC.

Uchino, B. N., Cacioppo, J. T., & Kiecolt-Glaser, J. K. (1996). The relationship between social support and physiological processes: A review with emphasis on underlying mechanisms and implications for health. *Psychological Bulletin, 119*, 488–531. doi: 10.1037/0033-2909.119.3.488

United States v. Windsor, 133 S.Ct. 2675 (2012).

Upchurch, D. M., Levy-Storms, L., Sucoff, C. A., & Aneshensel, C. S. (1998). Gender and ethnic differences in the timing of first sexual intercourse. *Family Planning Perspectives, 30*, 121–127. doi: 10.2307/2991625

Urquhart, V. V. (2014). What do we really mean when we say women are sexually "fluid"? *Slate.* Retrieved October 19, 2014, from http://www.slate.com/blogs/outward/2014/09/26/why_the_sexual_fluidity_trope_is_sexism_in_disguise.html

Valenti, J. (2009). *The purity myth: How America's obsession with virginity is hurting young women*: Berkeley, CA: Seal Press.

VanLaningham, J., Johnson, D. R., & Amato, P. (2001). Marital happiness, marital duration, and the U-shaped curve: Evidence from a five-wave panel study. *Social Forces, 79*, 1313–1341. doi: 10.2307/2675474

Van Lankveld, J. J. D. M., ter Kuile, M. M., de Groot, H. E., Melles, R., Nefs, J., & Zandbergen, M. (2006). Cognitive-behavioral therapy for women with life-long vaginismus: A randomized waiting-list controlled trial of efficacy. *Journal of Consulting and Clinical Psychology, 74*, 168–178. doi: 10.1037/0022-006x.74.1.168

Van Parys, A. S., Verhamme, A., Temmerman, M., & Verstraelen, H. (2014). Intimate partner violence and pregnancy: A systematic review of interventions. *PLoS ONE, 9*. doi: 10.1371/journal.pone.0085084 van Widenfelt, B., Hosman, C., Schaap, C., & van der Staak, C. (1996). The prevention of relationship distress for couples at risk: A controlled evaluation with nine-month and two-year follow-ups. *Family Relations, 45,* 156–165. doi: 10.2307/585286

Wainright, J. L., & Patterson, C. J. (2006). Delinquency, victimization, and substance use among adolescents with female same-sex parents. *Journal of Family Psychology, 20,* 526–530. doi: 10.1037/0893-3200.20.3.526

Wainright, J. L., & Patterson, C. J. (2008). Peer relations among adolescents with female same-sex parents. *Developmental Psychology, 44,* 117–126. doi: 10.1037/0012-1649.44.1.117

Waite, L. J., & Gallagher, M. (2000). *The case for marriage.* New York: Doubleday.

Wallen, K. (1982). Influence of female hormonal state on rhesus sexual behavior varies with space for social interaction. *Science, 217,* 375–376. doi: 10.1126/science.7201164

Wallen, K. (1995). The evolution of female sexual desire. In P. R. Abramson & S. D. Pinkerton (Eds.), *Sexual nature, sexual culture* (pp. 57–79). Chicago: University of Chicago Press.

Walsh, D. G., & Hewitt, J. (1985). Giving men the come-on: Effect of eye contact and smiling in a bar environment. *Perceptual and Motor Skills, 61,* 873–874. doi: 10.2466/pms.1985.61.3.873

Walster, E., Walster, G. W., & Berscheid, E. (1971). The efficacy of playing hard-to-get. *The Journal of Experimental Education, 39,* 73–77. doi: 10.2307/20157200

Walster, E., Walster, G. W., Piliavin, J., & Schmidt, L. (1973). "Playing hard to get": Understanding an exclusive phenomenon. *Journal of Personality and Social Psychology, 26,* 113–121. doi: 10.1037/h0034234

Walters, A. S., & Curran, M.-C. (1996). "Excuse me, sir? May I help you and your boyfriend?": Salespersons' differential treatment of homosexual and straight customers. *Journal of Homosexuality, 31,* 135–152. doi: 10.1300/J082v31n01_08

Walther, J. B. (1992). Interpersonal effects in computer-mediated interaction: A relational perspective. *Communication Research, 19,* 52–90. doi: 10.1177/009365092019001003

Walther, J. B. (1995). Relational aspects of computer-mediated communication: Experimental observations over time. *Organization Science, 6,* 186–203. doi: 10.1287/orsc.6.2.186

Walther, J. B. (1996). Computer-mediated communication: Impersonal, interpersonal, and hyperpersonal interaction. *Communication Research, 23,* 3–43. doi: 10.1177/009365096023001001

Walther, J. B., Anderson, J. F., & Park, D. W. (1994). Interpersonal effects in computer-mediated interaction: A meta-analysis of social and antisocial communication. *Communication Research, 21,* 460–487. doi: 10.1177/009365094021004002

Walther, J. B., Loh, T., & Granka, L. (2005). Let me count the ways: The interchange of verbal and nonverbal cues in computer-mediated and face-to-face affinity. *Journal of Language and Social Psychology, 24,* 36–65. doi: 10.1177/0261927X04273036

Ward, R. A., & Spitze, G. D. (2004). Marital implications of parent–adult child coresidence: A longitudinal view. *The Journals of Gerontology: Series B: Psychological Sciences and Social Sciences, 59B,* S2–S8. doi: 10.1093/geronb/59.1.S2

Washburn, C., & Christensen, D. (2008). Financial harmony: A key component of successful marriage relationship. *The Forum for Family and Consumer Issues, 13*(1). Retrieved November 2, 2014, from http://ncsu.edu/ffci/publications/2008/v13-n1-2008-spring/Washburn-Christensen.php

Wathen, C., & MacMillan, H. L. (2003). Interventions for violence against women: Scientific review. *JAMA, 289,* 589–600. doi: 10.1001/jama.289.5.589

Watson, D., & Clark, L. A. (1984). Negative affectivity: The disposition to experience aversive emotional states. *Psychological Bulletin, 96,* 465–490. doi: 10.1037/0033-2909.96.3.465

Watson, D., Klohnen, E. C., Casillas, A., Nus Simms, E., Haig, J., & Berry, D. S. (2004). Match makers and deal breakers: Analyses of assortative mating in newlywed couples. *Journal of Personality, 72,* 1029–1068. doi: 10.1111/j.0022-3506.2004.00289.x

Watson, J. B. (1913). Psychology as the behaviorist views it. *Psychological Review, 20,* 158–177. doi: 10.1037/h0074428

Weber, J. P. (2013). *Having sex, wanting intimacy: Why women settle for one-sided relationships.* Lanham, MD: Rowman & Littlefield.

Wedderburn, R. (1549/1979). *The complaynt of Scotland.* Edinburgh: Scottish Text Society. (Reprinted from: 1st ed.).

Weinstock, H., Berman, S., & Cates, W. (2004). Sexually transmitted diseases among American youth: Incidence and prevalence estimates, 2000. *Perspectives on Sexual & Reproductive Health, 36,* 6–10.

Weiss, R. L., & Heyman, R. E. (1990). Observation of marital interaction. In F. D. Fincham & T. N. Bradbury (Eds.), *The psychology of marriage: Basic issues and applications* (pp. 87–117). New York: Guilford.

Weiss, R. L., Hops, H., & Patterson, G. R. (1973). A framework for conceptualizing marital conflict: A technology for altering it, some data for evaluating it. In L. A. Hamerlynck, L. C. Handy, & E. J. Mash (Eds.), *Behavior change: Methodology, concepts, and practice* (pp. 309–342). Champaign, IL: Research Press.

Weisskirch, R. S., & Delevi, R. (2012). Its ovr b/n u n me: Technology use, attachment styles, and gender roles in relationship dissolution. *Cyberpsychology, Behavior, and Social Networking, 15,* 486–490. doi: 10.1089/cyber.2012.0169

Westerman, D. L. (2008). Relative fluency and illusions of recognition memory. *Psychonomic Bulletin & Review, 15,* 1196–1200. doi: 10.3758/PBR.15.6.1196

Whisman, M. A. (2007). Marital distress and DSM-IV psychiatric disorders in a population-based national survey. *Journal of Abnormal Psychology, 116,* 638–643. doi: 10.1037/0021-843X.116.3.638

Whisman, M. A., Uebelacker, L. A., & Weinstock, L. M. (2004). Psychopathology and marital satisfaction: The importance of evaluating both partners. *Journal of Consulting and Clinical Psychology*, 72, 830–838. doi: 10.1037/0022-006X.72.5.830

White, L. K., & Booth, A. (1985). The transition to parenthood and marital quality. *Journal of Family Issues*, 6, 435–449. doi: 10.1177/019251385006004003

White, L. K., & Edwards, J. N. (1990). Emptying the nest and parental well-being: An analysis of national panel data. *American Sociological Review*, 55, 235–242. doi: 10.2307/2095629

White, S. G., & Hatcher, C. (1984). Couple complementarity and similarity: A review of the literature. *American Journal of Family Therapy*, 12, 15–25. doi: 10.1080/01926188408250155

Whitehead, B. D. (1997). *The divorce culture: Rethinking our commitments to marriage and family*. New York: Alfred A. Knopf.

Whitty, M. T., & Carr, A. (2006). *Cyberspace romance: The psychology of online relationships*. Basingstoke: Palgrave Macmillan

Wichstrøm, L., & Hegna, K. (2003). Sexual orientation and suicide attempt: A longitudinal study of the general Norwegian adolescent population. *Journal of Abnormal Psychology*, 112, 144–151. doi: 10.1037/0021-843x.112.1.144

Williams, D. E., & D'Alessandro, J. D. (1994). A comparison of three measures of androgyny and their relationship to psychological adjustment. *Journal of Social Behavior & Personality*, 9, 469–480.

Williamson, H. C., Karney, B. R., & Bradbury, T. N. (2013). Financial strain and stressful events predict newlyweds' negative communication independent of relationship satisfaction. *Journal of Family Psychology*, 27, 65–75. doi: 10.1037/a0031104

Williamson, H. C., Rogge, R. D., Cobb, R. J., Johnson, M. D., Lawrence, E., & Bradbury, T. N. (in press). Risk moderates the outcome of relationship education: A randomized controlled trial. *Journal of Consulting & Clinical Psychology*, 83, 617–269. doi: 10.1037/a0038621

Wilson, J. Q. (2002). *The marriage problem: How our culture has weakened families*. New York: HarperCollins.

Wilson, W. J. (1987). *The truly disadvantaged: The inner city, the underclass, and public policy*. Chicago: University of Chicago Press.

Wilson, W. J. (2009). *More than just race: Being Black and poor in the inner city*. New York: Norton.

Witchel, A. (2001). "Rules" books sell millions, but Mr. Right takes a hike. *The New York Times*. Retrieved 16 September, 2014, from http://www.nytimes.com/2001/05/06/living/06COUN.html?smid=pl-share

Witherspoon Institute. (2012). Family, marriage, and democracy [program summary].RetrievedMarch13,2014,fromhttp://winst.org/programs/family-marriage-and-democracy/

Wood, R. G., Moore, Q., Clarkwest, A., & Killewald, A. (2014). The long-term effects of Building Strong Families: A program for unmarried parents. *Journal of Marriage and Family*, 76, 446–463. doi: 10.1111/jomf.12094

Wood, R. G., Moore, Q., Clarkwest, A., Killewald, A., & Monahan, S. (2012). *The long-term effects of Building Strong Families: A relationship skills education program for unmarried parents.* Princeton, NJ: Mathematica Policy Research, Inc.

Woody, E. Z., & Costanzo, P. R. (1990). Does marital agony precede marital ecstasy? A comment on Gottman and Krokoff's "Marital interaction and satisfaction: A longitudinal view." *Journal of Consulting and Clinical Psychology, 58,* 499–501. doi: 10.1037/0022-006X.58.4.499

Woolley, H. T. (1914). The psychology of sex. *Psychological Bulletin, 11,* 353–379. doi: 10.1037/h0070064

World Bank. (2014). Fertility rate, total (births per woman) [dataset]. Retrieved April 23, 2014, from http://data.worldbank.org/indicator/SP.DYN.TFRT.IN/

Wright, J. D. (2012). Introductory remarks. *Social Science Research, 41,* 1339–1345. doi: 10.1016/j.ssresearch.2012.08.006

Wu, P.-L., & Chiou, W.-B. (2009). More options lead to more searching and worse choices in finding partners for romantic relationships online: An experimental study. *CyberPsychology & Behavior, 12,* 315–318. doi: 10.1089/cpb.2008.0182

Yang, M.-L., & Chiou, W.-B. (2010). Looking online for the best romantic partner reduces decision quality: The moderating role of choice-making strategies. *Cyberpsychology, Behavior and Social Networking, 13,* 207–210. doi: 10.1089/cpb.2009.0208

Yuan, J. (2013). The state of seduction: A roundtable of pickup artists, some of whom would definitely not date each other. *New York.* Retrieved 16 September, 2014, from http://nymag.com/news/features/sex/pickup-artists-roundtable-2013-7/

Zajonc, R. B. (1968). Attitudinal effects of mere exposure. *Journal of Personality and Social Psychology, 9*(2), 1–27. doi: 10.1037/h0025848

Zimmer-Gembeck, M. J., Siebenbruner, J., & Collins, W. A. (2001). Diverse aspects of dating: Associations with psychosocial functioning from early to middle adolescence. *Journal of Adolescence, 24,* 313–336. doi: 10.1006/jado.2001.0410

Zimmer-Gembeck, M. J., Siebenbruner, J., & Collins, W. A. (2004). A prospective study of intraindividual and peer influences on adolescents' heterosexual romantic and sexual behavior. *Archives of Sexual Behavior, 33,* 381–394. doi: 10.1023/B:ASEB.0000028891.16654.2c

Zoroya, G. (2013, July 11). Special forces' marriages on shaky ground, survey shows. *USA Today.* Retrieved November 2, 2014, from http://www.usatoday.com/story/news/nation/2013/07/09/marriages-military-families-elite-troops-stress/2432243/

AUTHOR INDEX

Abbey, A., 36
Abma, J. C., 97
Agnew, C. R., 58
Agyei, Y., 81
Alderson, D. P., 106
Alexander, M. G., 9, 148
Allen, E. S., 104, 105
Allen, G., 163, 164
Allison, C., 148
Al Sughayir, M. A., 22, 24
Amato, P. R., 96, 106, 122, 170–172
Ambady, N., 54
Ambrosino, B., 73
American Psychiatric Association,
    68, 85
American Sociological Association, 89
Amsel, R., 22, 35
Anderson, J. F., 61
Anderson, N. H., 30
Andersson, G., 84
Andover, M. S., 165
Andrews, S. L., 37
Aneshensel, C. S., 163
Anglin, K., 154
Anisko, J. J., 10
Antheunis, M. L., 61, 62

Antill, J. K., 46
Archer, J., 148
Ariely, D., 52
Armstrong, E. A., 10, 16–19
Aronson, E., 41
Asch, S. E., 65
Asher, E. R., 185
Astone, N. M., 140
Atkins, D. C., 160
Aube, J., 45
Avishai, O., 106
Axinn, W. G., 99
Ayduk, O., 165

Bachman, J. G., 95
Back, K., 41
Bailey, A. E., 104
Bailey, J. M., 9, 76, 78, 81
Baldwin, S. A., 105, 159
Balsam, K. F., 82, 83
Bandura, A., 103, 109, 157
Blankenhorn, D., 105
Barber, J. S., 99
Barelds, D. P. H., 42
Bargh, J. A., 62, 64
Bar-Kalifa, E., 138

Great Myths of Intimate Relationships: Dating, Sex, and Marriage,
First Edition. Matthew D. Johnson.
© 2016 John Wiley & Sons, Inc. Published 2016 by John Wiley & Sons, Inc.

Bunde, M., 111, 120
Burchinal, M., 131
Burdick, C. A., 37
Burke, L. K., 84
Burnett, A. L., 8
Buss, D. M., 10, 12, 48–50
Buswell, B. N., 146, 148
Buunk, B. P., 81
Bzostek, S. H., 131

Caal, S., 162
Cacioppo, J. T., 52, 135
Cacioppo, S., 52
Caffrey, N., 4
Calabrese, S. K., 21
Cameron, J. J., 36
Campbell, D. T., 75, 168
Campbell, W. K., 123
Camperio-Ciani, A., 79
Campos, B., 129
Capaldi, D. M., 112
Capiluppi, C., 79
Caplan, G., 132
Caplan, R. D., 129
Caprariello, P. A., 51
Carden, M. L., 102
Caren, N., 89
Carlson, M. J., 122, 125, 131
Carnelley, K. B., 164
Carney, M. M., 153
Caron, S. W., 162
Carothers, B. J., 149
Carr, A., 65
Carrére, S., 122
Carroll, G. R., 61
Carroll, R. A., 77
Carver, K., 163
Cary, M. S., 33
Casey, J. J., 113
Casillas, A., 44
Casper, L. M., 99
Caspi, A., 52, 64
Castro, F. G. l., 159
Castro-Martín, T., 95

Catalano, S., 17
Catanese, K. R., 5, 12
Cate, R. M., 29
Cates, W., 17
Cauce, A. M., 130
Caughlin, J. P., 112, 123
Centers for Disease Control and
     Prevention, 17, 19
Chambers, A. L., 160
Chandek, M. S., 153
Chandra, A., 71, 97
Chase-Lansdale, P. L., 171
Chen, H., 43, 44
Cheng, C., 150
Cherlin, A. J., 171
Chernev, A., 57
Chiou, W.-B., 57, 58
Chivers, M. L., 8, 9, 75–79
Chorost, A. F., 120
Christensen, A., 46, 107, 109, 112,
     120, 132, 160
Christensen, D., 128
Chung, G. H., 130
Ciarocco, N. J., 39
Clark, A. E., 169
Clark, C. L., 150
Clark, L. A., 68
Clarkin, J. F., 69
Clarkwest, A., 106
Clausell, E., 83
Claxton, A., 125, 131
Claxton, S. E., 29
Claypool, H. M., 40
Clements, K., 155
Clements, M., 104
Clinton, H. R., 126
Coates, D., 168
Cobb, R. J., 104, 107, 108, 113, 122,
     165
Cochran, S., 83
Cochran, S. D., 82
Cohan, C. L., 96–100, 128–133
Cohen, D., 22
Cohen, J., 105, 145, 147, 148

SUBJECT INDEX

Great Myths of Intimate Relationships: Dating, Sex, and Marriage,
First Edition. Matthew D. Johnson.
© 2016 John Wiley & Sons, Inc. Published 2016 by John Wiley & Sons, Inc.

ceiling effect, 39
Centers for Disease Control and
    Prevention, 17, 19
chastity, 48, 49
child maltreatment, 156
choice overload, 57
cohabitation effect, the, 94–100
    causality hypothesis, 98–99
    inertia hypothesis, 99
    selection hypothesis, 98
    weeding hypothesis, 97–98
commitment, 58–59, 96–99, 104,
    123–124
    dependence, 58
    opportunity cost, 58
    satisfaction, association with, 58
communication, 109–120, 132, 148
    computer mediated (CMC), 59–65
    nonverbal, 35, 65
    problems, 158, 163
    skills, 96, 104, 106–114, 155
compatibility perspective, the, 69
complementarity see heterogamy
complex marriage, 101–102
computer-mediated communication
    see communication
conditioning see learning
conflict, 46, 104, 108, 111–115, 120,
    171–172, 174
    effects on children, 170–172
Connelly, Jennifer, 32
consummation of marriage see
    marriage consummation
couple therapy, 10, 25, 42, 103, 109,
    114, 120, 132, 151–161, 172
    behavioral marital therapy, 158–160
    cognitive-behavioral couple therapy,
    120, 160
    emotionally focused couple
    therapy, 160
    efficacy and effectiveness of,
    158–161
    history of, 157–158
    integrative couple therapy, 160

insight-oriented couple therapy, 160
    violence, and, 155
Cross, John, 21
cross-sectional data, 168, 170 see also
    longitudinal data
cross-validation, 93–94
Crowe, Russell, 32
culture, 5–7, 22–24, 43, 48–50, 130, 166
    Hook-up, 12–20

depression, 68, 120, 126, 138–139,
    162–163
discord see conflict
discrimination, 82, 90, 113, 130
distal predictors, 109–110 see also
    proximal predictors
divorce, 52, 68, 70, 88–112, 123–124,
    130, 133, 160, 166–172
    effects on children, 170–172
    rate, 157, 167
domestic violence see intimate partner
    violence
domestic violence shelters, 152, 155–156
dyspareunia, 22

effect size, 145–148
effectiveness, 28, 158–159 see also
    efficacy
efficacy, 28, 158–159 see also
    effectiveness
eHarmony, 66–69
Eliot, George, 20–24
Eros, 7, 10–12 see also libido
ethnicity, 70, 130
evolution, theory of, 10, 50, 79
expectations, 28, 63–64, 126, 167
eye contact, 33–39

Falloppio, Gabriele, 7
fantasy, 11
feminine see femininity
femininity, 33, 46, 143, 149–150
Fighting for your Marriage (book),
    116, 120

physical health, 1–2, 131, 170
playing hard-to-get, 34–35
plethysmograph, 8–9, 74–78
Popenoe, David, 157
Popenoe, Paul, 157
postdiction, 93
poverty, 105, 129–131
pratfall effect, the, 41
prediction
    of outcomes, 93–94 *see also*
      postdiction
    of self, 55
premarital cohabitation *see*
    cohabitation effect, the
premarital counseling, 100–109
    see also primary interventions
    PREP, 104–108
primary interventions, 103
primates, 9, 32
problem solving skills, 81, 94, 104,
    107–121
proceptivity, 33–36, 79
proximal predictors, 109–110, 114
    see also distal predictors
proximity, 41
psychodynamic psychotherapy *see*
    insight-oriented therapy
p-value *see p* < .05

quasi-experimental, 104–105

race, 2, 70, 130, 148, 164 *see also*
    discrimination and ethnicity
Regnerus, Mark, 86–91
relationship aptitude, 67–69
relationship education programs *see*
    premarital counseling
relationship quality, 1–2, 29, 43, 45,
    58, 65, 81, 83, 94, 96, 106,
    108–112, 117–125, 129–132,
    135, 140, 159–164 *see also*
    marital quality
relationship satisfaction *see* marital
    quality; relationship quality

repression
    of sexual minorities, 71–72, 124
    of women's sexuality, 5–8
restraining orders *see* intimate partner
    violence, orders of protection
Rules of the Game (book), 32
Ruskin, John, 21–22

Sade (musician), 30
salary *see* income; poverty
same-sex relationships, 38, 71–91, 124
    cultural and political
      considerations, 75
    definitions, 73–75
    marriage, 85–91
    relationship dissolution, 83–84
    sexual activity and satisfaction,
      82–83
    similarities between same-sex and
      other-sex couples, 80–85
    stress and support, 81–82
satisficers, 58
secondary interventions, 103
self-disclosure, 61–64, 135, 140
self-esteem, 36, 135, 146–150, 163
self-report data, 8–10, 74–78
separate evaluation mode, 55–56
sex, 4–29 *see also* Eros; gender; libido
    casual sex, 12–20
    development of sexuality, 165–166
    first time, 165
    marital, 10–11, 20–29
    older adults, 4
    oral sex, 16, 18, 76
sex role identity, 46, 143, 149
sexual arousal *see* arousal
sexual assault, 18
sexual desire *see* Eros; libido
sexual fluidity, 73–79
sexual functioning, 26, 29
sexual identity, 74, 79
sexual minorities *see* same-sex
    relationships
sexual orientation, 73–75, 79–82, 89